# STATE CIVIL JUSTICE REFORM: FUTURE CHALLENGES, PAST SUCCESSES

AUTHORS

Richard A. Bandstra
Mark A. Behrens
Samuel A. Brunelli
Susan Charlton
John Dorso
Joseph K. Doss
Matthew P. Eastus
Claudia Wilson Frost
Walter A. Graham
John Greene
Martin J. Hatlie
John L. Howard
David Hricik
Karla Kinderman
Christopher Landau
James D. Miller
John T. Montford
John Edward Porter
Marjorie E. Powell
Victor E. Schwartz
Kenneth W. Starr
Keith A. Teel

INTRODUCTION

by

The Honorable Dan Quayle
The Honorable Griffin B. Bell

EDITOR

Roger Clegg

The National Legal Center for the Public Interest is a tax-exempt, nonprofit public interest law foundation, duly incorporated under the law of the District of Columbia to provide nonpartisan legal information and services to the public at large. NLCPI is qualified to receive tax-deductible contributions under I.R.C. Sec. 501(c)(3).

Price $19.50

THE NATIONAL LEGAL CENTER
FOR THE PUBLIC INTEREST
1000—16th Street, N.W., Suite 301
Washington, D.C. 20036
Tel: (202) 296-1683


Library of Congress Catalog Card Number 94-067133
ISBN 937299-33-2
Published September 1994

# TABLE OF CONTENTS

# DETAILED TABLE OF CONTENTS

**Court Procedures**

## PART II
## STRATEGY AND TACTICS

# INTRODUCTION

DAN QUAYLE
GRIFFIN B. BELL

The need for civil justice reform is continuous. While the most recent debates on legal reform have seemed particularly pitched and partisan, that the legal system needs constant attention is hardly a recent conclusion. At the turn of the century, Dean Roscoe Pound examined the state of judicial administration and reported that "our system of courts is archaic and our procedure behind the times."* Dean Pound went on to enumerate many vexing problems—among them outdated and ineffective procedures and a poorly organized and administered court system—that had resulted in popular dissatisfaction with the legal system. Clearly, these observations also ring true today.

Given the evolutionary nature of law, it is perhaps not surprising that we face not only some of the same problems, but that we are also challenged by other, equally severe and crucial ones. The complex problems of access, efficiency, and fairness intersect daily in almost every lawsuit filed in every jurisdiction.

Our courts, our legislatures and, most importantly, our citizens are aware of this challenge. It would be almost impossible to ignore the consequences. Spiraling caseloads have resulted in dockets where delays of two to five years are common. Compounding the harm of delay is the ever increasing expense of a day in court. The high cost of litigation puts legal services beyond the financial wherewithal of too many Americans.

The tremendous burdens of cost and delay are real. They are borne not just by the individual litigants but by all Americans. A legal system that does not resolve disputes quickly, fairly, and finally is not delivering justice. All of society bears the costs, whether through the virtually unquantifiable costs of uncertainty and delay or the pinpoint accuracy of billings for legal services. The civil justice system imposes a "litigation tax" on us all—a tax that we pay both in dollars and in foregone opportunities and lost innovations. Our justice system once promoted and ordered our nation's commerce. Now it stifles the free-market economy that has provided a wealth of opportunity for generations of Americans.

We add our voices to paraphrase Dean Pound: our system is archaic and our procedures behind the times. Our legal system is

*The Causes of Popular Dissatisfaction with the Administration of Justice (1906), *reprinted in Proceedings Honoring Roscoe Pound*, 35 F.R.D. 273, 284 (1964).

in critical need. The necessity for improvement cannot be met by endless discussion and debate. Real reform requires new ideas, and a resolve to improve the system for all Americans.

This monograph documents some of the successful efforts to reform the civil justice system. It would be incorrect to say that these improvements are the only viable solutions, or that these reforms will be permanent. But each chapter explains how some of the best ideas are being or could be translated into action at the state and federal level.

The monograph is divided into two parts. The first part describes the specific reforms that are needed, and the second part discusses strategy and tactics.

The book begins by addressing the three sets of substantive reform issues. The first is how to define liability. Product liability is discussed by Victor Schwartz, probably the nation's foremost expert on the topic, and his colleague Mark A. Behrens; James D. Miller analyzes joint and several liability; and Marjorie Powell of the Pharmaceutical Research and Manufacturers of America, and Martin Hatlie and Karla Kinderman of the American Medical Association, discuss medical liability issues. In addition, U.S. Representative John Porter writes about his efforts to encourage states to enact laws providing better "volunteer immunity"—that is, laws limiting the liability of those voluntarily performing charitable and other humane work.

However liability is defined, there will be instances in which damages are appropriately awarded, but it is essential in those cases that the award be fair and not excessive. This principle frequently has been violated in recent years by the award of unsupportable noneconomic damages and punitive damages. These two issues are analyzed carefully by Keith A. Teel and Joseph K. Doss of Covington & Burling, and former Solicitor General and U.S. Court of Appeals Judge Kenneth W. Starr and his colleague Christopher Landau, respectively. Interestingly, Judge Starr concludes that the first and best line of defense is in the courts, and argues for more aggressive judicial review of juries' punitive damage awards. He recognizes, however, that there is also a role for the legislature; that role, by the way, is discussed in greater depth by Senator Graham in his chapter in part II.

Consideration also must be given to procedural issues. Discovery abuse and reform is discussed by Baker & Botts attorneys Claudia Wilson Frost, Matthew Eastus, and David Hricik; here, too, most of the needed corrective measures have been taken by bench and bar, rather than legislatively. John Howard of Tenneco concludes Part I of the monograph by discussing what is perhaps the most promising and important topic of all—ways to avoid litigation altogether by, for instance, improved settlement procedures and alternative dispute resolution.

Samuel A. Brunelli of the American Legislative Exchange Council begins part II of the monograph with his essay on "The Politics of Civil Justice Reform." He includes an impressive array of polling data, demonstrating the widespread grassroots support for stemming the litigation tide. His chapter makes clear that civil justice reform is politically possible.

Following this overview, five state legislators—two Democrats and three Republicans—describe how they succeeded in passing reform legislation in their respective states of Arizona, Michigan, Mississippi, North Dakota, and Texas. Each story is different, but there is a common theme: that carefully building coalitions and aggressively taking the case for reform directly to the people will overcome the narrow interests favoring the status quo. These success stories are included to show that reform is possible—not that the battle has been won, for it is far from over.

Moreover, should every approach or improvement discussed by the distinguished authors of this monograph be implemented, the need for civil justice reform would nonetheless continue. Every year more cases are filed than the year before and every day we call on our courts to resolve more problems. As was noted by Edmund Burke in Parliament before the American Revolution, Americans are a "litigious lot." The need for an effective and orderly legal system—one that protects the rights of the individual through fast, fair, and final dispute resolution—will always be present. Our obligation to maintain and improve the system will also endure.

# PART I

# SUGGESTED REFORMS

## Defining Liability

CHAPTER 1

# PRODUCT LIABILITY: MAKING THE LAW WORK THROUGH FAIR AND RATIONAL RULES

VICTOR E. SCHWARTZ
MARK A. BEHRENS

## I. Introduction

Product liability law must balance interests of both consumers and manufacturers to achieve socially optimal levels of safety in products. Fortunately, most courts and legislatures have developed fair and reasoned rules which, when applied consistently within traditional boundaries, promote innovation and provide consumers with safe, effective products.

This chapter will discuss the four primary bases of liability for product-related harms: liability for manufacturing defects, express representation, defective design, and failure adequately to instruct or warn. It will also describe important rules which have developed within each of these four theories to further good public policy in accord with principles of fairness and reason. Finally, this chapter will discuss the role of legislatures with respect to the legal issues described.

## II. The Need for Sound Principles of Liability

### *Manufacturing Defects*

A manufacturing defect occurs where a product contains an unintended deviation from the manufacturer's design specifications—for example, an automobile with a wheel[1] or steering gear[2] not in accord with the manufacturer's own specification, or a bottle of

[1]MacPherson v. Buick Motor Co., 111 N.E. 1050 (N.Y. 1916).

[2]Henningsen v. Bloomfield Motors, Inc., 161 A.2d 69 (N.J. 1960). *See also* Williams v. Volkswagenwerk Aktiengesellschaft, 180 Cal. App. 3d 1244, 226 Cal. Rptr. 306 (1986) (defective steel part fractured, causing loss of steering in automobile).

soda pop containing a foreign object.[3] These are classic examples of manufacturing defects.

The established rule for manufacturing defects is that liability will be imposed regardless of whether the manufacturer satisfied a duty of care with respect to its quality control. Thus, unlike design defect and failure to warn claims, liability in a manufacturing defect case can be determined by simply comparing the product at issue to other like products made by the same manufacturer.[4] Most practitioners and scholars are satisfied that such "super strict liability" is appropriate in this instance to assure consumers that goods they purchase are free from manufacturing defects.[5]

### *Express Warranty*

The tort of express warranty also is a "super strict liability" tort—i.e., it does not base liability on whether the manufacturer did the very best that was possible to make its product safe. In its traditional formulation, a plaintiff could establish a violation of express warranty by showing that he "relied" to his detriment on a promise or statement about a "specific" safety characteristic of a product.[6] These principles were incorporated in the *Restatement (Second) of Torts*, section 402B, under the label of innocent "misrepresentation."[7]

The tort of express warranty evolved out of contract law in the classic case *Baxter v. Ford Motor Co.*[8] In *Baxter*, Ford Motor Co.

---

[3]Coca-Cola Bottling Works v. Lyons, 111 So. 305 (Miss. 1927) (glass in Coke bottle).

[4]*See, e.g.*, Back v. Wickes Corp., 378 N.E.2d 964, 970 (Mich. 1984); Voss v. Black & Decker Mfg. Co., 450 N.E.2d 204, 207 (N.Y. 1983). *See also* Mississippi Product Liability Bill, signed by governor on Feb. 26, 1993 (Committee Substitute for House Bill 1270 § 1) (product "deviated in a material way from the manufacturer's specifications or from otherwise identical units manufactured to the same manufacturing specifications"; see chapter 12, below); WASH. REV. CODE ANN. § 7.72.030(2)(a) (West 1992); OHIO REV. CODE ANN. § 2307.74 (Anderson 1991).

[5]*See* David Owen, *The Moral Foundations of Products Liability: Toward First Principles*, 68 NOTRE DAME L. REV. 427, 500–06 (1993) (strict liability is morally defensible for manufacturing defects, but not for design and failure to warn).

[6]*See* Victor Schwartz, *Violation of Express Warranty: A Useful Tort That Must Be Kept Within Rational Boundaries*, 3 PROD. LIAB. L.J. 147 (1992).

[7]Section 402B states:

> One engaged in the business of selling chattels who, by advertising, labels, or otherwise, makes to the public a misrepresentation of a material fact concerning the character or quality of a chattel sold by him is subject to liability for physical harm to a consumer of the chattel caused by justifiable reliance upon the misrepresentation even though (a) it is not made fraudulently or negligently, and (b) the consumer has not bought the chattel from or entered into any contractual relationship with the seller.

RESTATEMENT (SECOND) OF TORTS § 402B (1965).

[8]12 P.2d 409 (Wash.), *aff'd*, 15 P.2d 1118 (Wash. 1932).

made a representation in its sales catalogs and advertising materials that its "Triplex" windshield "would not . . . shatter under the hardest impact."[9] After purchasing a Ford automobile on the basis of these statements, Baxter sustained severe injuries when a pebble flew off the road and broke the windshield of his car. Ford was held strictly liable in tort, without regard to whether its representations were made fraudulently or negligently.

Cases following *Baxter* and the comments to section 402B make clear that manufacturers should not be held liable for representations which are characterized as "sales talk," "puffing," or "loose general praise."[10] Rather, the representation must relate to a "material fact" concerning a "specific" characteristic of the product, such as the misrepresentation in *Baxter* that Ford Motor's windshield was shatterproof.[11]

Recent decisions suggest that most courts still follow the guidance provided by the established case law. For example, in *Berkebile v. Brantly Helicopter Corp.*,[12] the court found that a statement in a "colorful, persuasive" sales brochure for a helicopter, claiming generally that the pilot could be "assured of a safe, dependable helicopter," was nothing more than puffing and sales talk and not a warranty against specific defects. The court rejected the express warranty claim of the executrix of a deceased helicopter pilot based on the language of section 402B, finding that the manufacturer's statement did not constitute a misrepresentation of the safety of its helicopter. Similarly, in *Baughn v. Honda Motor Co.*,[13] television advertisements for a minibike that said, "You meet the nicest people on a Honda," described the bike as suitable for children and showed children riding the minibikes, were considered puffing. They did not create liability where the injured child failed to wear a helmet and ran a red light. As a result, the court dismissed an injured child's innocent misrepresentation claim based on the advertisements.[14]

Nevertheless, a few courts in recent years have diluted the traditional "specificity" requirement and allowed claims based on statements which some would consider mere puffing.[15] For instance, in

[9]12 P.2d at 410.

[10]*See* RESTATEMENT (SECOND) OF TORTS § 402B cmt. g (1965). *See generally* James Sales, *The Innocent Misrepresentation Doctrine: Strict Tort Liability Under Section 402B*, 16 HOUS. L. REV. 239 (1979).

[11]*See* Baxter v. Ford Motor Co., 12 P.2d at 410.

[12]337 A.2d 893, 903 (Pa. 1975).

[13]727 P.2d 655, 668 (Wash. 1986).

[14]*Id.*

[15]The other essential element of the express warranty (innocent misrepresentation) tort, "justifiable reliance," does not appear to have undergone similar dilution since the publication of section 402B. Section 402B expanded the "reliance" requirement to include indirect consumers who are injured by a product, yet were unaware of

one case, a salesman's oral statement that a decade-old automobile was a "good runner" was held to constitute a guarantee of its safety.[16] In another case, sunglasses advertised as providing "instant eye protection" constituted an express warranty violation because the glasses shattered when struck by a hard ball, even though the advertisement could have been interpreted to claim that the sunglasses provided "protection" from sun and glare.[17]

Courts should avoid this limited line of cases and apply consistently the carefully crafted judicial interpretations of section 402B and the principles established in *Baxter,* since express warranty claims pack a tremendous legal punch—they are virtually immune from traditional defenses, such as comparative fault,[18] and relatively straightforward and inexpensive to litigate (experts often are not required). Fair and settled law dictates that while manufacturers should not be permitted to avoid responsibility for specific misrepresentations, they also should not be held liable for generalized sales talk that is understood as such by ordinary, reasonable consumers of products.

### *Design Defect and Failure To Warn Claims*

As we have shown, the law applicable to manufacturing defects and express representations imposes liability without regard for fault. Whether the manufacturer exercised reasonable care in the marketing of its product is irrelevant. By way of contrast, design defect and failure to warn claims are generally considered, and should be, fault-based torts. That is, liability will be imposed only when the manufacturer's design specifications or warnings themselves create unreasonable risks, as measured by an objective standard outside the specifications. This usually requires a jury to weigh whether it was possible and practical for the manufacturer to know about a danger or make its product safer given the scientific knowledge available at the time the product left the manufacturer's control. Key principles applied in design defect and failure to warn cases follow.

---

misrepresentation in its promotion. *See* RESTATEMENT (SECOND) OF TORTS § 402B (1965).

[16]Crothers v. Cohen, 384 N.W.2d 562, 566 (Minn. App. 1986).

[17]Filler v. Rayex Corp., 435 F.2d 336, 338 (7th Cir. 1970).

[18]For instance, "state of the art" is no defense to an express warranty claim. *See, e.g.,* Spartanburg County Sch. Dist. Seven v. National Gypsum Co., 805 F.2d 1148, 1150 (4th Cir. 1986). Manufacturer negligence is irrelevant, and plaintiff fault, usually, is not a defense. *See* William Prosser, *The Fall of the Citadel (Strict Liability to the Consumer),* 50 MINN. L. REV. 791, 838–39 (1966) (citing cases).

## Design Liability

Sometimes a manufacturer, when it puts a product on the market, cannot discover a particular risk despite adequate testing of the product. Other times the manufacturer may discover a risk, but be prevented from making the product totally safe because of limited existing technology. It is unsound public policy to demand that manufacturers make their products safer than is possible given the available scientific and practical technology. Such a rule would discourage the innovation of important and socially beneficial products, such as pharmaceuticals and medical devices. Furthermore, manufacturers would find it difficult, if not impossible, to protect themselves adequately with insurance.[19]

Claimants who argue that a product contains a defective design should prove that there was a practical and technologically feasible alternative design available at the time of manufacture that would have prevented the harm.[20] The fact that liability should not be imposed for such "unavoidably unsafe" products is recognized in comment k to the *Restatement (Second) of Torts,* section 402A,[21] and in clear and unambiguous case law.[22] A five-year study conducted by Reporters of the American Law Institute came to the same conclusion.[23]

Similarly, courts have declined to impose liability for products where the risk cannot be eliminated without depriving the consumer of the usefulness or desirability of the product. An example of one such product is the ordinary kitchen knife. The fact that the knife

[19]Such "super strict design liability" would also make it impossible for a manufacturer to be judged by an objective standard of behavior to which it is reasonably possible for the manufacturer to conform.

[20]*See* Texas S.B. 4, signed by governor on Mar. 4, 1993, at § 82.005 (requiring that plaintiff prove the availability of a safer alternative design; see p. 228 below).

[21]Comment k states in relevant part:

> Unavoidably unsafe products. There are some products which, in the present state of human knowledge, are quite incapable of being made safe for their intended and ordinary use. These are especially common in the field of drugs . . . . Such a product, properly prepared, and accompanied by proper directions and warning, is not defective, nor is it unreasonably dangerous.

RESTATEMENT (SECOND) OF TORTS § 402A cmt. k (1965).

[22]*See, e.g.,* Brown v. Superior Court, 751 P.2d 470 (Cal. 1988); Grundberg v. Upjohn Co., 813 P.2d 89 (Utah 1991). Not all courts have followed the majority rule. In O'Brien v. Muskin Corp., 463 A.2d 298 (N.J. 1983), a case challenging the choice of material for the bottom of an above-ground swimming pool, the New Jersey Supreme Court imposed liability where there was no safer alternative way for the manufacturer to design the pool. The New Jersey legislature responded by enacting legislation reversing *O'Brien. See* N.J. STAT. ANN. § 2A-58C-3 (West 1991).

[23]*See* 2 THE AMERICAN LAW INSTITUTE, ENTERPRISE RESPONSIBILITY FOR PERSONAL INJURY—REPORTERS' STUDY 56 (1991).

is capable of slicing a finger does not make it defective or undesirable for use as a kitchen utensil.

The principle of "no liability for inherently unsafe products" is supported by comment i of the *Restatement (Second) of Torts,* section 402A.[24] Courts generally have supported this principle and have declined to impose liability regardless of whether the court thought it was a good idea for people to use such products as tobacco,[25] alcohol,[26] convertible automobiles,[27] and motorcycles.[28] Most every major court has recognized that legislatures and administrative agencies are better suited to decide whether products that are generally available, but considered socially undesirable for some segments of society, should be controlled or banned.[29]

### Failure To Warn

Similar to design liability law, warnings law has developed established and reasoned rules which promote product safety and encourage innovation. One of these rules holds that liability should not be imposed for failure to warn when the manufacturer neither knew nor reasonably could have known about a risk. Courts have recognized that a contrary rule would deter the introduction of new and useful products.[30] The Supreme Court of California recently came to the same conclusion in *Anderson v. Owens-Corning Fiberglas Corp.,*[31] a case of potentially huge significance since the Supreme

---

[24]Comment i reads in pertinent part:

> Unreasonably dangerous. The rule stated in this section applies only where the defective condition of the product makes it unreasonably dangerous to the user or consumer. Many products cannot possibly be made entirely safe for all consumption, and any food or drug necessarily involves some risk of harm, if only from over-consumption . . . . The article sold must be dangerous to an extent beyond that which would be contemplated by the ordinary consumer who purchases it, with the ordinary knowledge common to the community as to its characteristics.

RESTATEMENT (SECOND) OF TORTS § 402A cmt. i (1965).

[25]*See* Williamette Essential Oils, Inc. v. Harrold & Jensen Implement Co., 683 P.2d 1374 (Or. App. 1984).

[26]*See* Joseph E. Seagram & Sons, Inc. v. McGuire, 814 S.W.2d 385 (Tex. 1991).

[27]*See* Delvaux v. Ford Motor Co., 764 F.2d 469 (7th Cir. 1985).

[28]*See* Kutzler v. AMF Harley-Davidson, 550 N.E.2d 1236 (Ill. App.), *appeal denied,* 555 N.E.2d 377 (Ill. 1990); Camacho v. Honda Motor Co., 741 P.2d 1240 (Colo. 1987), *cert. denied,* 485 U.S. 901 (1988).

[29]An exception was Kelley v. R.G. Indus., Inc., 497 A.2d 1143 (Md. 1985) (holding handgun manufacturer strictly liable for injury resulting from properly functioning "Saturday Night Special"). *Kelley* was subsequently overruled by legislation. *See* MD. ANN. CODE art. 27, § 36-I(h) (West Supp. 1990).

[30]*See, e.g.,* Woodill v. Parke Davis & Co., 402 N.E.2d 194, 199–200 (Ill. 1980).

[31]810 P.2d 549 (Cal. 1991). In *Anderson,* the court held that not only could a jury consider whether the defendant knew or could have known about the risk involved at the time of manufacture, but the manufacturer would be entitled to an absolute defense in a duty to warn case when it neither knew of nor could have discovered a particular risk.

Court of California was the founder of strict product liability in tort law.[32]

On the other hand, the Supreme Judicial Court of Massachusetts, in *Simmons v. Monarch Machine Tool Co.,*[33] indicated that a manufacturer could be held liable for failure to warn even if it neither knew nor could have known about a particular risk. The *Simmons* case is a reemergence of the unsound public policy that surfaced briefly in the 1980s, one of super strict or absolute liability.[34] It represents unsound public policy—a policy that would discourage the development of good and useful products. In that regard, after the *Simmons* decision, a Massachusetts biopharmaceutical company, Biogen, Inc., halted its research for an AIDS vaccine.[35] The core problem with super strict liability is that it does not differentiate between publicly useful and harmful activities by manufacturers.[36] What makes the *Simmons* case even more of a travesty is that the issue of super strict liability was not before the court. The case involved a machine tool that a jury found was negligently made. The Supreme Judicial Court of Massachusetts affirmed the lower courts on this point. The issue of strict liability was not even argued before the court, and the public policy considerations of adopting it were not considered or discussed.

In the 1980s, state supreme courts in New Jersey and Louisiana ventured into the never-never land of super strict liability.[37] In each

---

[32]The *Anderson* decision is significant for several other reasons. First, *Anderson* was an asbestos case and courts in asbestos cases have shown a unique sympathy for claimants, which has been the predicate for super strict warnings liability. Second, the court based its decision on public policy reasons, noting that the imposition of liability for unknown risks would significantly deter innovation and create problems with insurability. Third, California has a well-known reputation as a tort law "farm system"; its law is often adopted by other states.

[33]596 N.E.2d 318 (Mass. 1992).

[34]*See* Beshada v. Johns-Manville Prods. Corp., 447 A.2d 539 (N.J. 1982) (asbestos); Halphen v. Johns-Manville Sales Corp., 484 So. 2d 110 (La. 1986) (asbestos). Both the New Jersey and Louisiana supreme courts later retreated from these decisions and suggested that the category of products which are subject to "super strict warnings liability" is quite limited. *See* Feldman v. Lederle Lab., 479 A.2d 374, 388 (N.J. 1984) (suggesting that *Beshada* was limited "to the circumstances giving rise to its holding"); Brown v. Sears, Roebuck & Co., 516 So. 2d 1154 (La. 1988) (category of products which fall within scope of "super strict liability" is quite limited). Moreover, the respective legislature in each state also acted to overrule the decision. *See infra* note 38 and accompanying text.

[35]*See The Product Liability Fairness Act: Hearing on S. 687 before the Consumer Subcomm. of the U.S. Senate Comm. on Commerce, Science and Transportation,* 102d Cong., 2d Sess. (Sept. 23, 1993) (statement of James L. Vincent, Chairman and Chief Executive Officer, Biogen, Inc.).

[36]*See generally* Victor Schwartz, *The Death of "Super Strict Liability": Common Sense Returns to Tort Law,* 27 GONZ. L. REV. 179 (1991/92).

[37]*See supra* note 34.

case, the state legislature acted swiftly and overruled the court.[38] The same result may soon occur in Massachusetts.[39]

One other established rule in warnings cases is that, in general, manufacturers are under no duty to warn about risks that should be obvious to foreseeable product users. This rule is supported by an overwhelming majority of jurisdictions.[40] There is a strong public policy behind this rule: social scientists have found that warnings about commonly known risks are not only likely to be ignored, but can dangerously diminish the significance of warnings about nonobvious dangers.

## III. The Role of Legislatures in Product Liability Law

Some may have the perception that product liability law advances primarily through judicial decision, but there is strong support for the proposition that legislatures can and should take an active role in creating fair and rational product liability law. For instance, legislatures have played an important role in overturning judicial decisions that expanded strict design defect and failure to warn liability law beyond traditional and reasoned boundaries.[41] In point of fact, legislatures, as contrasted with courts, are in a much better position to effectuate sound and effective reform.

First, courts are confined to the narrow issues before them in a case. If they go beyond those issues, they violate the concept of dealing with true "cases and controversies."

Second, courts do not have the benefit of learning about the full extent of the public policy issues that guide sound product liability reform. The ability of legislatures to call upon a wealth of knowledge and different perspectives gives them better insight than courts into the "total picture."

Third, courts, following the common law process, institute their rules on a *retroactive* basis. This results in expensive legal costs and sometimes unanticipated results. Fundamental fairness suggests that people who are potential plaintiffs or defendants should know

---

[38] *See* N.J. STAT. ANN. § 2A-58C-3 (West 1991) (overturning O'Brien v. Muskin Corp.); LA. REV. STAT. ANN. §§ 9:2800.53, :2800.56 (West 1991) (overturning Halphen v. Johns-Manville Sales Corp.). *See also* MD. ANN. CODE art. 27, § 36-I(h) (West Supp. 1990) (overturning Kelley v. R.G. Indus., Inc.).

[39] A major effort is underway to overrule the aberrant *Simmons* case in Massachusetts. *See* H.B. 2625, introduced by the Chairman of the Massachusetts House Judiciary Committee, Salvatore DiMasi (Jan. 1993).

[40] *See, e.g.*, Glittenberg v. Doughboy Recreational Indus., 491 N.W.2d 208, 214 n.15 (Mich. 1992) (providing comprehensive list of state court decisions supporting the position that a manufacturer owes no duty to warn about obvious dangers).

[41] *See supra* pp. 13–14 and note 38.

the rules in advance. Legislatures can and do act prospectively, telling us in advance what the rules are.[42]

## IV. Conclusion

The principles that have been discussed in this chapter generally have been applied consistently by courts. Some have been adopted by state legislatures. Strong public policy, as well as principles of fairness and reason, support each rule. Courts in future cases should continue to apply these established rules within their traditional boundaries. Legislatures also should play an important role in the law by enacting legislation to permit both plaintiffs and defendants to know in advance the standards of behavior to which each must conform.

[42]*See generally* Victor Schwartz & Mark Behrens, *Punitive Damages Reform—State Legislatures Can and Should Meet the Challenge Issued By The Supreme Court of the United States in* Haslip, 42 AM. U. L. REV. 1365, 1372–74 (1993).

CHAPTER 2

# JOINT AND SEVERAL LIABILITY: DOES JOINT LIABILITY VIOLATE DUE PROCESS?

JAMES D. MILLER

## I. Introduction

Joint liability is the legal rule that a defendant in some circumstances is liable for injury that was caused by someone else.[1] About forty of the states apply some version of joint liability, and it has been adopted widely under federal law as well.[2] The opposite of joint liability is individual or "several" liability, and the opposites are usually strung together to make the phrase "joint and several liability." The problem, however, is joint liability, not individual liability. Under a rule of individual liability, each defendant is held liable for the injury caused by that defendant. Individual liability thus creates no issue of equity for the civil justice system. Joint liability, in contrast, is unfair because it can make a defendant pay damages for injury caused by another person acting independently.[3]

---

[1]*See* RESTATEMENT (SECOND) OF TORTS § 875 (1977) ("Each of two or more persons whose tortious conduct is a legal cause of a single and indivisible harm to the injured party is subject to liability for the injured party for the entire harm.").

[2]*E.g.*, Edmonds v. Compagnie Générale Transatlantique, 443 U.S. 256, 260 & n.8 (1979) (maritime law); United States v. Monsanto Co., 858 F.2d 160, 171-72 (4th Cir. 1988) (Superfund), *cert. denied*, 490 U.S. 1106 (1989); Watts v. Laurent, 774 F.2d 168, 179 (7th Cir. 1985) (42 U.S.C. § 1983), *cert. denied*, 475 U.S. 1085 (1986). [Two other 1994 monographs by the National Legal Center for the Public Interest critique federal joint liability in the context of the securities laws: *Securities Class Actions: Abuses and Remedies* and *Accountants' Liability: The Need for Fairness*.—Editor's note.]

[3]There is an extensive literature on joint liability. *E.g.*, 2 AMERICAN LAW INSTITUTE REPORTERS' STUDY, ENTERPRISE LIABILITY FOR PERSONAL INJURY 127-57 (1991); Charles O. Gregory, *Contribution Among Joint Tortfeasors: A Defense*, 54 HARV. L. REV. 1170 (1941); 1 FOWLER V. HARPER & FLEMING JAMES, JR., THE LAW OF TORTS § 10.1 (1956); W. PAGE KEETON ET AL., PROSSER AND KEETON ON THE LAW OF TORTS §§ 46-52 (5th ed. 1984); John Izard & James D. Miller, *High Price-Fixing Awards Require Abolition of Joint & Several Liability*, NAT'L L.J., Aug. 27, 1979, at 22; Lewis A. Kornhauser & Richard L. Revesz, *Sharing Damages Among Multiple Tortfeasors*, 98 YALE L.J. 831 (1989); Lewis A. Kornhauser & Richard L. Revesz, *Apportioning Damages Among Joint Tortfeasors*, 19 J. LEGAL STUD. 617 (1990); WILLIAM M. LANDES & RICHARD A. POSNER, THE ECONOMIC STRUCTURE OF TORT LAW 190-93 (1987); Robert A. Leflar, *Contribution and Indemnity Between Tortfeasors*, 81 U. PA. L. REV. 130 (1932); William J. McNichols, *Judicial Elimination of Joint and Several Liability Because of Comparative Negligence: A Puzzling Choice*, 32 OKLA. L. REV. 1 (1979); Note, *Liability of Joint Tort-Feasors—Apportionment of Damages Between Joint Tort-*

Are state laws on joint liability, to the extent they produce this result, vulnerable to a challenge based on the Due Process Clause of the Fourteenth Amendment to the U.S. Constitution? No court has addressed this question,[4] but the answer should be yes, for two reasons: first, joint liability as applied today in the civil justice system has no historical foundation before this century and, second, joint liability is unfair and, when coupled with a comparative negligence rule, hopelessly irrational. Under the Supreme Court's current mode of due process analysis, these two reasons are sufficient to call joint liability into serious question.

The most striking feature of joint liability in the contemporary civil justice system is the wide range of different reforms enacted by state legislatures in recent years.[5] Although several states have simply abolished joint liability,[6] many more have only limited its application in some way.[7] While virtually any limitation of joint liability is better than nothing, the states that have merely limited joint liability have not squarely addressed the injustice of holding a defendant liable for injury caused by someone else. Thus, a due process challenge to joint liability would be viable even in many states that have adopted reforms of joint liability.

The Supreme Court has decided many cases that involved the constitutionality under the Due Process Clause of various legal rules that are applied in the context of private civil actions. The first task in assessing whether joint liability is vulnerable to a due process challenge is to distill from these cases some test or standard under

*Feasors by Verdict of Jury*, 14 VA. L. REV. 677 (1928); Note, *Modification of the Doctrine of Joint and Several Liability: Who Bears the Risk?*, 11 NOVA L. REV. 165 (1986); Note, *1986 Tort Reform Legislation: A Systematic Evaluation of Caps on Damages and Limitation on Joint and Several Liability*, 73 CORNELL L. REV. 628 (1988); Larry Pressler & Kevin V. Schieffer, *Joint and Several Liability: A Case for Reform*, 64 DENV. U. L. REV. 651 (1988); William L. Prosser, *Joint Torts and Several Liability*, 25 CAL. L. REV. 413 (1937); Joseph Sanders & Craig Joyce, *"Off to the Races": The 1980s Tort Crisis and the Law Reform Process*, 27 HOUS. L. REV. 207 (1990); Stephen D. Sugarman, *A Restatement of Torts*, 44 STAN. L. REV. 1185 (1992) (book review); John H. Wigmore, *Joint Tortfeasors and Severance of Damages: Making the Innocent Party Suffer Without Redress*, 17 ILL. L. REV. 458 (1923); Richard W. Wright, *Allocating Liability Among Multiple Responsible Causes: A Principled Defense of Joint and Several Liability for Actual Harm and Risk Exposure*, 21 U.C. DAVIS L. REV. 1141 (1988).

[4]*Cf.* Pacific Mut. Life Ins. Co. v. Haslip, 111 S. Ct. 1032, 1041 (1991) (holding that imposing liability on employer for fraud by employee under respondeat superior is consistent with due process).

[5]The Appendix to this chapter contains a survey of the joint liability rules in each of the states.

[6]*E.g.*, COLO. REV. STAT. § 13-21-111.5 (Supp. Oct. 1993) ("[N]o defendant shall be liable for an amount greater than that represented by the degree or percentage of the negligence or fault attributable to that defendant.").

[7]For example, New York's complex reform of joint liability is discussed in *In re* Brooklyn Navy Yard Asbestos Litig., 971 F.2d 831, 841-50 (2d Cir. 1992).

which joint liability is likely to be judged (while keeping in mind that few things in law are as fluid as the Supreme Court's thinking on due process). That threshold issue is addressed in part II of this chapter. The next task is to apply that constitutional test to the modern form of joint liability, which is the subject of parts III and IV.

## II. Due Process and Legal History

Under what circumstances does a rule applied in the civil justice system violate due process? The Supreme Court's recent consideration of this question has been in the context of punitive damages.[8] While the results in these cases so far have often disappointed those who favor reform of the civil justice system, the Court has followed a mode of analysis that could challenge some of the worst aspects of civil justice in this country, including joint liability. A challenge to joint liability should be analyzed as a procedural due process claim, not a substantive due process claim. At the most basic level, joint liability is about the rules used to mold a jury verdict into a judgment, and these rules are procedural in nature.

The Court's due process analysis has two dimensions: history and fairness. For a majority of the Court, those dimensions are conjunctive; for Justice Scalia, at least, they are disjunctive. A majority of the Court reasons that a civil justice rule that has long antecedents has a good claim to be consistent with due process, but even the oldest rule also must meet a standard based in some way on fairness. Justice Scalia, in contrast, considers a historical warrant for a rule to be dispositive of any due process challenge.[9] While Justice Scalia has not written directly on the applicable standard for a civil justice rule that lacks an historical warrant, there is at least a suggestion that he would then apply some fairness-based standard as well. To summarize this good news: a clear majority of the Court, and probably even Justice Scalia, believes that any new legal regime (including punitive damages) must meet a fairness-based standard.

[8]Pacific Mut. Life Ins. Co. v. Haslip, 111 S. Ct. 1032 (1991) (affirming award of punitive damages); TXO Prod. Corp. v. Alliance Resources Corp., 113 S. Ct. 2711 (1993) (same); Honda Motor Co. v. Oberg, 114 S. Ct. 2331 (1994) (reversing and remanding award of punitive damages).

[9]In Rutan v. Republican Party, 110 S. Ct. 2729, 2748 (1990), Justice Scalia dissented from the Court's holding that an officeholder discharged for political reasons could maintain an action under 42 U.S.C. § 1983 for violation of the First Amendment. He reasoned as follows: "[W]hen a practice not expressly prohibited by the text of the Bill of Rights bears the endorsement of a long tradition of open, widespread, and unchallenged use that dates back to the beginning of the Republic, we have no proper basis for striking it down."

The majority opinion in *Pacific Mutual Life Insurance Co. v. Haslip*[10] relied on the historical acceptance of punitive damages as an important factor in affirming the award of punitive damages. In *Haslip*, the Court reviewed the long legal tradition of awarding punitive damages and noted that "the common-law method for assessing punitive damages was well established before the Fourteenth Amendment was enacted. Nothing in that Amendment's text or history indicates an intention on the part of its drafters to overturn the prevailing method."[11] Yet the Court went on to write that the historical acceptance of punitive damages "is not the end of the matter. It would be just as inappropriate to say that, because punitive damages have been recognized for so long, their imposition is never unconstitutional."[12] The Court measured the punitive damages awarded in *Haslip* under a "constitutional calculus" standard based on "general concerns of reasonableness and adequate guidance from the [trial] court when the case is tried to a jury,"[13] and on the basis of that standard found that the award of punitive damages at issue in *Haslip* to be consistent with due process.

In his concurring opinion, Justice Scalia gave his fullest statement to date of his "historical tradition" model of procedural due process. He began by noting that all the Justices agreed that "[i]n 1868 . . . when the Fourteenth Amendment was adopted, punitive damages were undoubtedly an established part of the American common law of torts."[14] He then argued that this historical tradition, standing alone, should uphold the method of awarding punitive damages against any due process challenge.[15] Justice Scalia reasoned that "if the government chooses to *follow* a historically approved procedure, it necessarily *provides* due process, but if it chooses to *depart* from historical practice, it does not necessarily *deny* due process."[16] This argument raises the question of what standard applies to a civil rule that has no historical tradition. While Justice Scalia has given no direct answer to this question, he has recognized that the Court has

[10]111 S. Ct. 1032 (1991).

[11]*Id.* at 1043.

[12]*Id.*

[13]*Id.*

[14]*Id.* at 1048 (Scalia, J., concurring).

[15]Justice Scalia's leading authority for this proposition was Hurtado v. California, 110 U.S. 516, 528-29 (1884), where the Court stated that "a process of law, which is not otherwise forbidden [by the Constitution], must be taken to be due process of law, if it can show the sanction of settled usage both in England and in this country." Justice Scalia recently relied on *Hurtado* again for the same proposition in his concurring opinion in Weiss v. United States, 114 S. Ct. 752, 771 (1994).

[16]*Haslip*, 111 S. Ct. at 1050 (Scalia, J., concurring).

suggested a fairness-based standard to "a departure from historical practice."[17]

Moreover, in illustrating his thesis, Justice Scalia offered a striking hypothetical that is plainly pertinent to joint liability. He criticized the majority's reliance on appellate review of the amount of punitive damages, because this review, like the jury's verdict in the first instance, is "governed by no discernible standard."[18] The lack of standards could be justified, according to Justice Scalia, only by the approval of history. He then wrote:

> [I]t would surely not be considered "fair" (or in *accordance with due process*) to follow a similar procedure outside of this historically approved context [of punitive damages]—for example, to dispense with meaningful guidance concerning *compensatory* damages, so long as whatever number the jury picks out of the air can be reduced by the trial judge or on appeal. I can conceive of no test relating to "fairness" in the abstract that would approve this procedure . . . .[19]

This hypothetical indicates that, even for Justice Scalia, a change in a civil justice rule that takes it out of its "historically approved context" would trigger a fairness-based test for due process purposes: if juries were no longer given meaningful instructions on the appropriate calculation of compensatory damages, that change "would surely not be considered 'fair' (or in accordance with due process)." By the same token, the development of a once-innocuous legal rule away from its "historically approved context" should be measured for due process purposes under some fairness-based standard.

Only Justice Scalia has analyzed the due process standard for a "new" legal rule, and he has done so in discussions not necessary for deciding the cases before him. But since the majority in *Haslip* would require even an established legal rule to pass a fairness-based standard, there is a solid basis for predicting that, where a civil rule can make no historical claim, every member of the Court will judge it on a fairness-based standard for purposes of due process.[20]

## III. From Conduct to Injury

One of the most influential law journal articles ever published also is one of the shortest. In 1923, Dean Wigmore took two and a half pages of the *Illinois Law Review* to remake the doctrine of joint

[17] *Id.* (recognizing that *Hurtado* "merely suggested" that a departure from historical practice be assessed by reference to "those fundamental principles of liberty and justice which lie at the base of all our civil and political institutions") (quoting *Hurtado*, 110 U.S. at 535).

[18] *Haslip*, 111 S. Ct. at 1053 (Scalia, J., concurring).

[19] *Id.* (first emphasis added, second emphasis in original).

[20] *Cf. Honda*, *supra* note 8.

liability.[21] He argued in effect that the strict rules that limited joint liability to persons who were conspirators, or something close to conspirators, should be relaxed in order to give plaintiffs access to a broader range of pockets. This change was necessary, Dean Wigmore asserted, to help ensure that plaintiffs could obtain compensation for their injuries. The social policy of compensating plaintiffs had never before been an explicit rationale for joint liability.

Rarely has a law professor's analysis received such an enthusiastic reception in the courts. Within a few decades, the old rules limiting joint liability to conspiracy-like conduct were moldering in a corner. They were replaced by new rules that focused on *what* had happened to the plaintiff, not on *who* had done it.

Starting in the 1950s, when prompted by Melvin Belli's *Modern Trials*[22] the plaintiffs' bar began its development into a major business enterprise, Dean Wigmore's analysis became an essential element in the expansion of liability imposed by the civil justice system. Thus, while "joint liability" as a label has existed for hundreds of years in the common law, its contemporary shape is a product exclusively of this century. It has no historical claim that reaches back to the ratification of the Due Process Clause of the Fourteenth Amendment, let alone the Fifth Amendment.

Before Dean Wigmore's analysis in the 1920s, joint liability always had been directly linked to the rules governing joinder of defendants in a single action.[23] Traditionally at common law, a plaintiff could name as defendants (or "join") only those persons the plaintiff was able to allege had acted in concert. The rules of joinder were taken seriously by the courts. Consequently, where two or more defendants were joined in a single action, they were held jointly liable if the plaintiff succeeded in proving her allegations. Joinder was equated to joint liability in a way that was essentially appropriate.

As long as the joinder rules remained rigid and inflexible, joint liability was narrow in scope, and where the courts did allow joint liability, they did so based on the nature of the defendants' conduct. An illustration is *Grunder v. Tibbitts*,[24] where the plaintiff was

[21]John H. Wigmore, *Joint Tortfeasors and Severance of Damages: Making the Innocent Party Suffer Without Redress*, 17 ILL. L. REV. 458 (1923).

[22]MELVIN BELLI, MODERN TRIALS (1954) (3 vols.). This work is among the most influential law books ever published in America. Dean Prosser began his review of *Modern Trials* with the sentence, "This book frightens me." 43 CAL. L. REV. 556 (1955).

[23]The classic statement of this history is William L. Prosser, *Joint Torts and Several Liability*, 25 CAL. L. REV. 413 (1937). The thrust of Dean Prosser's analysis was that there should be no conceptual link between joinder and entire (i.e., joint) liability: "It is equally unreasonable to deny joinder because there is no entire liability, and to impose such liability because joinder is allowed." *Id.* at 443.

[24]55 N.E. 762 (Ind. 1899), discussed by Dean Prosser, *supra* note 23, at 417 n.28.

seduced by one defendant, and then the second defendant, a physician, performed an abortion. The physician and the seducer were joinded in a single action. The Indiana Supreme Court struggled to show that the defendants' conduct actually made them "joint tortfeasors," so that the physician became liable for the seduction.

This was the problem so successfully attacked by Dean Wigmore in his 1923 article. As joinder began to decay as a legal doctrine, and plaintiffs were permitted to join defendants without restriction, joint liability became much broader simply because more defendants could be joined in the same action. To the extent this fundamental change received any theoretical justification from the courts—and there was not much—the reasoning was that the harm inflicted on the plaintiff could not be, as a practical matter, divided among the defendants: the courts said that where the plaintiff's harm was *indivisible*, the persons responsible were jointly liable.[25] Thus, joint liability, which for centuries had been grounded on the conspiracy-like conduct of the persons responsible for the plaintiff's injury, now came to rest on the entirely new idea that the plaintiff's injury was indivisible.

Professor James described this change in thinking as follows:

> [J]oint tort-feasors could be joined at common law at plaintiff's option. This has remained the rule ever since. Its application has become broadened, however, at least in this country—not so much because of any innovation introduced by the [civil procedure] codes *as by a change in the concept of joint tort*. Originally only those who acted in concert were regarded as joint tort-feasors. But the prevailing, if not universal, modern American view has come to include the case where the tortious conduct of *each defendant has contributed to causing a single indivisible injury, even where there was no concert of action between them.*[26]

This was not an innocuous change: the new "indivisibility" rationale for joint liability meant that actors who had no connection with one another could, nonetheless, be jointly liable merely because the plaintiff's injury was said to be "indivisible." Put another way, a defendant could be liable for the entire amount of damages that were in fact caused by someone else, with whom the defendant had no connection.

Thus, this century has seen a fundamental change in the doctrine of joint liability. The law formerly allowed joint liability when the

[25] *E.g.*, Bosco v. Serhant, 836 F.2d 271, 280 (7th Cir. 1987) (Posner, J.) ("[W]hen tortfeasors inflict an indivisible injury, each is liable for the full amount."), *cert. denied*, 486 U.S. 1056 (1988); United States v. Alcan Aluminum Corp., 990 F.2d 711, 722 (2d Cir. 1993) ("[W]here each tortfeasor causes a single, indivisible harm, then damages are not apportioned, and each is liable in damages for the entire harm.").

[26] FLEMING JAMES, JR., CIVIL PROCEDURE § 10.8, at 459 (1965) (emphasis added).

conduct of the persons responsible for plaintiff's injury was done in concert; now joint liability is linked instead to the nature of the plaintiff's injury. Whether the persons responsible for that injury conspired or acted in concert is irrelevant, and indeed the jointly liable persons often did not even know of one another's existence. This change has had exactly the effects sought by Dean Wigmore: it has exploded the earlier limits on joint liability and thereby increased the plaintiff's chances of satisfying a judgment.

This change, however, has had another effect as well: it has cut off joint liability from any meaningful connection with its historic roots in the common law. For purposes of due process, the contemporary doctrine of joint liability lacks the shield of tradition and should be judged by whatever fairness-based standard is appropriate for any rank innovation in the civil justice system. Due process at the time the Fourteenth Amendment was adopted did not contemplate the expansive scope of joint liability we now take for granted.

## IV. Fairness and Coherence

Even a well-trained legal mind has trouble focusing simultaneously on joint liability and "comparative negligence." The former assumes that the plaintiff's damages cannot be apportioned; the latter assumes the exact opposite; and yet the doctrines are asked to work in tandem in tort cases.

Comparative negligence is the law in the majority of states, and, like joint liability, it is intended to help the plaintiff recover money.[27] The common law traditionally applied the doctrine of contributory negligence, so that any negligent conduct by a plaintiff that contributed to her own injury barred recovery. Whatever the disadvantages of contributory negligence, it was at least conceptually compatible with joint liability. The newer doctrine of comparative negligence does not bar the plaintiff from recovery; instead, the jury determines the degree of fault attributable to the plaintiff, whose judgment is then reduced by a proportionate amount.[28] Comparative negligence,

[27]RESTATEMENT (SECOND) OF TORTS § 463 (1977). The leading law journal article is another classic by Dean Prosser, *Comparative Negligence*, 61 MICH. L. REV. 465 (1965).

[28]An extraordinary application of comparative negligence is Walt Disney World Co. v. Wood, 515 So. 2d 198 (Fla. 1987). Plaintiff was injured at the bumper car attraction at Disney World when her fiancé rammed her bumper car with his own. Plaintiff married her fiancé (thus immunizing him from tort liability) and sued Disney World. The jury made comparative negligence findings that plaintiff was 14% at fault, the fiancé/spouse 85% at fault, and Disney World 1% at fault. Because the spouse was immune, Disney World was liable for 86% of plaintiff's damages, a result approved by the Florida Supreme Court. One of the dissenting opinions noted that the majority's application of comparative negligence for the plaintiff but joint liability for the defendant "defies legal logic." *Id.* at 202 (McDonald, C. J., dissenting). This

however, makes the fundamental assumption that the jury can appropriately and fairly determine the relative fault of the persons responsible for the harm. This fundamental assumption is flatly inconsistent with the rationale developed in this century for joint liability: the supposed "indivisibility" of the harm to the plaintiff.[29]

Contribution among tort-feasors, also a product of this century,[30] exhibits the same conceptual conflict with joint liability. Under a contribution regime, a defendant may force an equitable allocation of the plaintiff's damages among the tort-feasors responsible for the plaintiff's injuries. Although in some states each person at fault for the plaintiff's injuries is liable for a pro rata share of contribution (so that each tort-feasor's share is equal), the majority rule is that contribution shares are based on the relative fault of each tort-feasor. The *Restatement (Second) of Torts* notes that the relative fault approach is "almost required for the effective administration" of comparative negligence, so that the plaintiff's negligence can be built into the total negligence of all the parties.[31]

Thus, the notion that joint liability is justified because the plaintiff's injuries are "indivisible" is hopelessly incoherent. It is incompatible with comparative negligence and contribution, both of which operate to divide responsibility for the same injuries that joint liability assumes are "indivisible." This lack of coherence has an important due process dimension, because one relevant inquiry under a fairness-based standard should be whether a new civil justice rule fits logically into the law. Joint liability fails this test.

The fact is that joint liability in its contemporary form is merely a raw decision to favor plaintiffs over defendants.[32] Dean Wigmore spoke of favoring "innocent" plaintiffs over tort-feasor defendants,[33] but with the advent of comparative negligence, the plaintiff may

case was not subject to Florida's tort reform statute, which is described in the Appendix to this chapter.

[29]*See* Senator Larry Pressler & Kevin V. Schieffer, *Joint and Several Liability: A Case for Reform*, 64 DENV. U. L. REV. 651, 677 (1988) (note omitted):

> It does not follow that simply because the *harm* is indivisible there is no basis for apportionment. It is the *responsibility* for causing the harm that should be the focus of the inquiry. . . . Lack of ability to apportion damages, based on the indivisibility of *harm*, is not a sound basis for retaining joint and several liability.

[30]RESTATEMENT (SECOND) OF TORTS § 886A (1977); Theodore W. Reath, *Contribution Among Persons Jointly Charged for Negligence*, 12 HARV. L. REV. 176 (1898) (tracing history of common-law rule against contribution).

[31]RESTATEMENT (SECOND) OF TORTS § 886A cmt. i to subsec. 3, at 341 (1977).

[32]Richard W. Wright, *Allocating Liability Among Multiple Responsible Causes: A Principled Defense of Joint and Several Liability for Actual Harm and Risk Exposure*, 21 U.C. DAVIS L. REV. 1141, 1143 (1988) ("The fundamental issue . . . in the political debate should be whether the plaintiff, the tortfeasors, or both should bear the . . . risk of collecting from insolvent or otherwise unavailable tortfeasors.") (footnote omitted).

[33]Wigmore, *supra* note 21.

well have been more negligent than the defendant.[34] Thus, the supposed innocence of plaintiffs gives no support to joint liability, at least under a comparative negligence regime.

Joint liability is sometimes defended on the ground that it tends to deter wrongful conduct,[35] but one recent study concluded that it is impossible to arrive at a "general assessment" of the actual effect of joint liability on deterrence: "Under some circumstances joint and several liability may not affect tort law's promotion of optimal deterrence; under other circumstances the rule may generate undesirable consequences."[36] The best that can be said for the theoretical effect of joint liability in its modern form on deterrence is that it is indeterminate.

Joint liability certainly accomplishes the task of helping plaintiffs collect judgments against multiple defendants for money damages, but this violates everyday ideas of fairness where one defendant ultimately pays for injury caused by another person who acted independently. The classic statement of this principle was made by the Kansas Supreme Court:

> There is nothing inherently fair about a defendant who is 10% at fault paying 100% of the loss, and there is no social policy that should compel defendants to pay more than their fair share of the loss. . . . If one of the parties at fault happens to be a spouse or a governmental agency and if by reason of some competing social policy [the spouse or agency is immune], there is no compelling social policy which requires the codefendant to pay more than his fair share of the loss. The same is true if one of the defendants is wealthy and the other is not.[37]

There is no fairness rationale that justifies joint liability, especially when it is linked with comparative negligence.

## V. Conclusion

Does joint liability violate due process? There are five propositions that are relevant to this question: (1) joint liability, in its contemporary form, is fundamentally different from its ancestor that was applied by the courts when the Fourteenth Amendment was ratified in the last century; (2) joint liability is now dramatically broader than its ancestor, principally because the law in this century has

[34] *See, e.g., supra* note 28.

[35] Lewis A. Kornhauser & Richard L. Revesz, *Sharing Damages Among Multiple Tortfeasors*, 98 YALE L.J. 831 (1989) (concluding that joint liability provides optimum level of deterrence).

[36] 2 AMERICAN LAW INSTITUTE REPORTER'S STUDY, ENTERPRISE LIABILITY FOR PERSONAL INJURY 134 (1991).

[37] Brown v. Keill, 580 P.2d 867, 874 (1978) (interpreting Kansas comparative fault statute to abolish joint liability by implication).

abandoned the limitation that joint liability attaches only to conspiracy-like conduct; (3) the "indivisibility" justification for joint liability makes no sense when joint liability is applied in a regime of comparative negligence and contribution; (4) there is no social policy that justifies favoring plaintiffs over defendants in the dramatic fashion represented by joint liability; and (5) the civil justice system should not force any defendant to pay for injury caused by another person, especially in the absence of conspiracy-like conduct between them. These propositions, taken together, support the conclusion that joint liability is inconsistent with due process.

In considering the due process issues raised by joint liability, the variety and complexity of state law must be kept in the forefront of the analysis. Due process is most directly implicated by applying joint liability and comparative negligence in a situation where the remedies of indemnity and contribution are either not available or ineffective because the other responsible persons are insolvent, legally immune from liability, or unavailable. The conceptual contradiction between joint liability and comparative negligence supports a challenge to joint liability. Indemnity and contribution mitigate the inequitable effects of joint liability,[38] and so the unfairness of joint liability is more plain in cases where these doctrines do not apply or do not work.

The Supreme Court's treatment of punitive damages until *Honda* was disappointing in its results, but *Honda* and, especially, the Court's mode of analysis in *Haslip* will help challenge those aspects of the civil justice system that lack roots reaching back to the time the Fourteenth Amendment was ratified. Where a legal rule is without these roots, and operates unfairly, it is vulnerable to a due process challenge. Joint liability is such a rule.

[38]Hardy v. Gulf Oil Corp., 949 F.2d 826, 829 (5th Cir. 1992) ("[J]oint and several liability in its purest form can produce a seemingly inequitable result: one defendant might alone be required to bear the burden of several defendants' wrongs. The courts developed the principles of indemnity and contribution to alleviate this potentially unfair allocation of responsibility.").

# APPENDIX

## State Law of Joint Liability
(May 1994)

**Alabama:** Joint liability. Buchanan v. Collier, 555 So. 2d 134 (Ala. 1989); General Motors Corp. v. Edwards, 482 So. 2d 1176 (Ala. 1985).

**Alaska:** Joint liability abolished through a ballot initiative in 1988. ALASKA STAT. § 09.17.080(d) (Supp. 1991).

**Arizona:** Joint liability abolished except in cases of intentional torts and hazardous waste and solid waste disposal sites. ARIZ. REV. STAT. ANN. § 12.2506 (1993). Church v. Rawson Drug & Sundry Co., 842 P.2d 1355 (Ariz. Ct. App. 1992).

**Arkansas:** Joint liability retained. Bill C. Harris Constr. Co. v. Powers, 554 S.W.2d 332 (Ark. 1977); Missouri Pac. R.R. v. Star City Gravel Co., 452 F. Supp. 480 (E.D. Ark. 1978), aff'd, 592 F.2d 455 (8th Cir. 1979).

**California:** Joint liability abolished for noneconomic damages (Proposition 51). CAL. CIV. CODE §§ 1431.1-.5 (West Supp. 1990). Evangelatos v. Superior Court, 753 P.2d 585 (Cal. 1988); DaFonte v. Up-Right, Inc., 828 P.2d 140 (Cal. 1992).

**Colorado:** Joint liability abolished, except for concerted action to commit an intentional tort. COLO. REV. STAT. §§ 13-21-111.5 & 09-17-080 (Supp. Oct. 1993).

**Connecticut:** Joint liability retained, but collection of noneconomic damages prohibited where liable parties' share of judgment is uncollectible. CONN. GEN. STAT. § 52-572h (Cum. Supp. 1993). Gionfriddo v. Gartenhaus Cafe, 546 A.2d 284 (Conn. Ct. App. 1988), aff'd, 557 A.2d 540 (Conn. 1989).

**Delaware:** Joint liability. DEL. CODE ANN. tit. 10, § 6301 (1993).

| | |
|---|---|
| **District of Columbia:** | Joint liability. R. & G. Orthopedic Appliances & Prosthetics, Inc. v. Curtin, 596 A.2d 530, 544 (D.C. 1991); National Health Lab., Inc. v. Ahmadi, 596 A.2d 555 (D.C. 1991). |
| **Florida:** | Joint liability abolished as to noneconomic damages in negligence actions; also abolished as to economic damages for defendants less at fault than plaintiffs. The rule does not apply for economic damages from pollution, intentional torts, actions governed by a specific statute providing for joint liability, and actions involving damages no greater than $25,000. FLA. STAT. § 768.81 (Cum. Supp. 1993). Smith v. Department of Ins., 507 So. 2d 1080 (Fla. 1987); Conley v. Boyle Drug. Co., 570 So. 2d 275 (Fla. 1990). |
| **Georgia:** | Joint liability eliminated where plaintiff is partially responsible for damage. GA. CODE ANN. §§ 51-11-7 & 51-12-33 (Cum. Supp. 1993). |
| **Hawaii:** | Joint liability for noneconomic damages abolished for defendants responsible for 25% or less of fault. This limitation does not apply to automobile, product liability, intentional, or environmental tort cases. HAWAII REV. STAT. § 663-10.9 (Supp. 1993). |
| **Idaho:** | Joint liability abolished except in cases of intentional torts, hazardous waste torts, and medical device and pharmaceutical product liability actions. IDAHO CODE § 6-803(3)-(7) (Cum. Supp. 1993). |
| **Illinois:** | Joint liability abolished for defendants responsible for 25% or less of fault. This limitation does not apply to the award of medical expenses or to automobile, product liability, or environmental tort cases. ILL. REV. STAT. ch. 110, ¶ 2-1117-18 (Cum. Supp. 1993). Stifle v. Marathon Petroleum Co., 876 F.2d 552 (7th Cir. 1989). |
| **Indiana:** | No joint liability in actions based on fault. IND. CODE ANN. § 34-4-33-5(b) (Burns Supp. 1993). |

**Iowa:** Joint liability abolished for defendants who are less than 50% responsible for plaintiff's damages. IOWA CODE ANN. §§ 619.17, 668.1-668.4 (West Supp. 1993).

**Kansas:** No joint liability. Brown v. Keill, 580 P.2d 867 (Kan. 1978) (interpreting KAN. STAT. ANN. §§ 60-258a, 60-258b (Supp. 1993)).

**Kentucky:** Joint liability limited where jury apportions fault. KY. REV. STAT. ANN. § 454.040 (Michie/Bobbs-Merrill 1993). Dix & Assocs. Pipeline Contractors, Inc. v. Key, 799 S.W.2d 24 (Ky. 1990).

**Louisiana:** Joint liability applies only to the extent necessary to cover 50% of plaintiff's damages. When a defendant's fault is less than plaintiff's, that defendant is liable only for its share of damages. LA. CIV. CODE ANN. art. 2324 (Supp. 1993). Nance v. Gulf Oil Corp., 817 F.2d 1176 (5th Cir. 1987).

**Maine:** Joint liability. Paine v. Spottiswoode, 612 A.2d 235 (Me. 1992).

**Maryland:** Joint liability. MD. ANN. CODE art. 50, §§ 16-24 (1991). Huff v. Harbaugh, 435 A.2d 108 (Md. 1981).

**Massachusetts:** Joint liability. MASS. GEN. LAWS ANN. ch. 231 B, §§ 1-4 (West 1986).

**Michigan:** Joint liability abolished, except where plaintiff is not at fault and in product liability cases. In other actions, any uncollectible shares of the obligation are reallocated among the other parties in accordance with their percentage of fault. MICH. COMP. LAWS ANN. § 600.6304(6) (West Supp. 1993).

**Minnesota:** Joint liability except for any defendant found to be 15% or less at fault. Such a defendant is liable for a percentage of plaintiff's damages that is four times defendant's percentage of fault. MINN. STAT. ANN. § 604.02(1) (West Supp. 1993).

**Mississippi:** Joint liability limited to the extent necessary for the plaintiff to recover 50% of "recoverable" damages. Full joint liability continues to apply to intentional torts and conspiracy. MISS. CODE ANN. § 85-5-7(2), (6) (1993).

**Missouri:** Joint liability, except where plaintiff is contributorily negligent. If any defendant's equitable share is determined to be "uncollectible," it is reallocated to the remaining parties. MO. REV. STAT. § 32.07 (1978). Missouri Pac. R.R. v. Whitehead & Kales Co., 566 S.W.2d 466 (Mo. 1978).

**Montana:** No joint liability for defendants who are 50% or less at fault, except for defendants acting in concert. MONT. CODE ANN. § 27-1-703(2)-(3) (1993).

**Nebraska:** No joint liability for noneconomic damages. Joint liability applies to economic damages if plaintiff is less than 50% responsible for damages.

**Nevada:** Joint liability abolished when plaintiff's negligence exceeds defendant's, except for strict liability, product liability, toxic torts, and intentional torts. NEV. REV. STAT. § 41.141 (Supp. 1991).

**New Hampshire:** No joint liability for defendants who are less than 50% at fault. N.H. REV. STAT. ANN. § 507: 7-e (1993).

**New Jersey:** Joint liability based on degree of fault: if the defendant is less than 20% at fault, the defendant is liable for the share of damages attributable to it; if defendant is 20-60% liable, the defendant can be held responsible for full economic damages and its share of noneconomic damages; if defendant is responsible for greater than 60% of the damages, that defendant can be held liable for all damages. N.J. REV. STAT. § 2A:15-5.3 (1992).

**New Mexico:** No joint liability, except in cases involving intentional torts, vicarious liability, product liability, and "situations . . . having a sound basis

| | |
|---|---|
| | in public policy." N.M. STAT. ANN. § 41-3A-1 (Supp. 1989). Bartlett v. New Mexico Welding Supply, 646 P.2d 579 (N.M. Ct. App.), *cert. denied,* 648 P.2d 794 (N.M. 1982). |
| **New York:** | Joint liability, except that defendants 50% or less at fault are jointly liable only for economic damages. This limitation does not apply in cases of intentional torts, actions requiring proof of intent, actions taken in concert, workers' compensation, or administrative proceedings. N.Y. CIV. PRAC. L. & R. § 1601 (McKinney Cum. Supp. 1993). |
| **North Carolina:** | Joint liability. N.C. GEN. STAT. § 1B (1983). |
| **North Dakota:** | No joint liability, except for intentional torts and product liability cases. N.D. CENT. CODE § 32-03.2-02 (Supp. 1993). Kavadas v. Lorenzen, 448 N.W.2d 219 (N.D. 1989). |
| **Ohio:** | No joint liability for noneconomic damages when plaintiff is partially at fault. OHIO REV. CODE ANN. § 2315.19 (1992). |
| **Oklahoma:** | Joint liability limited to cases where damages cannot be apportioned or where plaintiff is not at fault. Boyles v. Oklahoma Natural Gas Co., 619 P.2d 613 (Okla. 1980). |
| **Oregon:** | No joint liability for noneconomic damages. No joint liability for economic damages when defendant is less than 15% at fault. This limitation does not apply to some environmental torts. OR. REV. STAT. §§ 18.470 & 18.485 (Supp. 1991). |
| **Pennsylvania:** | No joint liability when plaintiff's negligence is greater than defendant's. 42 PA. CONS. STAT. § 7102(b) (1993). |
| **Rhode Island:** | Joint liability. Roberts-Robertson v. Lombardi, 598 A.2d 1380 (R.I. 1991). |
| **South Carolina:** | Joint liability. Scott v. Fruehauf Corp., 396 S.E.2d 354 (S.C. 1990). |

**South Dakota:** Joint liability limited for defendants who are 50% or less responsible for damages. Such defendants are liable for a maximum of twice their share of fault. S.D. CODIFIED LAWS ANN. § 15-8-15.1 (Supp. 1993).

**Tennessee:** Joint liability abolished by state supreme court as part of adoption of comparative fault. McIntyre v. Balentine, 833 S.W.2d 52 (Tenn. 1992).

**Texas:** Full joint liability applies to cases involving exposure to toxic substances. Joint liability also applies where the defendant's share of fault is greater than 20% and, in a negligence action, is greater than the claimant's share of fault. Finally, joint liability applies where the claimant is not at fault, and the defendant's share of fault is greater than 10%. In other cases, there is no joint liability. TEX. CIV. PRAC. & REM. CODE ANN. § 33.013(a)-(c) (Supp. 1993).

**Utah:** No joint liability. UTAH CODE ANN. § 78-27-38-40 (Supp. 1987).

**Vermont:** No joint liability. VT. STAT. ANN. tit. 12, § 1036 (1992).

**Virginia:** Joint liability. VA. CODE ANN. § 8.01-35.1 (1992).

**Washington:** No joint liability, except where plaintiff is free of fault, defendants acted in concert, business torts are involved, or hazardous or solid waste disposal sites are involved. WASH. REV. CODE § 4.22.070 (Cum. Supp. 1993). Gerrard v. Craig, 836 P.2d 837 (Wash. Ct. App. 1992), *rev'd on other grounds,* 857 P.2d 1033 (Wash. Ct. App. 1993)

**West Virginia:** Joint liability, except where "medical professionals" and "political subdivisions or their employees" are found to be less than 25% at fault. W. VA. CODE § 55-7B-9 (Cum. Supp. 1993). Miller v. Monongahela Power Co., 403 S.E.2d 406 (W. Va.), *cert. denied,* 112 S. Ct. 186 (1991).

**Wisconsin:** Joint liability. McDonough v. Van Eerden, 650 F. Supp. 78 (E.D. Wis. 1986); Connar v. West Shore Equip., Inc., 227 N.W.2d 660 (Wis. 1975).

**Wyoming:** No joint liability. WYO. STAT. § 1-1-109(d) (Cum. Supp. 1993).

CHAPTER 3

# HEALTH CARE LIABILITY: REFORM IN A CHANGING ENVIRONMENT

MARTIN J. HATLIE*
KARLA KINDERMAN
MARJORIE E. POWELL

## I. Introduction

In Tulsa, Oklahoma, a female patient is mistakenly taken for an ultrasound test after surgery, but the error is discovered before the test is complete, and she is taken back to her room. She claims to have ruptured an incision during the move. A jury awards her $10 million, reduced to $5 million on appeal. Half of the award goes to her attorney for fees and expenses. This example is, unfortunately, "typical of a legal system out of control."[1]

The total cost of the medical liability system, including physicians' and hospitals' liability premiums, defensive medicine, and coverage for makers of medicines and medical devices, is more than $45 billion annually. These costs and other problems associated with medical liability are reflected in every aspect of the practice of medicine and the delivery of health care, particularly the escalating costs of medical services. The ultimate victims are, of course, the patients.

This chapter first briefly reviews the basis for medical liability[2] and the defects in the current system.[3] Following this discussion, various proposals for reforming the existing system are discussed.[4]

## II. Overview of Medical Liability

"Liability" has been defined as "an obligation one is bound in law or justice to perform." Those who are "liable" are "responsible,

*This chapter draws heavily on publications and documents of the American Medical Association, to which the AMA retains its copyright.

[1]Rowland Evans & Robert Novak, *America's Most Powerful Lobby*, READER'S DIG., Apr. 1994, at 132.

[2]*Infra* part II, pp. 35—42.

[3]*Infra* part III, pp. 43—49.

[4]*Infra* part IV, pp. 49—62.

chargeable, answerable, compellable to make satisfaction, compensation, or restitution . . . [and are] bound to respond because a wrong has occurred."[5]

Historically, physicians were the only parties held liable for negligent patient care. Today, however, liability has been extended to other health care workers (for example, emergency medical technicians, nurses, and pharmacists); health care entities like hospitals and managed care organizations; third-party payors (health care insurers); and manufacturers of medical products. Notwithstanding these additional defendants, courts have made it clear that physicians must retain the authority to make medical decisions and remain primarily liable for them.

*Physicians and Health Care Professionals*

Health care workers not traditionally named in liability cases are liable for negligence. For example, nurses may be held liable for falls and burns, and for failures to communicate effectively, make a "nursing diagnosis," notify the physician when necessary, and perform procedures appropriately. Emergency medical technicians employed by health care institutions, fire departments, ambulance companies, and other private and public organizations may be held liable for transportation, equipment used, and procedures employed. And pharmacists may be held liable for dispensing the wrong drug or the wrong dosage or strength, compounding the wrong prescription, and mislabeling or providing inadequate directions to the patient.

Notwithstanding the addition of possible defendants, in most situations the physician remains primarily liable for patient care. The basis for liability stems from principles of medical ethics supporting a physician's moral commitment to the patient, reflected in the Hippocratic Oath, the Declaration of Geneva, and elsewhere. Physicians are expected to perform actions that will benefit their patients and to refrain from performing procedures that could harm them.[6] Physicians are also contractually liable for their patients' care. When

---

[5] BLACK'S LAW DICTIONARY 473 (5th ed. 1983).

[6] American Medical Association, Report A of the Council on Ethical and Judicial Affairs, Proceedings of the House of Delegates 218 (Interim 1986). The AMA Code of Medical Ethics, adopted in 1847 and revised in 1903, 1912, 1927, and 1955, provides in part: "The principal objective of the medical profession is to render service to humanity with full respect for the dignity of man. . . . Physicians should merit the confidence of patients entrusted to their care, rendering to each a full measure of service and devotion." *See also* Jerry J. Phillips, Comments on the American Law Institute Study of Enterprise Liability for Personal Injury 27 (Apr. 1991); Edward B. Hirshfeld, *Should Third Party Payors of Health Care Services Disclose Cost Control Mechanisms to Potential Beneficiaries?*, 14 SETON HALL LEGIS. J. 115, 143-44 (1990).

the patient comes to a physician with complaints and the physician in turn initiates care, the law implies that a contract has arisen.[7]

These ethical and contractual obligations to the patient provided the tort common-law basis for physician liability, and the physician's common-law duties in tort are much the same today as they were nearly a century and a half ago.[8] Courts repeatedly have required the physician to possess and exercise that degree of knowledge, judgment, and skill which other physicians of good standing possess and exercise in like or similar circumstances.

Courts have upheld and protected from interference the medical profession's unique role in determining what is appropriate medical care. This point is well made in perhaps the most often cited and notorious case of third-party decisionmaking, *Wickline v. California*.[9] That case involved a patient who required the replacement of an abdominal artery, surgery that involved a significant risk of mortality. The patient was covered under the California Medicaid program (Medi-Cal), which approved a ten-day hospital stay for the surgery. The patient developed postsurgical complications, and her physicians wanted to keep her in the hospital for another eight days to ensure against infection or a blood clot threatening the loss of her legs. Her three physicians filed the appropriate paperwork to request an eight-day extension from Medi-Cal, but only a four-day extension was approved. Although in disagreement with Medi-Cal's decision, the physicians went along with it and discharged the patient after four additional days. After discharge, her condition worsened, requiring her to be readmitted to the hospital for an above-the-knee amputation of her leg. The court stressed that ultimately the responsibility for medical decisions belongs to physicians: "[w]hile we recognize, realistically, that cost consciousness has become a permanent feature of the health care system, it is essential

---

[7]George L. Priest, *The Current Insurance Crisis in Modern Tort Law*, 96 YALE L.J. 1521, 1550-56 (1987).

[8]In 1853, a New Hampshire court stated in Leighton v. Sargent, 27 N.H. 460:

> [A physician] contracts with his employer (1) that he possesses that reasonable degree of learning and skill and experience which is ordinarily possessed by the professors of that same art or science . . . (2) . . . that he will use reasonable and ordinary care and diligence in the exertion of his skill and the application of his knowledge to accomplish the purpose for which he is employed . . . (3) to exert his skill and apply his diligence and care, the medical and other professional men contract to use their best judgment.

Forty-five years later, in Pike v. Honsiger, 49 N.E. 760 (N.Y. 1898), the principles established by the *Leighton* court were expanded. The *Pike* court added the much disputed "locality rule" and an obligation to "keep abreast of the times." These cases are discussed in IAIN HAY, MONEY, MEDICINE AND MALPRACTICE IN AMERICAN SOCIETY 7-9 (1992).

[9]192 Cal. App. 3d 1630 (1986).

that cost limitation programs not be permitted to corrupt medical judgment."[10]

### *Hospitals and Managed Care Organizations*

Traditionally, most hospitals were viewed as workshops for physicians, and because they typically were run by the government or religious organizations, they were provided sovereign and charitable immunity, respectively. By the late 1950s, however, most state legislatures and courts had lifted the immunities,[11] and by the mid-1960s courts no longer construed hospitals merely as physician workshops.

This is clearly enunciated by the landmark decision in *Darling v. Charleston Community Memorial Hospital*.[12] That case involved the amputation of an athlete's leg following improper emergency treatment by a nonemployed staff physician. In holding the hospital liable for the loss of the leg, the court stated:

> The conception that the hospital does not undertake to treat the patient, does not undertake to act through its doctors and nurses, but undertakes instead simply to procure them to act upon their own responsibility, no longer reflects the fact. Present-day hospitals, as their manner of operation plainly demonstrates, do far more than furnish facilities for treatment .... Certainly, the person who avails himself of "hospital facilities" expects that the hospital will attempt to cure him, not that its nurses or other employees will act on their own responsibility.[13]

The effect of *Darling* was the emergence of corporate liability. Hospitals now owe a duty to patients to use reasonable care to ensure their safety. This includes providing and maintaining safe physical premises; furnishing patients with properly functioning and up-to-date equipment and supplies;[14] and selecting, retraining, and monitoring medical staff.[15]

---

[10]*Id.* at 1645.

[11]The doctrine of charitable immunity appeared in McDonald v. Massachusetts Gen. Hosp., 120 Mass. 432 (1876), and now exists only in a limited capacity—that is, allows recovery up to the hospital's liability coverage limits (e.g., Etheridge v. Medical Ctr. Hosps., 376 S.E.2d 525 (Va. 1989)), and limits liability to nonpaying (charity) patients (e.g., Cutts v. DeKalb Hosp. Auth., 385 S.E.2d 436 (Ga. Ct. App. 1989)). Sovereign or governmental immunity, another common-law doctrine, is virtually nonexistent. The Federal Tort Claims Act, 28 U.S.C. §§ 1346(b), 2671-2680 (1988), generally has waived the federal government's immunity, and many states have waived their immunity through similar state statutes.

[12]211 N.E.2d 253 (Ill. 1965).

[13]*Id.* at 257 (citing Bing v. Thunig, 143 N.E.2d. 3, 8 (N.Y. 1957)).

[14]For example, in Washington v. Washington Hosp. Ctr., 579 A.2d 177 (D.C. 1990), a hospital was held liable for not having the latest monitoring technology for anesthesia. In Pearce v. Feinstein, 754 F. Supp. 308 (W.D.N.Y. 1990), a hospital was held liable for supplying defective instruments.

[15]For example, in Johnson v. Misericordia Community Hosp., 301 N.W.2d 156 (Wis. 1981), the hospital was liable for failing to make an adequate inquiry of the physician's credentials. If the hospital had made an adequate inquiry, it would have

Theories of corporate negligence have been extended to managed care entities. For example, in *Harrell v. Total Health Care*,[16] the plaintiff asserted that an independent practitioner association had a duty to the health plan's subscribers to select the plan's physicians carefully. The court concluded that the plaintiff had stated a cause of action for negligent selection and failure to prevent a foreseeable risk of harm because the health plan had not conducted an investigation of the negligent physician's credentials.

Under the principle of respondeat superior, meaning "Let the master answer," health care institutions and managed care organizations are also *secondarily* liable for the torts committed by their employees within the scope of employment. Under this theory, health care entities are clearly liable for employee physicians, like residents. Moreover, under agency principles, the actions of emergency room physicians, anesthesiologists, and radiologists—who typically are not employed by the health care entity[17]—will nonetheless give rise to liability for that entity if the patient reasonably believes that they are employees.[18] Thus, Section 429 of the *Restatement (Second) of Torts* provides:

> One who employs an independent contractor to perform services for another which are accepted in the reasonable belief that the services are being rendered by the employer or his servants, is subject to liability for physical harm caused by the negligence of the contractor in supplying such services, to the same extent as though the employer were supplying them himself or by his servants.

Similarly, Section 267 of the *Restatement (Second) of Agency* provides:

> One who represents that another is his servant or other agent and thereby causes a third person justifiably to rely upon the care or skill of such apparent agent is subject to liability to the third person for harm caused by the lack of care or skill of the one appearing to be a servant or other agent as if he were such.

---

discovered that the physician had falsified information in his application for staff privileges.

This responsibility has been codified in both state and federal statutes. For example, the Health Care Quality Improvement Act of 1986, Pub. L. No. 99-660, 100 Stat. 3784 (1986), requires health care institutions to check the National Practitioner Data Bank (containing information about disciplinary actions against physicians) prior to making staff appointments, to review periodically information about their staff physicians, and to report disciplinary actions involving a suspension of 30 days or more.

[16]781 S.W.2d 58 (Mo. App. 1989).

[17]Whether the health care institution will be held liable for the torts of the individual physician or other health care worker does not depend on whether the relationship is characterized as one between independent parties; instead, actual "control" is determinative. *See* Keller v. Missouri Baptist Hosp., 800 S.W.2d 35 (Mo. App. 1990).

[18]Pamperin v. Trinity Memorial Hosp., 423 N.W.2d 848 (Wis. 1988).

Many courts have applied these principles to find the health care institution liable for nonemployee physicians.[19]

*Third-Party Payors*

Third-party payors (i.e., health care insurers) may be held liable if denying benefits causes harm to the patient. The leading case in this area is *Wilson v. Blue Cross*,[20] which involved a hospitalized patient who suffered from severe depression, drug dependency, and anorexia. Although the admitting physician submitted a treatment plan that required four weeks of inpatient care, the utilization review (UR) firm employed by Blue Cross denied coverage for care beyond ten days. The patient was discharged from the hospital and committed suicide less than three weeks later. The court expressly rejected the payor's claim that its action was a "benefit determination" as opposed to a "medical treatment" decision, and decided as a matter of law that insurers and UR firms may be held liable for refusals to pay benefits where the payment decision was a substantial factor in causing injury to the person denied coverage.

Although cases like *Wilson* provide injured patients legal remedies against a third-party payor, including the right to recover compensation for the negligent deprivation of necessary care, the federal Employee Retirement Income Security Act of 1974 (ERISA)[21] preempts and supersedes state law. By doing so, it effectively allows self-insured employer-provided plans (more than two-thirds of employer-provided plans) to escape liability for negligent UR decisions.[22] Although there have been no reported cases of physician liability for negligent UR decisions, it can be anticipated that if the UR firm/

[19]*See, e.g.*, McDowell v. NKC, Inc., No. 89-CA-2221-S (Ky. Ct. App. 1990); Hardy v. Brantley, 471 So. 2d 358 (Miss. 1985).

[20]222 Cal. App. 3d 660 (1990).

[21]Pub. L. No. 93-406, 88 Stat. 829 (1974) (*see* 29 U.S.C. § 1002(1)).

[22]The best illustration is Corcoran v. United Healthcare, Inc., 965 F.2d 1321 (5th Cir. 1992). When Mrs. Corcoran came close to her pregnancy due date, her physician decided that she should be admitted to the hospital so that she and the fetus could be monitored around the clock. Her hospital stay had to be approved by United Healthcare, a UR firm hired by Mrs. Corcoran's employee insurance plan, which was administered by Blue Cross/Blue Shield. Despite considerable effort on the part of her physician to get her hospital stay approved, United determined that it was not necessary to hospitalize Mrs. Corcoran. Instead, United authorized 10 hours per day of home nursing care. During a time period when no nurse was on duty, the fetus went into distress and died. Mrs. Corcoran and her husband filed a wrongful death action against both BC/BS and United in a Louisiana state court, alleging that the unborn child died as a result of their negligence. This action was removed to federal court on the grounds that it was preempted by ERISA. The Fifth Circuit concluded that the claim was indeed preempted by ERISA and that ERISA provided the Corcorans' exclusive remedy. The remedies under ERISA do not include compensation or punitive damages for medical negligence.

payor is not liable for them, then the physician, who may be the only deep pocket left, will be the patient's only potential source of a remedy.

*Manufacturers of Medical Products*[23]

Manufacturers of medical products are typically liable under one of three legal doctrines: negligence, breach of warranty, or strict liability.

To sue successfully for negligence in product liability, a plaintiff must show that the defendant breached his or her responsibility to exercise reasonable care in the design, manufacture, assembly, testing, or inspection of the product. A drug manufacturer would likely be found negligent if a drug was not manufactured in accordance with product specifications and "current good manufacturing practices," and the specific failure was causally linked to the injury. Currently, drug and medical device manufacturers almost always follow current good manufacturing practices, which prevent manufacturing defects, so traditional product liability suits are rare. Most suits invoking the negligence doctrine base their claim on the duty to warn, although increasingly plaintiffs allege failure to conduct adequate general safety testing and sometimes improper design.

The duty to warn can be applied in suits invoking either the negligence or strict liability doctrines. Generally, the legal duty is to warn medical professionals, as "learned intermediaries," about the inherent dangers in the use of the product. Once warned, learned intermediaries are presumed to understand the risks and weigh them against the expected benefits to be derived from the use of the product. If a manufacturer's package contains inserts, or the manufacturer distributes any other promotional materials, that are misleading, insufficient, or ambiguous, then the manufacturer would be held liable.

Warranties can be express or implied. Liability under express warranty allows recovery from a manufacturer whose product did not conform to an assertion by the manufacturer when the plaintiff relied on the assertion and, as a result of this nonconformance, was injured. Express warranties are based on oral or written statements and can be absolute. For example, if a drug company specifically stated that there were no contraindications to a drug but an individual was later shown to have a contraindication to that drug (even if the contraindication was discovered subsequent to the statement),

[23]The issues raised in this section are discussed more generally in chapter 1, *supra.*—Editor's note.

the manufacturer could be held liable. Liability under implied warranties arises if the product is distributed in a truly defective state or not fit for the intended purpose.

Manufacturers are held strictly liable for certain products regardless of fault. Almost all states recognize that prescription drugs and vaccines cannot be made completely safe, and manufacturers of them are specifically protected from strict liability by those states that have adopted comment k of Section 402A in the *Restatement (Second) of Torts*, which addresses such products. Comment k provides that when an unavoidably unsafe product is not unreasonably dangerous, its manufacturer is not liable for injuries resulting from its use, if the product is properly manufactured and contains an adequate warning. Thus, the comment does not provide absolute liability, but directs the claimant to challenge the adequacy of the drug's warning. Perhaps the most often-cited case is one in which California's supreme court expressly adopted comment k and applied it to all prescription drug products.[24] In earlier cases, courts in other states had reached the same conclusion and also applied comment k to all prescription drugs.[25]

Some state courts have held, however, that under certain circumstances a drug may not be afforded protection by comment k. For instance, in *Feldman v. Lederle Laboratories*, New Jersey's supreme court stated: "We see no reason to hold as a matter of law that all prescription drugs that are unsafe are unavoidably so. Drugs, like other products, may contain defects that could have been avoided by better manufacturing or design."[26] Thus, even though a drug may have been through the rigorous FDA approval process and found to be safe and effective, some courts have decided that it is truly a jury question whether drugs contain "defects" that could have been avoided.

Manufacturers of medical devices have another defense in California and elsewhere. The statute authorizing the federal Food and Drug Administration (FDA) to regulate medical devices contains a clause preempting state "requirements" that are different from or inconsistent with the federal regulatory requirements. Courts have read this clause to preempt state tort law claims based on aspects of medical devices that have been approved by the FDA.

[24]Brown v. Superior Court, 751 P.2d 470 (Cal. 1988). For a recent California case following *Brown*, see Artiglio v. Superior Court, 27 Cal. Rptr. 2d 589 (1994).

[25]*See, e.g.*, McKee v. Moore, 648 P.2d 23, 24 (Okla. 1982); Terhune v. A.H. Robbins Co., 577 P.2d 975, 977-79 (Wash. 1978).

[26]479 A.2d 374, 383 (N.J. 1984).

## III. Problems with the Current System

For decades, the United States has struggled with the growing inability of the existing civil justice system to resolve medical liability claims. Studies conducted by the Bush administration's Council on Competitiveness, the Reagan administration's Tort Policy Working Group, Congress's General Accounting Office, and the Department of Health and Human Services Task Force on Medical Malpractice and Insurance, to name just a few, agree that the current tort system, without substantial modification or reform, cannot resolve medical liability claims effectively and efficiently. Patients are denied access to the legal process, and the process itself entails great delay and expense. The system does not effectively deter negligent conduct and provide corrective justice and adequate compensation for those injured. As Jeffrey O'Connell, a noted expert on torts, has observed:

> The determination in a malpractice case of a health care provider's fault requires complex and unpredictable litigation which attempts to unravel the often largely unknown mysteries of causation of injury and illness and to determine the appropriateness of treatment procedures about which experts are often bitterly divided. The process is lengthy, and the results are erratic. Some injured patients recover nothing. Some receive less than fair compensation, some recover amounts far in excess of their actual losses. Large portions of the awards depend on subjective and emotional considerations. The results are often fortuitous, yet society pays high costs for operating this unsatisfactory lottery.[27]

The specific results of the "unsatisfactory" system are briefly summarized below.

### *Unpredictable Awards and "Junk Science"*

Because the current tort system relies heavily on juries, it is not optimally suited for resolving medical negligence issues. Many scholars blame the jury system for the wide variance of both damage awards and recoveries. And because juries are not required to provide reasons for their verdicts, these decisions offer little guidance to physicians, patients, product manufacturers, or attorneys for resolution of future claims. Consequently, they discourage many non-negligent actions while failing to deter actual negligence. Finally, most jurors lack the ability to resolve technical disputes or evaluate expert testimony about what the duty of care is, whether a possible breach of the duty caused the injury in question, or whether a warning adequately conveyed a product's risks.

[27]Jeffrey O'Connell, The Case Against the Current Malpractice System (Feb. 21, 1984) (paper presented at National Medical Malpractice Conference).

"Expert testimony" itself has been called into question. Concerns specifically with the appropriate role, responsibilities, and qualifications of medical expert witnesses continue to be raised frequently in debate on professional liability issues. Much of the discussion has focused on the "professional" expert witness who earns a substantial portion of his or her income from medical-legal consulting activities. These witnesses bear much of the blame for the proliferation of "junk science" in the courtroom.[28]

Other questions have been raised about witnesses from academic settings who, while highly trained, may be unfamiliar with practice settings that have limited resources or other circumstantial factors that bear on the care that can be rendered. The relaxation in courts of foundational standards for qualifying medical expert testimony also has been identified as one of many factors distorting the standard of care by which physician defendants are judged.

The common denominator for all of these concerns is the conclusion that the legal process for resolving liability claims is being abused through the introduction of biased, overly partisan, or unqualified medical testimony.[29]

### *Cost of Liability Insurance*

The medical-professional liability insurance industry has gone through two "crisis" periods. The first crisis, in the 1970s, is referred to as the availability crisis; the second, in the 1980s, as the affordability crisis. Before the insurance crisis of the mid-1970s, large multiline property and casualty insurance companies provided the majority of medical liability coverage. In the late 1960s and early 1970s,

[28] *See, e.g.*, PETER W. HUBER, GALILEO'S REVENGE: JUNK SCIENCE IN THE COURTROOM (1991).

[29] In 1992, the AMA, together with numerous medical societies participating in the AMA/Specialty Society Medical Liability Project, filed an amicus curiae brief with the U.S. Supreme Court in Daubert v. Merrell Dow Pharmaceuticals, Inc., 113 S. Ct. 2786 (1993). The brief argued that the Federal Rules of Evidence require judges to make a determination that expert opinion offered by a party was based upon scientific knowledge, as evinced by publication in a peer-reviewed journal or other reliable indicator of a sound scientific methodology. The Supreme Court held that judges had an obligation in every case to conduct a "preliminary assessment" that expert opinion was in fact based on scientific knowledge.

The Pharmaceutical Manufacturers Association also filed an amicus curiae brief in the *Daubert* case, arguing that there is an important public health interest in the availability of medicines that have been shown to be safe and effective. The FDA makes safety and effectiveness decisions based on generally accepted scientific principles, but its scientific decisions can be negated by a tort system that allows experts to testify based on individual views that have not been subjected to the scrutiny of the scientific community.

however, the number of claims filed against physicians (the frequency of claims) and the size of awards and settlements (the severity of claims) began to accelerate dramatically. This phenomenon made it difficult to predict future claims experience and to calculate the amount of premium income that needed to be raised. As a result, every major multiline carrier, with the notable exceptions of the St. Paul Companies and the Medical Protective Company, ceased or greatly curtailed its underwriting of medical liability coverage, thereby creating an acute "insurance availability" crisis. For most of the nation's physicians in private practice, insurance simply could not be purchased at any price.

As these commercial insurers withdrew from the professional liability insurance market and the premiums charged by the remaining insurers rose dramatically, groups of physicians, often working through their state medical societies, began to establish their own medical liability insurance companies. In contrast to the commercial companies, which are organized as profit-making entities, most of the physician-owned insurance companies are not-for-profit enterprises. Since the mid-1970s, these physician-owned and -directed insurance companies have become a major force in the malpractice insurance market, and now insure more than half of the physicians in this country who purchase their own insurance.

The malpractice liability crisis of the 1970s appeared to have been resolved by the end of that decade. The growth in frequency and severity of claims reached a plateau. Liability insurance was available, at rates that were higher than in the early 1970s but relatively stable. But during the 1980s another crisis shook the insurance industry, as the frequency and severity of claims spiraled again. Premiums that had leveled off in the 1970s and early 1980s rose rapidly in the mid-1980s.

This affordability crisis dramatically affected the practices of some physicians. Physicians in some specialties, notably obstetrics and gynecology, cut back on the performance of high-risk procedures and the treatment of high-risk patients to keep the cost of their premiums down and to avoid liability.

The insurance crises, which in hindsight appear to be cyclical, have been attributed to a number of interrelated factors, including longer statutes of limitation; changes in the attitudes of patients toward their physicians, including an increased willingness on the part of patients to sue; inflation; increasingly liberal court decisions; and larger settlements and judgments.

Premium costs ultimately are passed on to patients. For each baby delivered in Florida, for instance, $1,119 goes to pay liability insurance. Physicians in some states pay hundreds of thousands of dollars annually for liability coverage. Liability costs for obstetrician-gynecologists are so high that in some states more than half the family physicians have discontinued obstetrics altogether. Many rural counties no longer have even one doctor who provides obstetric care.

The estimated annual cost of physicians' and health care facilities' liability insurance—not including cost of insurance for other health care workers and manufacturers of medical products—is more than $9 billion. This figure is just the tip of the iceberg. It does not take into account the costs of defensive medicine, discussed next.

### *Defensive Medicine and Other Costs to Patients*

"Defensive medicine" is practiced when physicians and health care providers, fearing malpractice claims, protect themselves by ordering redundant laboratory exams or consultations. The pervasive threat of a liability dispute disrupts clinical decisionmaking, encouraging a defensive posture among physicians and adding billions of dollars in defensive-medicine costs to the bill for health care services. In 1991, the cost of defensive medicine was estimated to be as high as $25 billion.[30]

Seventy-eight percent of all physicians report that the threat of professional liability encourages them to order tests that they might not otherwise consider necessary. Among hospital-based physicians and surgeons, the figure is 87% and 86%, respectively, and among young physicians, 84%. If these practices were eliminated, the U.S. health care system could save approximately $35.8 billion over the next five years.[31]

For patients, liability creates a significant obstacle to affordable health care—and, in some instances, to receipt of health care at all.[32] As of 1990, 12% of physicians who practiced obstetrics had given up this portion of their practices for liability-related reasons. Another 24% had reduced the number of high-risk pregnancies they handled. As Otis Bowen, former Secretary of the U.S. Department of Health and Human Services, said, a physician used to treat a child's bump on the head with advice to "go home and put ice on it. Now you give him $100 worth of X-rays and tell him to go home and put ice on it." These costs have adversely affected some health insurers' ability to continue to provide full benefits.

The liability costs borne by makers of medicines and medical products contribute additional billions to the national health care

---

[30]Lewin-VHI, Inc., Estimating the Costs of Defensive Medicine (Jan. 27, 1993).
[31]*Id.*
[32]Patricia M. Danzon, *Liability for Medical Malpractice*, 5 J. Econ. Persp. 51 (1991).

bill. In 1990, $10.8 billion was paid to claimants in all medical product-liability cases in the U.S.—and that does not include associated administrative and legal defense costs. This liability burden results in more hidden costs for patients, increases the cost of developing and manufacturing medicines, and has forced companies to take some needed medicines off the market. Even more troubling, it discourages companies from pursuing some research projects that could lead to medical breakthroughs.

Two good examples of these problems involve pertussis and AIDS. Until an effective vaccine was developed in the late 1940s, pertussis, or whooping cough, was a leading killer and crippler of children. Later, although no sound scientific study ever confirmed any cause-and-effect relationship between the pertussis vaccine and any adverse neurological reactions, many lawsuits were filed against vaccine manufacturers. Between 1960 and 1985, seven of the eight vaccine manufacturers withdrew from the market. To prevent a dangerous shortage of the vaccine, a liability fund was established and financed by an increase in the cost of the vaccine.

Similarly, the climate of uncertainty created by liability exposure has discouraged AIDS vaccine research. Several companies have abandoned research projects or postponed clinical trials of promising vaccines because of liability concerns, according to an April 1992 report in *Science* magazine. While some drugs that treat AIDS and other diseases associated with AIDS have been approved, liability remains one concern that has discouraged research into and official testing of possible vaccines.

### *Suits Do Not Correspond with Negligent Events*

The 1990 Harvard Medical Practice Study of patient charts in New York hospitals shows that the medical records of 1% of the patients admitted in 1984 reflect a "negligent adverse event," but only 8 of the 306 patients so identified filed liability claims. Conversely, 80% of all liability claims filed did not show evidence of negligence.[33] In sum, the physician's chance of being sued bears little relation to whether he or she is negligent; the correlation between negligent adverse events and actual claims was minimal.

Other studies show that physicians ultimately are exonerated in the majority of claims filed, but only after years of litigation and thousands of dollars in defense costs.[34] For instance, they indicate

[33] HARVARD MEDICAL PRACTICE STUDY, PATIENTS, DOCTORS, AND LAWYERS: MEDICAL INJURY, MALPRACTICE LITIGATION AND PATIENT COMPENSATION IN NEW YORK (1990).

[34] GENERAL ACCOUNTING OFFICE, MEDICAL MALPRACTICE: CHARACTERISTICS OF CLAIMS CLOSED IN 1984 (1987).

only one percent of patients are injured by negligent care, yet the frequency of medical malpractice claims doubled between 1982 (3.2 claims per 100 physicians) and 1988 (6.4 claims per 100 physicians). In 1989, this figure increased again to 7.4 per 100 physicians.[35] These findings strongly suggest that the tort system is functioning poorly as a screen for identifying meritorious claims. Moreover, this inefficient process is a costly one. The General Accounting Office estimates that 43% of total insurer defense costs are spent on claims that ultimately are closed in the defendant's favor.

*Inadequate and Untimely Compensation of Patients*

Only about forty cents of every dollar spent on medical liability litigation actually reaches injured patients. The majority is spent on attorney fees for both sides, litigation expenses, and insurance administration costs. Studies show that 60% to 75% of cases are ultimately closed with no payment going to the claimant; these nonmeritorious cases are expensive and add significantly to the liability system's administrative costs. Thus, when a patient pursues a legitimate claim, the remedy is extremely reduced, by approximately 38%, because of attorney fees and other expenses.[36]

Studies also show that most people injured by medical negligence do not gain access to the liability system at all. Despite its inflated costs, the liability system is inaccessible to most injured patients. In any other part of the insurance or medical services sector, this would be unconscionable, but it is business as usual in the medical liability system.

Thus, a small percentage of claimants are handsomely compensated by a system that places no upward limit whatsoever on jury awards, but most people are undercompensated.

The compensation is not only inadequate but also untimely. On average, it takes more than two years from the filing of a medical liability claim to its resolution. More complex cases involving large sums are resolved on an even more protracted basis; typically it takes from six to ten years in urban areas to resolve a claim. Complex pretrial procedures, the convoluted process of discovery, and overcrowded dockets account for the delay that characterizes the legal process as it now functions.

Who pays for this waste and inefficiency? In the end, we all do—as patients. We pay a price for the unreasonable fear created by a system that, in effect, transmits the message that every patient is

---

[35]Source: American Medical Association Center for Health Policy Research.

[36]TILLINGHAST, A TOWERS & PERRINS CO., TORTS COST TRENDS: AN INTERNATIONAL PERSPECTIVE (1992).

a potential plaintiff, whether or not one practices good medicine or produces a safe drug. We pay the insurance premiums for physicians, hospitals, and medical product producers, all of which have been passed on to us in the cost of health care services. Most importantly, patients injured by medical negligence "pay" if they are not adequately compensated.

## IV. Reform of the Current System

Although many agree that the civil justice system as it applies to medical liability disputes does not optimally serve the interests of injured patients, health care providers, or the public, there is less consensus about how to fix it. No one is recommending that negligent health care providers and medical product manufacturers be let off the hook. They should be held accountable for their actions. But what both patients and health care providers deserve is a dispute resolution and compensation mechanism that works fairly, quickly, and cost-consciously for everyone.

Recent polls show that the American public is quite aware of the toll that excessive and often unfounded liability suits have taken on the cost, availability, and quality of health care. A poll conducted by the American Medical Association in 1992 revealed that 63% of U.S. adults think the number of malpractice suits against doctors is higher than justified, and 55% think the amount of money awarded to patients by juries in these suits is usually too much. The same survey indicated that 71%, the highest response ever, favor a ceiling on pain and suffering awards. According to a 1991 Gallup poll, 77% think malpractice lawsuits and awards are an important reason why health care costs are rising. The *Los Angeles Times* found that, when given seven possible reasons why health care is so expensive, people are most likely to name malpractice suits. A recent survey of citizens in five states shows that the average voter would not elect a candidate endorsed by plaintiffs' lawyers.[37]

Alternatives to the existing system have been proposed and employed in various states.[38] For instance, voluntary arbitrations and specific modifications in the existing tort system designed more or less to control or supplant juries have been enacted. There is

[37]Similar polling data are discussed in chapter 9.—Editor's note.

[38]For a summary and discussion of state initiatives, see AMERICAN TORT REFORM ASS'N, STATE LAWS ON MEDICAL LIABILITY (1994); OFFICE OF TECHNOLOGY ASSESSMENT, U.S. CONGRESS, IMPACT OF LEGAL REFORMS ON MEDICAL MALPRACTICE COSTS (1993); AGENCY FOR HEALTH CARE POLICY & RESEARCH, DEP'T OF HEALTH & HUMAN SERVICES, COMPENDIUM OF STATE SYSTEMS FOR RESOLUTION OF MEDICAL INJURY CLAIMS (1991); AMA, TORT REFORM COMPENDIUM (1989). [*See also infra* chapter 11.—Editor's note.]

empirical evidence that "alternative dispute resolution" has been effective. Such reforms are discussed below.

*Alternative Dispute Resolution*

Alternative dispute resolution (ADR) could ameliorate the problems of delay, expense, and access to the civil justice system, and warrants further study as a viable means of mitigating problems that pervade the traditional strategies for deciding medical liability claims.

A number of states experimented with ADR programs in the 1970s and 1980s, with mixed results. Arbitration and mediation constitute the primary forms of ADR that are being pursued both at state and federal levels, along with a variety of other procedural options—for example, summary jury trials, minitrials, early neutral evaluation, outcome-determinative mediation, and "settlement weeks."[39] The problems detailed earlier in this chapter, which appear to be inherent in the traditional jury-based civil justice system, have led to the development of these procedural options for resolving claims.

A more efficient procedure than litigation, ADR is designed both to expedite claims resolution and to lower transaction costs. Studies have shown that attorneys spend considerably less time preparing cases for arbitration than they would spend preparing them for trial. The hearings take less time and, therefore, when attorneys charge by the hour, their fees are substantially lower than fees charged for cases that go to trial.

Researchers have also studied whether parties view such procedures as an inferior form of justice, representing denial of due process and procedural fairness. The findings on this issue have been very positive as well. In every jurisdiction in which court-ordered arbitration has been studied, both plaintiffs and defendants, and their attorneys, whether winners or losers, reported high satisfaction with the arbitration process and its outcome.

Adherents of ADR frequently call for the substitution of neutral scientific experts for lay decisionmakers at some stage of the litigation process and with respect to some issues. While few of the ADR procedures currently operating within courts mandate this option,

[39]"ADR" is the term applied to a number of different substitutes for traditional courtroom litigation. It is being used increasingly in many sectors, with demonstration experiments being conducted in the states and at various levels in the judicial system. ADR may be either voluntary on the part of the parties or mandatory. If mandatory, it is usually imposed as a precursor to bringing a claim in the civil justice system. The ADR decision or result may be either binding (barring the subsequent pursuit of a claim in the courts) or nonbinding. [Many of these reforms are discussed more generally in chapter 8.—Editor's note.]

experts may participate by stipulation of both parties or through discretionary authority of the judge. It has been suggested that better opportunities for using neutral scientific experts, or others with specialized knowledge, may exist outside of court settings. Within the court setting, medical malpractice panels have been recommended as an obvious mechanism for involving experts in resolving medical disputes, particularly with respect to complex cases, such as neurologically-impaired infant claims.

More dramatic alternatives than ADR, such as no-fault insurance and enterprise liability, also have been proposed. They are discussed next.

*No-Fault*

Proposals for a no-fault system, much like that in place for automobile accidents, raise an immediate and reasonable concern: its potential cost and the effect it will have on deterrence. The basic no-fault idea as employed in the automobile context is not perfectly suited to the unique problems which arise in medical liability cases. No one knows how many more claims might require compensation under a no-fault system for medical liability. Moreover, it is generally accepted that physicians should not be responsible for compensating "injuries" that are a natural consequence of treatment or disease, as opposed to negligence. Thus, although a no-fault system for medical liability would be free of the expense of proving negligence, there would remain the significant costs associated with proving the complex element of causation.

The reason no-fault is attractive to some is that it satisfies an essential requirement for abolishing the common-law malpractice action—namely, that there be a significant quid pro quo provided to the patients in order to justify withdrawing their claims from the civil justice system. No state legislature or court will be favorably disposed to approve a solution which appears to take rights from patients, especially those suffering from iatrogenic injuries (i.e., those alleged to have been the fault of a health care professional).

*Enterprise Liability*

Among the proposals the Clinton administration has recommended is one that would transfer medical liability exposure from individual health care professionals to a single defendant—Accountable Health Plans (AHPs).[40] Although it is well accepted that the

[40]The Health Care Security Act of 1993, also known as the Clinton Health Plan, does contain some modest tort reform proposals: a medical specialist would have to certify for any claim that the care provided deviated from the standard of care; all claims would be submitted to alternative dispute resolution; contingency fees would be capped at 33-1/3%; evidence of payments received from third parties would be

current system must be reformed, enterprise liability cannot substitute for proven tort reform efforts. Shifting the cost of insurance and defense does precious little to resolve the inherent problems of the system, in addition to running afoul of current ethics, policy, and law.

On the surface, enterprise liability, as it is called, may seem to be an attractive alternative, because it would relieve physicians of direct premium costs. But it is not real tort reform. Enterprise liability will not contain liability costs, since it merely shifts them from one part of the health care system (doctors) to another (AHPs). This system would in fact likely lead to increased health care prices, since the AHP would be the ultimate faceless "deep pocket," making people more likely to sue and juries more likely to make extravagant awards, regardless of whether a health care professional was actually at fault.

Moreover, transferring all liability exposure to the AHPs and empowering them to micromanage the medical staff tells physicians that the most important thing is to follow the rules—the rules of a large business with its own incentives to cut costs.

Finally, the cost of professional liability insurance would not be eliminated, but simply shifted to the enterprise from the physician. This increased financial burden placed on already financially insecure hospitals may lead even more of them to close their doors. To minimize this effect, it has been suggested that physicians pay surcharges to the enterprise in which they practice.[41] One could foresee that the amount paid would reflect the enterprise's cost of liability insurance and the implementation and maintenance of enterprise-based activities required to ensure that physicians do not act in a negligent manner. And, in addition to paying surcharges, physicians would still have to purchase insurance to cover their exposure for nonenterprise-related activity.[42]

### *MICRA-Like Reforms*

In 1975, California doctors apparently faced an unpleasant choice: should they close their doors altogether, face the prospect of practicing without insurance, or dramatically raise their fees? California

admissible at trial; and either party could request that the payment of the award be spread out in periodic installments. In addition, the use of practice guidelines would be expanded.

[41] Kenneth S. Abraham & Paul C. Weiler, Organizational Liability for Medical Practice (1993).

[42] *See, e.g.*, Physician Insurers Association of America, Enterprise Liability: A Mechanism for Shifting Costs? (1993); Patricia M. Danzon, Enterprise Liability (May 4, 1993) (unpublished draft) (physicians who practice in a number of different plans would be covered by different insurance companies, and the information on their overall claims experience would be fragmented).

physicians faced the highest malpractice insurance premiums in the world, with rates increasing by a staggering 300% to 400% in a single year. Consumers, doctors, hospitals, and insurance carriers across the state demanded legislative relief. The solution was the Medical Injury Compensation Reform Act of 1975, or MICRA.[43]

MICRA ensures full and adequate compensation for all actual losses, yet contains costs by placing various controls on the "lottery" aspects of the medical liability system. It contains four key provisions. The first is a cap on noneconomic damages. Patients can still recover 100% of their medical bills, lost wages, and other out-of-pocket expenses resulting from medical negligence, but a $250,000 limit is placed on noneconomic damages awards above and beyond those basic losses. The second key provision is a limit on attorney fees. A new sliding-scale contingency-fee schedule ensures that patients, not lawyers, receive the bulk of awards. MICRA's third key provision is a double-recovery disclosure. A jury must be notified if a plaintiff has already received payment for economic losses from other sources, such as workers' compensation, disability, or health insurance. Finally, MICRA requires the periodic payment of future damages. These installments preserve funds for medical treatment or income that may become necessary in the future.

MICRA's four key provisions have the strongest impact on very large claims, where the contingency-fee system has the potential to make a lawyer a millionaire with a single case. Even for these large claims, MICRA ensures that patients are fully compensated for all out-of-pocket losses. By reducing contingency fees as awards rise, MICRA guarantees that the most seriously injured patients keep more of any award. MICRA's $250,000 ceiling on noneconomic damages is still very generous, much more than any other country in the world allows. In practice, MICRA affects less than two percent of the cases filed, yet it saves a tremendous amount of money by screening out "lottery" awards.

Eighteen years after its passage, MICRA continues to be a model for liability reform across the country. It has provided stability and predictability in California's insurance system. It also ensures that patients will be covered if they suffer medical negligence, and encourages quick settlement of valid claims. The limits on contingent fees, along with limits on noneconomic damages, encourage

[43]1975 Cal. Stat. 3949, codified at CAL. BUS. & PROF. CODE § 6146 (West 1990) (attorney fees); CAL. CIV. PROC. CODE §§ 340.5 (statute of limitations), 667.7 (periodic payment), 1295 (voluntary arbitration), 3333 (damage caps), 3333.1 (collateral source rule) (West 1982). MICRA was the most comprehensive reform enacted during the height of the "availability" malpractice crisis of the mid-1970s.

attorneys to settle cases out of court rather than pursuing costly, lengthy litigation with the hope of a "lottery" award from the jury.

Moreover, MICRA has contained medical malpractice premiums, which have risen sharply in other states. Thanks to MICRA, California ob-gyn premiums, which were the highest in the nation in 1975, now rank fifteenth. Internal-medicine premiums rank seventeenth, and surgical premiums nineteenth. In fact, medical malpractice premiums paid by California physicians are one-third to one-half the cost of premiums in those states which have not enacted similar reforms. This is especially remarkable because the cost of living in many areas of California is well above the rest of the nation. While a California obstetrician pays $40,000 annually to obtain the typical level of malpractice insurance coverage, the average Florida obstetrician pays an astounding $152,000, and the average New York obstetrician pays $94,000.

As a result, a recent "Families USA" study cites the average New York family's health care costs in 1991 as $5,585, while in California it was $4,433. MICRA has given patients access to high-tech, high-risk but essential medical products and procedures. Without the stability that MICRA provides, most doctors could not survive the liability exposure of performing these procedures.

While the MICRA reforms do not apply to medical products (such as drugs and devices), but only to medical providers, other aspects of California's law have served to provide some stability to the litigation climate in California for medical products. Perhaps most important is the *Brown* decision, which holds that prescription drugs are unavoidably unsafe and therefore not defective if properly manufactured and accompanied by an adequate warning.[44] Another California law, applicable to all personal injury cases including claims against medical product manufacturers, has eliminated joint and several liability for both economic and noneconomic damages. Even with these limits on liability and recoverable damages, lawyers involved in defending suits against medical-product manufacturers report that in some cases the plaintiff's lawyer, or the judge, has demanded a higher settlement from the manufacturer to compensate for limits on the plaintiff's recovery from the medical provider.

### *AMA Strategy*

Besides immediate implementation of MICRA-like reforms,[45] there needs to be a more fundamental alternative that can serve as

[44]*See supra* p. 42 & n.24.

[45]Some federal legislative initiatives should create uniform standards of medical liability law like those contained in MICRA. *See, e.g.*, The Federal Health Care Liability Act of 1994 (June 1994) (Health Care Liability Alliance (*see infra* note 54) model legislation).

a model for those states that seek to halt the recurring crises in medical liability which periodically have threatened the average person's access to quality health care. The American Medical Association's Specialty Society Medical Liability Project (AMA/SSMLP) recommends a comprehensive reform approach with three major components.[46] Developed in conjunction with thirty-one national medical specialty societies and first published in 1986, the AMA/SSMLP model has since been extensively reviewed and analyzed by legal and economic scholars. It would deliver more compensation dollars to more patients equitably and efficiently without increasing total system costs, and has the potential to reduce the incidence of negligent injuries by better coordinating physician oversight and patient-safety systems.

The first major component of the model is a replacement of the common-law cause of action for medical malpractice with an administrative claim for medical negligence. This breaks no new ground. State legislatures abolished the common-law cause of action for personal injury in the workplace just after the turn of the century. In its place, states enacted workers' compensation schemes.[47] Thus, as a possible alternative to the jury system, AMA/SSMLP proposes that an administrative, fault-based system be employed. Such a system can be structured so that it provides patients and the public with significant advantages over the existing tort system. It can provide access to recovery that is currently unavailable, incentives

[46]The AMA/SSMLP is a coalition of more than 30 medical and specialty organizations and societies, including: American Academy of Family Physicians; American Academy of Orthopaedic Surgeons; American College of Cardiology; American College of Obstetricians and Gynecologists; American College of Physicians; American College of Radiology; American College of Surgeons; American Medical Association; American Society of Anesthesiologists; Council of Medical Specialty Societies; Society of Thoracic Surgeons; American Academy of Allergy and Immunology; American Academy of Dermatology; American Academy of Facial Plastic and Reconstructive Surgery; American Academy of Neurology; American Academy of Ophthalmology; American Academy of Otolaryngology—Head and Neck Surgery; American Academy of Pediatrics; American Association of Thoracic Surgery; American Association of Neurological Surgeons; American Association of Plastic Surgeons; American College of Chest Physicians; American College of Emergency Physicians; American College of Gastroenterology; American College of Legal Medicine; American Psychiatric Association; American Society of Clinical Pathologists; American Society of Cytology; American Society for Dermatologic Surgery; American Society of Plastic and Reconstructive Surgeons; American Society for Surgery of the Hand; American Urological Association; College of American Pathologists; Congress of Neurological Surgeons; International Society for Cardiovascular Surgery; Society of Nuclear Medicine; and the Society for Vascular Surgery.

[47]Similarly, no-fault mechanisms have replaced the civil justice system with respect to injuries caused by automobiles. A no-fault, administrative system for medical liability is already in place in Virginia and Florida for the limited category of cases involving newborns. Nonetheless, for the reasons discussed above at p. 51, there are serious problems with using the no-fault approach in the medical liability area.

and mechanisms to enhance the quality of medical care, and more predictable determinations of liability and damages. It can also resolve medical liability disputes more quickly and at less expense.

The other two components of the AMA/SSMLP approach are modification of the substantive legal rules for medical liability cases, and reform of the procedures for monitoring and disciplining physicians and encouraging patient-safety initiatives in a variety of sectors. All three components are discussed in greater detail below.

### Administrative Process

Under the AMA/SSMLP proposal, juries would be replaced by a state administrative agency, or Medical Board, possessing both rulemaking authority and the responsibility to adjudicate claims. The size of the Board most likely would vary with the size of the implementing jurisdiction; in the typical state, the Board would be governed by seven full-time members. Physicians and other representatives of the health care community would serve on the Board, but it is recommended that the majority of members be drawn from outside the medical community. Members would be nominated by a committee representing a number of societal interests and selected by the governor, subject to approval by the state legislature.

The Medical Board would act as a prehearing and initial hearing body. Claims would be resolved according to a staged process with conferences between the parties to encourage settlement at every stage. Parties who refuse reasonable settlement offers would be subject to responsibility for the opposing party's legal fees and expenses in proceeding. The process would begin when a simple form completed by the claimant, or his or her attorney, is filed with the Board.[48]

The first stage involves examination of a claim by a trained claims reviewer who has the power to order and review the medical record and any supplementary materials provided by the parties. Claims that clearly have no merit could be rejected at this stage, triggering immediate "appellate" review by a member of the Board. If the claims are found to have possible merit, the claims reviewer would arrange for expert review by up to two practitioners in the relevant specialty who would have the ability to interview both patients and providers. If both experts found no merit, the claim would be rejected, again triggering the right to review by a Board member. If

[48]The proposal includes a two-year "reasonable discovery" statute of limitations with a four-year statute of repose and a special exception for minors that would allow up to four years for children under six to initiate claims.

at least one expert found potential merit, a settlement conference would be held.

If settlement is not reached at the first settlement conference, the second stage would then ensue. At this point, the claim would be assigned to a hearing examiner or administrative law judge (ALJ). A distinguishing feature of the AMA/SSMLP proposal is that claimants would have the option to be represented by their own private counsel, with statutorily limited fees, or by counsel appointed and renumerated by the Medical Board, thereby providing access to claimants who cannot find affordable counsel on their own. During stage two, the ALJ would supervise an expedited discovery process, culminating in a second settlement conference. The ALJ would be authorized to make settlement recommendations at this juncture, when in most cases all the information needed to estimate the value of a claim should be available.

If no settlement is reached, stage three would proceed with a formal hearing before the same ALJ who supervised the stage two proceedings. Parties would be able to present evidence and cross-examine witnesses. The ALJ would render a written decision on liability and damages within ninety days of the hearing.

As a final stage, a losing party would have a right to review of the ALJ's decision by a three-member panel of the Board. The panel can adopt, modify, or reject the ALJ's decision. If the Board finds that the physician is liable, the physician would be required to pay damages within thirty days. If no Board review is formally requested, the Board has the responsibility to review the ALJ's decision to ensure that it does not contradict earlier decisions and to certify it as binding precedent for future cases.

Although the administrative process outlined in the AMA/SSMLP proposal is a substantial one, its emphasis on expeditiously identifying nonmeritorious claims and encouraging settlement at every stage suggests that, in operation, it would be faster and more cost-effective for all parties. The decision to provide legal counsel to claimants at no cost to them addresses the reality of the legal access problem. Efficiencies should be achieved as claims reviewers and ALJs develop institutional memory and expertise to apply to complex issues of medical science, causation, the standard of care, and the calculation of damages. In contrast, the jury must be educated with each case.[49]

[49]The AMA/SSMLP plan seeks to limit both plaintiffs' and defendants' efforts routinely to seek de novo review of the Board's decision before a jury, and recommends only limited judicial review of the Medical Board's decision in the intermediate appellate court of the state. Such review would be confined to determining whether the Board acted arbitrarily or capriciously, failed to follow its own rules, or otherwise abused its discretion.

### Modification of Substantive Rules

A second component of the AMA/SSMLP proposal recommends numerous changes to the substantive law governing medical liability.

Under the current proposal, the "locality rule"—allowing the standard of care to be based on customary local geographical practices—would no longer apply. Instead, the rule would be replaced by a standard of reasonableness determined by reference to the standards of the "prudent and competent practitioner" working under similar circumstances. The Medical Board would consider the physician's expertise, the state of medical knowledge, the availability of health care facilities, and the impact of the patient's other medical problems upon available treatment options. Many states already are moving in this direction in reforming the medical standard of care.

The proposal also recommends the modification of the causation standard to permit patients to recover if the physician's negligence represents a "contributing factor to the injury."

Informed consent, traditionally measured from the perspective of a reasonable physician, would instead be gauged from the point of view of the reasonable patient, consistent with the growing trend in a number of states.

Damages then could be apportioned according to the degree of the physician's fault, as determined by the ALJ.[50] Under the doctrine of joint and several liability, joint tort-feasors—for example, a physician and a health care institution—can be held liable independently for payment of the entire judgment. Where joint liability is eliminated, each defendant is liable for only the fault that is attributable to him. A relatively small number of states have abolished the doctrine for both economic and noneconomic damages, and a few more have limited its application to certain situations.[51]

The proposal also recommends a number of specific monetary guidelines for the payment of damages. If claim settlements are to be successfully encouraged, all parties must be given greater direction as to the value of a claim. Currently, many cases which clearly arise from negligent care go to trial because the parties cannot agree on the damages owed. The problem is particularly acute with respect to noneconomic damages—i.e., pain and suffering, loss of consortium, and emotional distress—where consistency is lacking from case to case. The size and variance of a small number of awards for

[50]Traditional tort doctrine denies recovery unless the physician was more than 50% responsible for the loss, if there is more than one possible cause for the injury.

[51]The constitutional problems with joint and several liability are discussed in chapter 2.—Editor's note.

noneconomic damages has made the cost of professional liability premiums skyrocket. For this reason, a number of states have limited the amount of noneconomic damages that are recoverable in medical injury lawsuits.[52] The damage caps range from $250,000 in California and many other states to $1 million in Wisconsin.

The AMA/SSMLP model also would permit the offset of payments from collateral sources. Currently, the collateral source rule prohibits the defense at trial from introducing evidence that the plaintiff has been compensated or reimbursed for his or her injury from any source other than the defendant (for example, private health insurance or workers' compensation). The absence of this evidence allows a "double recovery" and a windfall to the plaintiff. A number of states have enacted legislation to prevent such an occurrence. Some of the states have mandated that the court deduct third-party payments from any award, while others have left any reduction to the jury's or the court's discretion.

Periodic payment would be required for large awards, with noneconomic damages calculated according to a formula based on the average annual wage in the state and the life expectancy of the patient before the injury. Under a periodic payment system, damage payments are made over the actual lifetime of the plaintiff for the actual period of disability. This prevents a windfall to the plaintiff's beneficiaries if the plaintiff dies sooner than anticipated, and the insurer is able to fund these payments at a much lower cost than an equivalent lump sum. Other mechanisms exist to ensure that the damages compensate the patient rather than the attorney.[53]

### Patient Safety

A third component of the AMA/SSMLP proposal calls for increased coordination and analysis of information on substandard performances by physicians.

The medical community certainly recognizes that bad doctors exist and strongly supports efforts to identify them and stop them

[52]*See* Fein v. Permanente Medical Group, 695 P.2d 665 (Cal. 1985).

[53]For instance, attorney contingency fees can be based on a sliding scale, so that as the amount of the award increases, the percentage that is permitted as a contingency fee decreases. Many states, including California, Connecticut, Delaware, Florida, Illinois, Maine, Massachusetts, New Hampshire, New Jersey, New York, Pennsylvania, and Wisconsin, have adopted this approach. Thus, California's statute (CAL. BUS. & PROF. CODE § 6146 (West 1990)) provides:

> An attorney shall not contract for or collect a contingency fee for representing any person in an action against a health care provider based upon alleged professional negligence in excess of the following: (1) 40% of the first $50,000 recovered; (2) 33-1/3% of the next $50,000 recovered; (3) 25% of the next $500,000; and (4) 15% of any amount on which the recovery exceeds $600,000.

from practicing. Even one incident of medical malpractice is too much. For that reason, the AMA/SSMLP believes a strong effort to promote patient safety and injury prevention must be an essential component of medical liability reform.[54] This will not completely solve the medical liability system's problems or eliminate adverse outcomes, but any comprehensive tort reform effort should include effective monitoring and detection systems to rid the profession of physicians who endanger patient safety.

A 1984 Harvard medical malpractice study of injuries in New York hospitals found that only one percent of patients suffered avoidable "adverse events" during their stays. Despite this low percentage, however, the study indicates that numerous injuries could be avoided annually if additional, proactive patient-safety programs were implemented.

Essential elements of the patient-safety effort should include strengthening state licensing boards and the peer review process to better identify and discipline incompetent and unethical health care providers. The authority and power of state licensing or disciplinary boards to investigate and act on cases where there is evidence of substandard conduct also would be bolstered.

One option would be to use the ADR process outlined above to prosecute disciplinary actions as well. Under this scenario, a disciplinary hearing would be conducted by an ALJ, appealed to the Board, and then to the intermediate appellate court. Even if states choose to keep their disciplinary and liability claim-processing functions separate, assignment of the liability dispute-resolution system to the executive branch may foster the communication of information important to patient safety between agencies. For example, better data collection by the ADR Board may provide the basis for early warning systems that alert disciplinary authorities to a practitioner who has sustained more than the expected number of claims. In this respect, the ADR agency would better accomplish some of

[54]As a member of the Health Care Liability Alliance (HCLA), the AMA/SSMLP advocates that patient-safety measures be implemented at the federal level as part of health system reform. HCLA is a national coalition that supports effective federal health liability reform as an integral component of health system reform. In addition to promoting patient safety, HCLA supports the federal implementation of MICRA-like reforms and opposes enterprise liability. Other members of HCLA include: American Home Products; American Hospital Association; American Society of Healthcare Risk Managers; Biotechnology Industry Organization; Californians Allied for Patient Protection; Council of Community Blood Centers; The Doctor's Company; Health Industry Manufacturers Association; Health Insurance Association of America; Medical Protective Company; Medical Mutual Liability Insurance Society of Maryland; MEDMARC Insurance Company; MMI Companies, Inc.; National Association of Manufacturers; National Council of Community Hospitals; Pharmaceutical Research & Manufacturers of America; Physician Insurers Association of America; and the Physician Insurance Company of Michigan.

the goals underlying the establishment of the National Practitioner Data Bank.[55]

The patient-safety effort also should bolster confidentiality and immunity provisions to encourage witnesses to come forward; expand research to improve the ability to measure outcomes, accurately diagnose illnesses and injuries, and reduce medication errors; require health care delivery systems to have coordinated patient-safety programs in every hospital, clinic, and doctor's office; establish programs to improve communication between patients, physicians, and other health care professionals, and ensure that patients understand their treatment options so they can make informed decisions; and expand drug-use review programs to identify patients who are overtreated or reacting badly to a combination of prescription drugs.

### Georgetown Summary of Advantages of the AMA/SSMLP Project Model

An intensive analysis of the AMA/SSMLP project model was completed by the Georgetown University medicine and law centers. Their analysis revealed that this model would be fairer to both claimants and defendants, more cost-effective, and more systematic in deterring medical negligence and promoting patient safety than the present system.

According to the analysis, savings would be achieved through early identification and dismissal of frivolous cases, more efficient claims processing, lower legal fees, and the incorporation of effective damage guidelines. In particular, deadlines for each stage of the proceedings will result in improved efficiency, and ceilings on noneconomic damages and reduction in damage awards for payments from collateral sources will control costs and more fairly distribute noneconomic damage awards. There will also be broader access to the system since claimants will be able to receive legal representation at no cost.

During the prehearing and initial hearing phases, according to the analysis, expert personnel will be involved at each level of the decisionmaking process. Over time, their experience is expected to result in better evaluation of medical negligence claims than a jury could provide. Administrative law judges will be able to inject more fairness into the process as well. Medical Board involvement will

[55]Franklin M. Zweig, Seymour Perry, & Sandra S. Thurston, *Forcing a Truce Between Medicine and Justice*, *in* 1 COURTS, HEALTH SCIENCE & THE LAW 492 (1991); AMA/Specialty Society Medical Liability Project, A Proposed Alternative to the Civil Justice System for Resolving Medical Liability Disputes: A Fault-Based, Administrative System (Jan. 1988).

serve to increase consistency in the decisionmaking process in both liability determinations and the size of damage awards.

In addition, the model predicts that the performance-monitoring function will act as a constructive tool for education and rehabilitation. The reporting requirements incorporated into this aspect of the proposal will also substantially increase the amount of information available on physician performance, and the Medical Board will have broader authority to enforce discipline.

## V. Conclusion

The present liability system is broken and needs to be fixed. Reforms are necessary and available to meet the needs of injured patients who deserve fair compensation; to be fair to the health care sector, which is willing to assume its share of the responsibility for avoidable patient injury; and to achieve a better balance of litigation costs and benefits for society. Without strong support for reform, the "unsatisfactory lottery" will likely continue at enormous cost to us all.

CHAPTER 4

# VOLUNTEER IMMUNITY: PRODDING THE STATES

U.S. REPRESENTATIVE JOHN EDWARD PORTER

## I. Introduction

Legislative efforts at reform of our tort system can engender fierce controversy and extensive debate. Various interest groups will seldom agree even on the problems with our tort system. Small wonder, then, that there is no consensus on solutions.

I have experienced this debate firsthand through my work on issues of medical malpractice liability, product liability, and volunteer and nonprofit liability. Like many other members of Congress, I have been fortunate enough to work in two different legislative bodies: in my case, the Illinois General Assembly and the United States House of Representatives. In the general assembly, I learned how to go to work to solve problems—carrying sixty bills to final passage in the house in six years without ever suffering a single defeat—but I have learned that in Washington a great deal of time is devoted to blocking proposals and other defensive maneuvers.

The Volunteer Protection Act takes account of both considerations—the obstacles to tort reform and the unwillingness of Washington to take proactive steps on controversial and deep-seated problems. Thus, the Act addressed an area where there was a fair amount of consensus that liability protection was warranted, namely the services of volunteers. But the legislation also placed the onus for action on the state legislatures, conditioning certain federal funds on the enactment of state legislation. Identifying a small, discreet part of tort reform—that benefitted the nonprofit community and allowed states to address the problem in their own ways—was a realistic, achievable objective.

The Volunteer Protection Act was first introduced in 1985 and has never been enacted into law. Yet the story of this legislation is not a story of failure, but of success. When the bill was introduced, only a handful of states had addressed, or even considered, the question of volunteer and nonprofit liability. Today, virtually every state has a law on the books addressing this subject. Indeed, the simple existence of federal legislation and the efforts made to enact it set off a brushfire of legislative activity at the state level—exactly what I was seeking.

The Volunteer Protection Act is thus best understood as a model for how advocates of civil justice reform can make progress through pursuing limited and incremental objectives with primary emphasis at the state level.

## II. Development of the Volunteer Protection Act

### *Problems with Volunteer and Nonprofit Liability*

If you asked the average citizen about lawsuits, she would likely tell you about medical malpractice, automobile injuries, airplane crashes, and product liability. Chances are, she would not tell you that volunteers and the organizations they serve face liability issues.

But in fact there is such a problem—albeit not of the level facing manufacturers and medical providers—and the problem is a serious one. It begins with a number of lawsuits against volunteers and volunteer organizations, some of which have been highly publicized. One of the most widely reported of such horror stories involved Little League coaches in Runnymeade, New Jersey, who were sued when a fly ball injured a young player in the outfield. The central allegation in the cause of action was that the boy was a born infielder, not an outfielder, and the coaches knew it. This case was settled for $125,000.

The above example is one where direct service volunteers—the Little League coaches—were drawn into litigation. More common, perhaps, are suits against volunteers serving on boards of directors of nonprofit organizations rather than providing direct services. Such actions should come as little surprise to those familiar with the "deep pocket" syndrome which infects our legal system. Frequently, charitable organizations will seek out established and esteemed members of the community to serve on their boards. Such individuals help to lend visibility to the good works of the charity and can be very helpful in the fundraising so vital to any nonprofit organization. As a result, however, they are also ripe targets for plaintiffs' lawyers.

More serious perhaps than these individual suits, and the problems they have created for the particular defendants involved, is the public perception of volunteering as a risky undertaking. This fear of lawsuits has affected volunteer programs nationwide by discouraging individuals from coming forward to pledge their time for good causes.

In 1988, the Gannett Organization conducted a study using a database provided by the American Society of Association Executives. The study disclosed that approximately twenty percent of association executives of Section 501(c) nonprofit organizations were having trouble recruiting volunteers because of the fear of liability exposure. Volunteer board members approach the request to serve on an organization's board with caution, investigating the organization's history of lawsuits and its potential for liability risk. It is not that volunteers have been sued *successfully* in large numbers. The problem is that they have been named in many lawsuits and the costs of legal defense can be staggering.

In 1983, a man climbing Box Springs Mountain, overlooking Riverside, California, slipped on a boulder and plummeted some ninety feet, sustaining severe spinal injuries. Teammates from the volunteer Riverside Mountain Rescue Unit scrambled to aid a physician and a paramedic in mounting a ticklish nighttime helicopter evacuation. The unit's volunteers had saved hundreds of lives over the past thirty years. For their trouble, those involved in the emergency mission were sued two years later by the victim, who asked $12 million in damages. Despite the fact that the climber had been under the influence of alcohol at the time of the accident, he claimed that reckless and negligent rescue techniques had caused him to be a quadriplegic. The lawsuit was eventually dropped, but not before those involved had made a huge investment in their defense.

Thus, the exposure of volunteers to tort liability can be a serious, as well as expensive, problem. It is sometimes said that there is no problem at all—that the individual volunteer need only carry homeowner's or other general renter's insurance to protect himself from any liability. But these policies do not necessarily provide the needed protection and not everyone has such insurance. Such an attitude also ignores the reality of our judicial process—that the process of being hauled into court is traumatic and time-consuming, and that it is small comfort to be told that he or she probably will not be held personally liable in the end.

### *The Concept of Volunteer Protection*

The approach I have worked to develop is the concept of "volunteer protection"—quite simply, *the provision of tightly circumscribed civil liability immunity for individual volunteers*. To understand the approach embodied by volunteer protection, it is useful first to understand what it does *not* do.

First, it is not "charitable immunity"—that is, it does not revive the long-abandoned doctrine that charitable *organizations* should be immune from tort liability. Quite to the contrary, it clarifies that it is the organizations who must answer for tort claims.

Volunteer protection limits itself to the *individual* volunteer and, in so doing, serves a channelling function, directing legal action away from the individual volunteer and toward the organization. There are sound reasons for making a distinction between the liability of the volunteer and that of the organization. It encourages the organization to adopt risk-management practices that teach volunteers to avoid injuries, and allows an individual to volunteer services without fear of placing personal assets at risk. The organization itself is also, of course, usually in a better position to satisfy a judgment.

Second, volunteer protection is not protection for *paid* employees of charitable organizations. Such persons would continue to be treated under longstanding rules governing the liability of employee and employer. Considerations related to employees are different than those that pertain to volunteers, and the law should recognize this.

Third, it is also important to understand that volunteer protection does not provide immunity to child molesters, drunk drivers, and other bad actors. Volunteers who behave willfully or wantonly are not afforded protection from answering in court for their conscious or reckless misdeeds. Only what is called "simple negligence" is protected.

What volunteer protection *does* do is prevent the individual volunteer—whether board member or direct service volunteer—from being individually named in a cause of action and forced to defend herself against an allegation connected with her charitable activity. It is the premise of volunteer protection that the organization utilizing the volunteer—not the volunteer herself—should recompense any injury.

In so doing, volunteer protection makes a societal judgment that liability for simple negligence should be channeled away from individual volunteers and to the organization employing the volunteer. It recognizes that the organization should be responsible for its conduct and in so doing encourages organizations to behave safely and carefully.

### *The Volunteer Protection Act*

The federal Volunteer Protection Act reflects these principles.

Some advocates of tort reform believe that tort law should be federalized. This might make sense for product liability because those cases so often involve interstate commerce, conflicts of law, and choice of law. But that is usually not the case in volunteer litigation and, generally, I think it is fair and correct to recognize that, in our federal system, the states have preeminence in tort matters barring an overriding justification for federal treatment.

Nonetheless, the federal government can and should still play a role in prompting action by the states. The issue providing a model is the twenty-one-year-old drinking age. Responding to the problem of "blood borders" between states with different legal drinking ages in the mid-1980s, Congress conditioned federal highway funding on states raising their drinking age. As a member of Congress who represented a district with a blood border between Wisconsin and Illinois, I was very active in this fight. A similar approach was used to create the fifty-five mile per hour national speed limit, and it is an approach which has been upheld by the Supreme Court against constitutional challenge.[1]

The Volunteer Protection Act borrows from this idea. It outlines a model state law and then applies an incentive structure, qualifying states which adopt such a law for an increase of one percent in their Social Services Block Grants funds. These funds are expended on useful and cost-effective social service programs which depend heavily on volunteer participation, making them an appropriate subject for federal encouragement of state reform. The Act also allows an appropriate amount of time—two years—for a state to enact a volunteer protection law. In sum, the Volunteer Protection Act provides a gentle prod to encourage states to enact limited liability protection for volunteers at the state level.

The Volunteer Protection Act exempts volunteers from individual liability except in extreme circumstances. It states that individuals who are acting within their official capacity, whose behavior is neither willful nor wanton, are protected from having to answer in court individually for a lawsuit alleging any injury. States are allowed substantial latitude in crafting their statutes, and are permited, in particular, discretion with respect to five optional provisions in the model bill that were included to address specific concerns which have been raised over the years.

First, a state may include in its volunteer protection law the requirement that a volunteer organization abide by stipulated risk-management procedures, which may include the mandatory training of volunteers. Risk management is the logical analog to volunteer protection: there is no better protection from lawsuits than adherence to practices, policies, and procedures that minimize the likelihood of injury. Risk-management training is particularly important where volunteers work in high-risk areas, such as hospitals or youth sports programs, where proper procedures can significantly reduce

[1]South Dakota v. Dole, 483 U.S. 203 (1987).

the potential for damage or injury. Many states have readily adopted this qualification when drafting their volunteer protection bills.

Second, state volunteer protection laws may stipulate that the organization is liable for the acts and omissions of the volunteer to the same extent that an employer is liable, under the laws of that state, for the acts or omissions of its employees. This provision allows states to clarify that the doctrine of respondeat superior (the master responds for the torts of the servant) applies in the context of the volunteer and the organization. Generally, under this doctrine, the master (the volunteer organization) is liable where the acts or omissions of the servant produce injury or damage if the servant (the volunteer) is acting within the scope of his duties to the master. Similarly, a servant volunteer acting outside the scope of his duties is not protected. Thus, the effect of respondeat superior combined with limited volunteer immunity in the volunteer organization context is to ensure that an injured party can pursue an action against either the organization or the volunteer.

Third, the model law allows states to exclude from liability protection any volunteer operating a motor vehicle or vessel for which a pilot's license is needed. The purpose of this provision is to allow the states to ensure that volunteer immunity does not interfere with well-developed state law and insurance systems designed to compensate motor-vehicle injuries and damage and to deter unsafe driving. Ordinarily, motor vehicle insurance covers a driver regardless of whether he is operating his own vehicle or someone else's. Volunteers might, however, still face liability without insurance coverage in situations where they are operating a van or truck, but are insured only for operating a car. Also, if the volunteer were compensated for driving beyond expenses, standard auto policies might not apply (of course, in this situation, the volunteer is not acting as a volunteer).

Fourth, the model law allows an exemption in the case of a suit brought by an appropriate officer of the state or local government to enforce a federal, state, or local law. An example is an injunction or an action alleging conversion or tax evasion.

Fifth and last, states may also include in their volunteer protection law the stipulation that protection from liability applies only if the organization has a financially secure source of recovery for individuals who suffer injury as a result of actions taken by a volunteer on behalf of the organization or entity. A "financially secure source of recovery" may be an insurance policy within specified limits, comparable coverage from a risk-pooling mechanism, equivalent assets, or alternative arrangements that satisfy the state that the entity will be able to pay for losses up to a specified amount. Separate standards for different types of liability exposure may be specified.

This provision is intended to prevent the unfairness that would result to an injured party if the volunteer would be immune and the organization judgment-proof. The states can provide that, where the organization could not satisfy a judgment, the volunteer would remain personally liable.

Because these five provisions are optional, states that have enacted suitable volunteer liability laws, but that do not include all of the suggested provisions, will not be penalized if and when the federal volunteer protection law is passed. In addition, nothing in the Volunteer Protection Act preempts the laws of any state governing tort liability actions. It would, after all, be counterproductive to preempt state laws addressing volunteer liability that have been crafted to address the needs of that state, or to propound a model law that is so inflexible that it cannot be readily adopted by states.

The Volunteer Protection Act is a modest and balanced effort to encourage states to encourage volunteerism by providing limited liability protection for volunteers. The bill is a limited piece of legislation that allows states considerable latitude in designing their own laws. It is not a federal mandate, but a gentle nudge to encourage state action. Its purpose is neither to solve the liability crisis nor to assign blame for it, but solely to encourage Americans to keep volunteering and to assure them that they can do so without inordinate fear of ending up in court.

The nonprofit community has overwhelmingly endorsed this bill. Over 250 organizations—as diverse as the Big Brothers/Big Sisters of America, the American Red Cross, the General Federation of Womens' Clubs, and the Air Force Association, for instance—have expressed their support for the Volunteer Protection Act.

## III. Accomplishments and Status of the Act

### *What the Act Has Accomplished*

Although the Volunteer Protection Act has not been enacted into law by the U.S. Congress, its very existence, coupled with its strong grassroots support, has prodded the development of state laws. Indeed, the Act has set off a wave of volunteer-friendly legislation in the states.

Early volunteer protection laws were volunteer-specific. States responded narrowly to the liability concerns of the specific volunteers that were brought to the attention of state legislatures. Later on, more comprehensive statutes were passed.

For example, Wyoming granted partial immunity for amateur rodeo sponsors to protect them from the tort claims of injured cowboys. The Wyoming law stated that nonprofit organizations were not liable for injuries in connection with sponsorship of an amateur rodeo if the injured party was a contestant who voluntarily participated in the event and the injury was not the result of the willful, wanton, or reckless act of the sponsoring organization or its employees.[2] Years later, the state responded to growing liability concerns of volunteers and nonprofit organizations by enacting additional legislation. The current Wyoming law provides limited liability protection for volunteers exclusive of willful or wanton misconduct, gross negligence, or damages resulting from the negligent operation of a motor vehicle.[3]

Several years ago, Tennessee enacted a law to protect referees, umpires, linesmen, or persons serving in a similar capacity at a sports event who are registered with a local, state, regional, or national organization that provides training and educational opportunities for sports officials. This law excludes injury or damage inflicted intentionally or by gross negligence.[4] The same year, the Tennessee state legislature passed a law granting limited liability protection to directors and trustees of nonprofit organizations.[5] These laws improved the tort climate in Tennessee, but left the person filling the bowls in the soup kitchen still vulnerable.

Hawaii has responded to the liability crisis by granting limited immunity to volunteer firefighters who in good faith render firefighting services. The Hawaii law also states that, for the purposes of ratemaking, all insurers must treat a volunteer firefighter the same as a firefighter employed by a county fire department.[6] Nonetheless, Hawaii still does not have a general statute regarding volunteers.

While it is laudable that every state now has a law pertaining to legal liability of at least some types of volunteers, it is unfortunate that all of this legislation has contributed to a false impression that volunteers nationwide are immune from suit. To the contrary, many volunteers remain fully liable for any harm they cause and all volunteers remain fully liable for some actions. Only about half of the states protect volunteers other than directors and officers. Legislatures came to the aid of board members because they faced the worst insurance problems when most of the volunteer protection statutes were enacted. The resulting anomaly is greater protection for the volunteers who make policy than for the ones who carry it out.

---

[2]WYO. STAT. § 1-1-118 (1986).
[3]*Id.* § 1-1-125 (1992).
[4]TENN. CODE ANN. § 62-50-201 to -203 (Supp. 1989).
[5]*Id.* § 48-58-601.
[6]1993 Haw. Sess. Laws 269.

Moreover, every volunteer protection statute has exceptions. The most common and understandable are exclusions for claims based on a volunteer's willful or wanton misconduct, an exclusion allowed by the model bill of the Volunteer Protection Act. Several laws also include gross negligence or some other category above simple negligence. Unfortunately, a few laws even permit suits based on simple negligence, which nullifies the protection they purport to offer.

Beyond these intentional exclusions are gaps that result from the ambiguity in much of the legislation passed hastily at the height of the insurance crunch. Some of these laws are confusingly worded, exceptionally complicated, designed for profit-making corporations, or otherwise problematic. Even the very best laws require careful analysis to determine which volunteers they cover and what exceptions they contain.

To some extent, the diversity of the laws reflects legislatively varying conclusions of state legislatures that weighed the competing equities inherent in volunteer protection. Reasonable people can differ over the choice of protecting a volunteer from personal liability or providing compensation to the innocent victim of the volunteer's negligence. It is not necessary that there be a comprehensive, nationwide response to the broad issue of how individuals who suffer harm from volunteer activity should be compensated.

But the variation will, ideally, be within reasonable bounds. With the laws varying so radically from state to state, individuals who volunteer across state lines may be unknowingly at risk. Attorneys will, of course, forum shop when they have multiple jurisdictions from which to choose. This used to be a major problem for the Washington, D.C., and Maryland area. The growing fears of volunteers and volunteer organizations in suburban Maryland caused many volunteer agencies literally to shut their doors and close down programs. The Maryland legislature responded to these fears by enacting laws granting limited liability protection to volunteers with specific statutes protecting coaches, nonprofits' directors and officers, and volunteers on councils of condominium owners. But despite Maryland's legislation, the District of Columbia had no volunteer protection act until this past year.

Passage of the Volunteer Protection Act would help fill in the unreasonable state-to-state gaps. Over the years, we have seen many states use the model in the Volunteer Protection Act to craft their own state laws.

This effort was further advanced when President Bush, who hailed the volunteer sector as "a thousand points of light," adopted the Volunteer Protection Act in his own model state volunteer service act. In 1990, moreover, the Bush administration's Office of National Service promoted several initiatives to protect volunteers from unwarranted exposure to legal liability and to make insurance protecting against such liability more affordable and easily available. The President also called for the establishment of a privately funded, nongovernment-controlled center to address the concerns of volunteer organizations about tort liability.

This surge of federal action on the issue spotlighted the need for states to take the initiative to prevent the chilling effect on volunteerism. Many states responded and enacted effective volunteer protection laws, but others did not. Enactment of a federal volunteer protection act would provide an additional push to encourage the states that have not passed volunteer protection laws to do so.

### *Status of the Act*

With strong grassroots and state support, the cosponsorship of over two hundred U.S. Representatives in each of the last three Congresses, and the support of the past administration, one would think that the Volunteer Protection Act would be law. Instead, my legislation has been sitting in the House Judiciary Committee in bill form since 1985 without even a hearing.

The plaintiffs' trial bar traditionally has opposed liability reform in areas like medical malpractice and product liability and, unfortunately, it also opposes my legislation. This lobby has proved to be very successful at encouraging certain key committees to withold action on tort reform legislation. Given the difficulties of reaching the House floor by the traditional course of hearings and a reported bill, I have twice sought to attach it as an amendment to other legislation.

In 1993, the President's proposal for a national service program was introduced in the House of Representatives as the National Service Trust Act. The bill proposed to create a national service program which would grant education awards to participants for community service. It is certain that the execution of national service programs will create personal liability exposure for acts or omissions of the program participants. The National Service Trust Act envisions participants and programs being involved in a wide variety of activities, many of which are known for giving rise to litigation—e.g., addressing unmet environmental needs, disaster relief, and a professional corps program that recruits, trains, and places qualified participants in positions such as teachers, nurses, police officers, and early childhood development staff. These are all worthwhile activities, and they should not be undertaken without proper liability protection. Program participants should be exempt from individual liability except in extreme circumstances, thereby taking the fear of being sued out of this program.

When the National Service Trust Act came to the House floor for consideration, I proposed a modified version of the Volunteer Protection Act as an amendment. The amendment attempted to encourage states to enact limited liability protection to volunteers on behalf of nonprofits whose actions are directly related to the administration of a National Service Trust Act program. The amendment propounded the volunteer protection model law and proposed a trigger of a five percent decrease in the money that states otherwise would receive under the National Service Trust Act, with a reallocation of that money to states which had met the volunteer protection standard.

Despite some intriguing twists and turns, the National Service Trust Act was ultimately passed into law with no provision addressing the potential tort liability of its participants. The results of my efforts came as no surprise. This episode echoes 1990, when I was able to amend the National Service Act with my volunteer protection legislation by a unanimous vote in the House, but unfortunately the amendment was quietly stripped out in conference.

## IV. Conclusion

Efforts to promote volunteer liability protection have paid important dividends, although more remains to be done. The states have taken notice. Many states already have passed volunteer protection laws, additional states are in the process of passing such laws, and still others have improved existing laws because of the federal law's model bill. Members of Congress also have taken notice, and the Volunteer Protection Act is gaining additional congressional support. Eventually the Volunteer Protection Act will pass, and the remaining states will be encouraged to pass sound legislation, too.

# Fair Compensation

CHAPTER 5

# PUNITIVE DAMAGES: JUDICIAL AND LEGISLATIVE REFORMS

KENNETH W. STARR
CHRISTOPHER LANDAU

## I. Introduction

Few tendencies are more dangerous to a federal republic than parochialism. Indeed, the federal Constitution was adopted in large measure to check this danger: under the Articles of Confederation, Justice Joseph Story long ago explained, each state acted "according to its view of its own interests, or its local prejudices." The resulting discrimination stoked "the resentments of the States against each other, . . . daily increasing the mass of disaffection . . . [and thereby endangering] the peace and safety of the Union."[1]

Neither the adoption of the Constitution nor the passage of two centuries has eliminated parochial pressures. What *has* changed is the form in which the vice is manifested: as overt discrimination has become increasingly rare, indirect and subtle discrimination has flourished. The latter's appeal, of course, lies in its relative invisibility. Occasionally, however, it is clearly exposed.

Justice Richard Neely of the West Virginia Supreme Court of Appeals recently cast light on one particularly pernicious strain. In a book on the law of product liability, the justice pointed out that one modern-day engine of parochialism is punitive damages, long a creature of the common law. And he candidly admitted aiding and abetting their transformation by routinely affirming large punitive damages awards against out-of-state corporations. Bleeding such defendants, he unapologetically explained, enhanced both his sleep and his job security because "in-state plaintiffs, their families, and their friends will reelect me."[2]

When a local plaintiff (and, even more dramatically, an *injured* local plaintiff) stands up in court and points the finger at a faceless

---

[1]Joseph Story, A Familiar Exposition of the Constitution of the United States § 33 (1859). *See also* The Federalist No. 7 (Hamilton) (interstate commercial discrimination inevitably leads to discontent, outrages, reprisals, and wars).

[2]Richard Neely, The Product Liability Mess: How Business Can Be Rescued From the Politics of State Courts 4 (1988).

out-of-state corporation, there is little question where a jury's sympathies and prejudices will lie. Punitive damages awards provide an enticing avenue for acting on those improper instincts. As Justice Neely's comments highlight, however, state courts currently feel little or no responsibility to check these tendencies. It is the thesis of this chapter that this judicial abdication is not only unwise as a matter of law and policy, but represents a sharp break with our legal traditions.

In the current debate over punitive damages, those who favor virtually unconstrained jury discretion unfortunately have succeeded in seizing the legitimizing mantle of history and tradition. Current conventional wisdom maintains that the common law reserves questions regarding the availability and amount of punitive damages for the jury, and that the judicial role in evaluating such awards (and particularly the role of appellate judges) is accordingly very narrow. Thus, appellate courts now rarely afford challenges to punitive damages awards more than cursory treatment. "Punitive damages do not survive court scrutiny because they can be accurately measured and adjusted by court imposed guidelines. They survive . . . because of their historical acceptance."[3] Indeed, courts routinely chastise would-be judicial tort reformers for their impertinence, lecturing them to direct their policy-based appeals to the political, not the judicial, branch of government.[4]

This chapter contends that such conventional wisdom is, in no small measure, wrong. The common law traditionally imposed substantial restraints, both procedural and substantive, on jury awards of punitive damages. Because these restraints were an integral part of the punitive damages remedy at common law, the analogy between traditional common-law awards and the unconstrained awards of modern times is at best facile and at worst false. Contemporary punitive damages awards differ from their common-law ancestors not only in *degree* (i.e., size and frequency), but also in *kind*. Far from a result-oriented or counter-historical venture, careful judicial supervision of punitive damages awards in fact would amount to a *reaffirmation* of traditional legal principles, and one that can be accomplished by relying on time-honored judicial tools. A return to supervision by the courts—whether undertaken on their own initiative or, failing that, at the command of state legislatures—is not only consistent with but dictated by our legal traditions.

[3]Hospital Auth. of Gwinnett County v. Jones, 409 S.E.2d 501, 503-04 (Ga. 1991), *cert. denied*, 112 S. Ct. 1175 (1992).

[4]*See, e.g.*, Dunn v. Hovic, 1 F.3d 1371, 1385-89 (3d Cir.), *cert. denied*, 114 S. Ct. 650 (1993).

## II. Historical Background

Punitive damages, at least in their present, explicitly extracompensatory form, have always been something of an aberration in Anglo-American jurisprudence. As every first-year law student learns, the purpose of damages in our civil law is to *compensate* a party for an injury.[5] Punitive damages depart radically from this scheme. Although civil in nature, they share the criminal law's goals of punishment and deterrence, and its corresponding focus on a *defendant's conduct* rather than a *plaintiff's injury*.[6] They are, for all intents and purposes, criminal fines.[7]

Indeed, the historical evidence strongly suggests that punitive damages in their contemporary, explicitly extracompensatory, form arise not from hallowed legal tenets, but rather from a mundane semantic mistake.[8] Some early cases upholding compensatory damages awards used loose language that, taken out of context, was later used to justify punitive damages. These early cases fall into four general categories: (1) cases involving an injury deemed impervious to precise quantification, so that the calculation of (*compensatory*) damages was declared largely within the jury's discretion;[9]

[5]*See, e.g.*, 2 WILLIAM BLACKSTONE, COMMENTARIES *438; CHARLES T. MCCORMICK, HANDBOOK ON THE LAW OF DAMAGES § 1 (1935); *cf.* Hawkins v. McGee, 146 A. 641 (N.H. 1929).

[6]*See, e.g.*, MCCORMICK, *supra* note 5, § 77; DAN B. DOBBS, LAW OF REMEDIES § 3.9 (1973); WILLIAM PROSSER, LAW OF TORTS § 2, at 9 (calling punitive damages in the civil law "rather anomalous"); KENNETH REDDEN, PUNITIVE DAMAGES § 2.1 (1980); Electrical Workers v. Foust, 442 U.S. 42, 48 (1979).

[7]Indeed, as a practical matter, punitive damages often entail far more severe punishment than fines. Under federal law, for example, a motor-vehicle manufacturer may be fined $1000 per vehicle for a design defect, up to a maximum of $800,000 for a nationwide fleet. 15 U.S.C. §§ 1397, 1398 (1988). A jury applying state law, however, may award—and in fact has awarded—more than *$100 million* in punitive damages in a single case. *See* General Motors v. Moseley (appeal pending, Georgia Court of Appeals).

[8]*See, e.g.*, 2 SIMON GREENLEAF, LAW OF EVIDENCE 235 n.2 (John Wilder May ed., 13th ed. 1876); *see generally* Pacific Mut. Life Ins. Co. v. Haslip, 499 U.S. 1, 25-26 (1991) (Scalia, J., concurring in judgment).

[9]Thus, for example, in Huckle v. Money, 95 Eng. Rep. 768 (C.P. 1763), an early case often cited as the fountainhead of punitive damages, the court sustained a large verdict against a government officer for ordering an unlawful arrest under a general verdict. The court denied the defendant's motion for remittitur of the verdict, however, *not* on the ground that the large award was proper *as punishment*, but rather because in a case involving such an amorphous injury, "damages were properly left at large to the jury, [which was] at liberty to consider all the circumstances of oppression and arbitrary power by which the great constitutional right of the plaintiff was violated, in this attempt to destroy the liberty of the kingdom." GREENLEAF, *supra* note 8, at 235 n.2. As the Lord Chief Justice explained: "Upon the whole, I am of opinion the damages are not excessive; and that it is very dangerous for the Judges to intermeddle in damages for torts; it must be a glaring case instead of outrageous damages in a tort, and which all mankind at first blush must think so, to induce a Court to grant a new trial for excessive damages." 95 Eng. Rep. at 768-69.

(2) cases involving compensation for a variety of injuries (including mental anguish, hurt feelings, shame, degradation, and injury to standing and credit) that early common law did not recognize as *legally* compensable;[10] (3) cases involving compensation to a plaintiff, contrary to the traditional rule under American law,[11] for his legal costs and expenses;[12] and (4) cases where the plaintiff's injury was regarded as being more severe, and thus deserving greater compensation, because of the egregious nature of the defendant's misconduct.[13]

The cases, then, suggest that the practice of awarding truly extracompensatory punitive damages grew out of "the general language of some judges, and [from] remarks gratuitously made in delivering judgment on other questions."[14] Those early courts that actually paused to consider the legitimacy of punitive damages, rather than citing snippets of dicta, tended to reject them in no uncertain terms. As the New Hampshire Supreme Court lamented, extracompensatory punitive damages stemmed from "a perversion of language and ideas so ancient and so common as seldom to attract attention."[15]

---

[10]*See, e.g.*, 2 J.G. SUTHERLAND, A TREATISE ON THE LAW OF DAMAGES § 404, at 1314 (John R. Berryman ed., 4th ed. 1916); 2 THEODORE SEDGWICK, MEASURE OF DAMAGES, at 326 (Arthur G. Sedgwick & G. Willett Van Nest eds., 7th ed. 1880). As the court explained in Stuart v. Western Union Tel. Co., 18 S.W. 351, 353 (Tex. 1885): "[T]he whole doctrine of punitory or exemplary damages has its foundation in a failure to recognize as elements upon which compensation may be given many things which ought to be classed as injuries entitling the injured person to compensation."

[11]*See, e.g.*, Alyeska Pipeline Serv. Co. v. Wilderness Soc'y, 421 U.S. 240, 258-59 (1975).

[12]*See, e.g.*, SUTHERLAND, *supra* note 10, § 404, at 1313.

[13]Milwaukee & St. Paul R.R. v. Arms, 91 U.S. 489, 493 (1876) ("The tort is aggravated by the evil motive, and on this rests the rule of exemplary damages."); *see also* Scott v. Donald, 165 U.S. 58, 65 (1897) ("exemplary [damages are] allowable in excess of the actual loss, where a tort is *aggravated* by evil motive, actual malice, deliberate violence or oppression") (emphasis added); Hawes v. Knowles, 114 Mass. 518 (1874) (Gray, C.J.).

In a similar vein, some courts held that the defendant's socioeconomic status was relevant to the plaintiff's injury on the ground that, where the defendant was wealthy or prominent, the insult to the plaintiff was greater. SUTHERLAND, *supra* note 10, § 404, at 1315. *See also* Fay v. Parker, 53 N.H. 342, 355 (1873) (inquiry into the precise nature of the conduct of the defendant, his position or station, and wealth determined the indignity suffered by the plaintiff at his hands); *cf.* Huckle v. Money, 95 Eng. Rep. at 768-69 (contrasting the station of the plaintiff, a journeyman printer, to that of the defendant, a powerful government officer).

[14]GREENLEAF, *supra* note 8, at 235 n.2. *See also id.* at 245 n.2 ("[t]he obscurity in which this subject has been involved has arisen chiefly from the want of accuracy and care in the use of terms, and from a reliance on casual expressions and *obiter dicta* of judges, as deliberate expositions of the law, instead of looking only to the point in judgment").

[15]Fay v. Parker, 53 N.H. 342, 343 (1873). The New Hampshire court was far from alone:

> I have always regretted that this court adopted the rule of punitory damages in actions of tort. In the controversy between Prof. Greenleaf and Mr. Sedgwick, I cannot but think that the former was right in principle, though the weight of

Despite this checkered pedigree, explicitly extracompensatory punitive damages have become, at least since the late nineteenth century, an established part of the American common law of torts.[16] But to say that their roots run deep is not to say that they run broad. The background rule at common law always has been that a plaintiff's recovery is limited to compensation for his injury,[17] and that "[p]unitive damages are not a favorite in the law, and should be allowed only with caution and confined within narrow limits."[18]

Until relatively recently, of course, the legal and policy implications of punitive damages "merited scarce attention" outside the rarified universe of appellate courts and law classrooms.[19] Complaints seeking punitive damages were relatively rare, trial courts often refused to allow them to be presented to the jury, only rarely did juries actually award punitive damages, and in any event the amounts actually awarded were small.[20] Indeed, a recent study found that the largest punitive damages award in the United States in the nineteenth century—*including* verdicts set aside as excessive by reviewing courts—was $4,500 (a sum amounting to the grand total of *$58,000* in 1987 dollars).[21] In 1930, punitive damages awards of

> authority may be with the latter. It is difficult on principle to understand why, when the sufferer by a tort has been fully compensated for his suffering, he should recover anything more.

Bass v. Chicago & N.W. Ry. Co., 42 Wis. 654, 672 (1877); *see also* Spokane Truck & Dray Co. v. Hoefer, 25 P. 1072, 1075 (Wash. 1891) ("we believe that the doctrine of punitive damages is unsound in principle, and unfair and dangerous in practice . . .").

[16]*See, e.g.*, GEORGE FIELD, LAW OF DAMAGES 66 (1876) ("[The] doctrine [of punitive damages] seems to be sustained by at least a great preponderance of authorities, both in England, and in the general jurisprudence of this country.").

While relatively widespread, acceptance of punitive damages in this country never has been universal. Four states (Michigan, Nebraska, New Hampshire, and Washington) do not currently allow them. *See* RICHARD L. BLATT ET AL., PUNITIVE DAMAGES: A STATE BY STATE GUIDE TO LAW AND PRACTICE § 3.2, at 55 (1991). And, despite the language in the early cases, the law in England never evolved to the point of accepting expressly extracompensatory punitive damages; they are generally prohibited at modern English common law. *See, e.g.*, Rookes v. Barnard, 1 All E. R. 367, 407 (House of Lords 1964).

[17]*See, e.g.*, Milwaukee & St. Paul R.R. v. Arms, 91 U.S. 489, 492 (1876).

[18]Kemner v. Monsanto Co., 576 N.E.2d 1146, 1154 (Ill. App.), *appeal denied*, 584 N.E.2d 130 (Ill. 1991) (citations omitted); *see also* Smith v. Wade, 461 U.S. 30, 87 (1983) (Rehnquist, J., dissenting); Williams v. Bone, 259 P.2d 810, 812 (Idaho 1953); Cays v. McDaniel, 283 P.2d 658 (Or. 1955); *see generally* 25 C.J.S. *Damages* § 117(1), at 1114 n.18.5 (1966).

[19]*See* Dorsay D. Ellis, *Fairness and Efficiency in the Law of Punitive Damages*, 56 S. CAL. L. REV. 1, 2 (1982).

[20]BLATT ET AL., *supra* note 16, § 1.2, at 5-6.

[21]*See* Brief of the American Institute of Architects et al. at 14, Pacific Mut. Life Ins. Co. v. Haslip, 499 U.S. 1 (1991) (No. 89-1279) (citing New Orleans, J. & G. N.R.R. v. Hurst, 36 Miss. 660 (1859)). This particular award, notably, was criticized by common-law commentators. "[W]e think, with deference, that the verdict might with great propriety have been set aside. The amount warranted the presumption of undue bias." ARTHUR SEDGWICK, MEASURE OF DAMAGES § 388, at 756 (9th ed. 1912).

$12,650, $33,333, and $50,000—the latter of which would have a 1990 value of some $332,000—were described by a leading commentator as "startlin[g]."[22] And as of 1955, just before the current explosion, the largest punitive damages verdict in the history of California, and one of the two largest in the history of the United States, was $75,000.[23]

## III. Punitive Damages and Federal Law

Those numbers, of course, seem quaint by today's standards. If the law of punitive damages awards "seldom attract[ed] attention" in the late nineteenth century,[24] nothing could be further from the truth today. As awards underwent a breathtaking inflation both in size and frequency in the 1970s and 1980s, and their impact on the American economy became increasingly obvious, they gave birth to a fervent tort reform movement—and to a correspondingly fervent anti–tort reform movement.

Until recently, however, would-be tort reformers expended much of their energy at the *federal* level, and in particular on the federal *courts*. Those choices were understandable. A uniform, national policy regarding punitive damages has much to commend it, particularly in an age of increasingly national commerce and relaxed restraints on judicial jurisdiction—a company that can be sued *anywhere* can be sued virtually *everywhere*. The state court judiciary, as Justice Neely's comments underscore, has few structural incentives to halt the degenerative trend.

Despite fervent entreaties, however, the United States Supreme Court has displayed a consistent reluctance to enter the fray. The Court first declined to regulate punitive damages through the Eighth Amendment's Excessive Fines Clause, holding that provision inapplicable to disputes between private parties.[25] The Court subsequently has suggested that the Due Process Clause provides some, but by all appearances not overly searching, restraints.[26]

---

22 Charles T. McCormick, *Some Phases of the Doctrine of Exemplary Damages*, 8 N.C. L. REV. 129, 149 & n.114 (1930).

23 See AIA Brief, *supra* note 21, at 16.

24 *Fay*, 53 N.H. at 243.

25 Browning-Ferris Indus. Inc. v. Kelco Disposal, Inc., 492 U.S. 257 (1989). The *Browning-Ferris* Court, however, expressly left open the question whether the same result would obtain when a punitive damages award is paid, at least in substantial part, to a governmental entity. *Id.* at 263-64, 265, 275-76 & n.21. Given the increasing number of jurisdictions that thus allocate awards—*see, e.g.*, COLO. REV. STAT. § 13-21-102(4) (1993); FLA. STAT. ANN. § 768.73(2)(b) (West 1992); ILL. ANN. STAT. ch. 110, ¶ 2-1207 (1993); IOWA CODE ANN. § 668A.1(2)(b) (West 1992); MO. STAT. ANN. § 537.675 (Vernon 1992)—this avenue of attack may hold promise, particularly in light of the Court's recent and unprecedented application of the Excessive Fines Clause in a *civil* case, Austin v. United States, 113 S. Ct. 2801 (1993).

26 Pacific Mutual Life Ins. Co. v. Haslip, 499 U.S. 1 (1991); TXO Prod. Corp. v. Alliance Resources Corp., 113 S. Ct. 2711 (1993).

The Supreme Court recently made good on repeated threats to use the Due Process Clause to limit punitive damages awards in *Honda Motor Co. v. Oberg*.[27] But in many ways that case may only underscore how narrow is the scope of the federal due process protection in this area. Oregon's supreme court had declared that the federal Constitution did not require any judicial review of punitive damages awards—a position at odds not only with traditional common law but with contemporary practice in all the other states.[28] The case thus raised the question whether, and to what extent, a state could reduce the protection against punitive damages awards afforded at common law. This contrasts sharply with the questions presented in *TXO* and *Haslip*, where the Supreme Court was asked to announce affirmative limitations on punitive damages based on the Due Process Clause.

*Honda*, therefore, is unlikely to be a harbinger of a broad federal constitutional attack on punitive damages, but is instead a model of judicial restraint. Noting that "traditional practice provides a touchstone for constitutional analysis,"[29] the Court held only that due process prevents the states from dispensing altogether with judicial review of punitive damages awards—an essentially negative, not affirmative, view of the Clause's function. But having decided that some review is necessary, the Court sidestepped the narrower (and, from a practical point of view, more significant) question of how much review is necessary—i.e., the standard of review.[30] On this point, the Court merely hinted that the traditional, deferential standard of review fully satisfies constitutional norms.[31]

While *Honda* confirms that the Supreme Court prefers to wield the Due Process Clause as a shield rather than as a sword, it also underscores the importance of understanding the traditional common-law restraints on punitive damages. The questions of state law explored in this chapter thus may well overlap with federal due process concerns: to the extent that state courts have allowed traditional common-law protections to erode, and to the extent that erosion compromises "fundamental fairness," punitive damages awards may be unconstitutional. At the very least, *Honda* highlights the long-overdue need for states (and in particular state courts) to reconsider the extent to which their current tort law, in substance as well

[27]114 S. Ct. 2331 (1994). [For additional discussion of *Honda* and other recent punitive damages decisions of the Supreme Court, see Theodore B. Olson & Theodore J. Boutrous, Jr., *The Supreme Court's Developing Punitive Damage Jurisprudence*, 1994 PUB. INTEREST L. REV. 17 (also published by NLCPI). —Editor's note.]

[28]851 P.2d 1084, 1099 (1993).

[29]114 S. Ct. at 2339.

[30]*Id.* at 2340–41.

[31]*Id.*

as form, departs from traditional norms. In light of *Honda*, state courts have a unique opportunity to correct the serious distortions in their common law detailed in this chapter—by returning tort law to its traditional moorings, state courts will not only rationalize their own law, but now, in light of *Honda*, avoid serious federal constitutional questions.

Even if the federal Constitution ultimately provides some basis for overturning particularly large or otherwise egregious awards, however, it would be a mistake to miss the recent cases' central message: the federal Constitution is the wrong vehicle and the federal courts the wrong forum for effecting meaningful affirmative tort reform. Tort law has long been the province of the states, and for the federal courts to impose a comprehensive and searching regulatory scheme over punitive damages would defy the nation's basic federal structure. Because review of punitive damages awards is inherently fact-intensive, it would in any event be impractical for the Supreme Court of the United States to impose a uniform code binding on every court in the land.

What the federal Constitution *permits*, of course, it by no means necessarily *encourages*. The fact that the United States Supreme Court has declined to engage in exhaustive and intrusive substantive and procedural review of punitive damages awards hardly means that it *favors* such awards—indeed, Justices from across the political and jurisprudential spectrum have suggested quite the contrary.[32] Rather, it means only that to date the Court has not been persuaded of any principled constitutional justification for any such involvement, except to the limited extent recognized in *Honda*. As Justice Scalia has emphasized, "*[s]tate legislatures and courts* have the power to restrict or abolish the common-law practice of punitive damages, and in recent years have increasingly done so. . . . It is through those means—State by State, and, at the federal level, by Congress—that the legal procedures affecting our citizens are improved."[33]

The principles of federalism and judicial restraint that militate strongly against intrusive *federal* court regulation of punitive damages awards, of course, apply not at all with respect to *state* court regulation. To the contrary, those principles in fact favor aggressive state court review. As Justice Story implicitly recognized long ago,

[32]*See, e.g.*, TXO Prod. Corp. v. Alliance Resources Corp., 113 S. Ct. 2711, 2728-42 (1993) (O'Connor, J., joined by White, J., and Souter, J.); Browning-Ferris Inds. Inc. v. Kelco Disposal, Inc., 492 U.S. 257, 280-82 (1989) (Brennan, J., joined by Marshall, J.); *id.* at 282-83 (O'Connor, J., joined by Stevens, J.); Bankers Life & Casualty Co. v. Crenshaw, 486 U.S. 71, 87-89 (1988) (O'Connor, J., joined by Scalia, J.); *see also* Aetna Life Ins. Co. v. Lavoie, 475 U.S. 813, 828-29 (1986).

[33]*Haslip*, 499 U.S. at 39 (opinion concurring in judgment) (emphasis added).

federalism is a two-way street. Just as the national government must remain conscious and respectful of its proper sphere, so too must the states; participation in a federal system implies, on behalf of the states, acceptance of a responsibility to check the natural tendency to favor parochial over out-of-state and national interests. If a jury in one state imposes ruinous penalties against a corporation from another, it will not be long before the latter state reciprocates, undermining the entire cooperative system. The federal system imposes on its component states responsibilities beyond those expressly commanded by the central government.

It is on this implicit premise that the United States Supreme Court to date has refused aggressively to curb punitive damages awards, despite their present-day manifest unfairness and irrationality. Perhaps, as Justice Neely's "stop-me-before-I-kill-again" plea for federal intervention suggests, the state courts are not up to the task of providing meaningful supervision over punitive damages awards. But our federal system prohibits any such assumption. The state courts now have the opportunity (and the duty) to address the problem on their own. Should they fail to do so, the United States Supreme Court might well be persuaded to reconsider its essentially noninterventionist stance—and at that point any invocation of federalism plainly will ring hollow.

Rather than viewing state law and the state courts as the problem, therefore, tort reformers must view them as an essential part of the solution. But no such solution is likely to be forthcoming unless the issues are properly framed. Defendants who simply regurgitate a conclusory complaint that a particular award is unconstitutional simply because it is "unreasonably large" and "unfair" can fully expect to see their claims summarily rejected with citations to *Haslip*, *TXO*, and perhaps a state-law case or two noting the jury's broad discretion in assessing punitive damages.

It is vital, then, for state courts to reconsider the premise that punitive damages awards fashioned by a jury in an exercise of virtually absolute discretion comply with their common law. The most promising avenue for tort reform, as *Honda* suggests, is not to ask the courts to create new rights in this area, but to ask them to restore traditional rights that in recent decades have gradually, but no less surely, been undermined.

## IV. Traditional Common-Law Restraints on Punitive Damages

The judges who fashioned our common law over the centuries were not naive. They well understood the propensity of juries to become inflamed with passion or prejudice, particularly in cases pitting an injured individual against a faceless corporation. Thus, while common-law authorities occasionally described jury discretion in sweeping and near-absolute terms—terms that the present-day opponents of tort reform are quick to cite—those descriptions must be read in context. A careful reading of the cases shows, and the *Honda* Court confirmed,[34] that the common law assigned courts significant powers over punitive damages to the *courts*.

Indeed, common-law authorities typically emphasized the fundamental role of *both* jury and judge in the same breath. Judicial supervision over punitive damages awards was regarded not merely as incidental to, but as an essential element of, punitive damages awards. As Sedgwick explained in his influential treatise, "In general . . . *in cases proper for exemplary damages*, it would seem impracticable to set any bounds to the discretion of the jury, though, in cases where the wrong done, though with malicious intent, is greatly disproportioned to the amount of the verdict, *the court may exercise the power it always possesses to grant a new trial for excessive damages*."[35]

That passage from Sedgwick's treatise highlights not only the background norm of jury discretion but also two distinct areas where the common law assigned the *court* significant responsibility: (1) evaluating whether, as a matter of law, the defendant's conduct was sufficiently deliberate or otherwise culpable to authorize punitive damages *before* submitting the issue to the jury; and (2) scrutinizing the award *after* it is calculated by the jury. The following sections discuss each of these areas in turn.

### *State of Mind*

As noted above, punitive damages have more in common with criminal fines than with other forms of civil damages. At common law, therefore, they were strictly reserved for a limited class of cases—torts[36] involving "intentional and deliberate [misconduct], and ha[ving] the character of outrage frequently associated with crime,"[37] or, as an early common-law case put it, conduct "of the

[34]114 S. Ct. at 2335–38.

[35]SEDGWICK, *supra* note 10, at 333 note (emphasis added).

[36]At common law, punitive damages were available *only* in actions sounding in tort, and prohibited in those sounding in contract. *See, e.g.*, RESTATEMENT (SECOND) OF CONTRACTS § 355 (1981). A majority of jurisdictions, however, now recognize their availability in at least some actions in contract. *See, e.g.*, Gruenberg v. Aetna Ins. Co., 510 P.2d 1032, 1037 (Cal. 1973); Kilgore v. National Life & Accident Ins. Co., 138 S.E.2d 397 (Ga. App. 1964). *See generally* PUNITIVE DAMAGES: A CONSTRUCTIVE EXAMINATION-REPORT OF THE SPECIAL COMMITTEE ON PUNITIVE DAMAGES OF THE AMERICAN BAR ASSOCIATION SECTION ON LITIGATION 43-54 (1986).

[37]PROSSER, *supra* note 6, § 2, at 9.

most atrocious and dishonorable nature."[38] These judges did not condone hypersensitivity, and to them the "most atrocious" conduct was *very* unusual and extreme. The extremely culpable state of mind the common law classified under the rubrics "willful" and "wanton."

At its core, such extreme culpability refers to misconduct undertaken with specific intent to injure. But it was not strictly limited thereto. Rather, the common law took the apparently small but fateful step of allowing a jury to *presume* evil intent in the narrow class of cases where a defendant manifested a "conscious and deliberate disregard" of the interests of others. (An obvious example is shooting a loaded gun into a crowded room; even if the defendant did not specifically intend to injure anyone, his action is sufficiently deliberate to be classified as "willful" or "wanton.") Such misconduct, often (but oxymoronically) termed "conscious indifference," was deemed to be of equivalent moral reprehensibility to specifically intentional misconduct, and thus presumptively intentional.

Accordingly, it is well settled at common law that some form of "guilty intention"—whether actual or presumptive—"is required in order to charge [defendant] with exemplary or punitive damages."[39] That limitation is hardly surprising. "[I]n morals, and the eyes of the law, there is a vast difference between the criminality of a person acting mistakenly from a worthy motive, and one committing the same act from a wanton and malignant spirit, and with a corrupt and wicked design."[40] Thus, "[t]he allowance of exemplary damages depends upon the bad motive of the wrong-doer as exhibited by his acts. Where, therefore, the acts fall short of 'willful misconduct, or that entire want of care which would raise the presumption of a conscious indifference to consequences,' exemplary damages should not be given."[41] Extending the concept of "willful or wanton" to encompass "conscious indifference" in addition to specifically intentional misconduct was, to common-law judges, not a particularly big step, for both categories of intent were understood to apply only to a limited range of extremely culpable conduct.

The line separating "gross negligence" from "conscious indifference," then, was understood to demarcate categories different in

[38]Coryell v. Colbaugh, 1 N.J.L. 77 (1791).

[39]Lake Shore & M.S. Ry. Co. v. Prentice, 147 U.S. 101, 107 (1893). *See also id.* at 111 ("criminal intent [is] necessary to warrant the imposition of [punitive] damages"), 114 ("unlawful and criminal intent" required for punitive damages). *See generally* Smith v. Wade, 461 U.S. 30, 78-79 n.12 (1983) (Rehnquist, J., dissenting) (describing state of mind required for punitive damages in the nineteenth century).

[40]Simpson v. McCaffrey, 13 Ohio 508, 522 (1844).

[41]SEDGWICK, *supra* note 10, at 328 note.

*kind*, not just *degree*, and drawing that line was deemed an appropriate endeavor for courts as a matter of law, not juries as a matter of fact. "[W]hile the measurement of punitive damages is a jury question, the preliminary question of whether the facts of a particular case justify the imposition of punitive damages is properly one of law."[42] Although the jury had broad discretion to determine whether punitive damages should be awarded in any particular case, then, at common law that discretion operates only *after* the trial court determined, *as a matter of law*, that there was sufficient evidence of a "willful or wanton" state of mind to justify sending the case to the jury in the first place.[43]

However justified in theory, and despite the diligent efforts of judges to perform their screening function, expansion of the concepts of "willful" and "wanton" to encompass "conscious indifference" was nonetheless to transform punitive damages in practice. Having breached the bright line provided by specific intent, the unfortunate fact is that the common law never developed any effective replacement rule to delineate the culpability necessary to sustain a punitive damages award. Indeed, that culpability was often defined more by what it was *not* than by what it *was*: it was *not* mere "negligence," or even "gross negligence." In contrast to "willful" and "wanton" misconduct, negligence in all its forms is characterized by inadvertence.[44]

Unfortunately, neither "gross negligence" nor "conscious indifference" is a precise concept, so the line between the two was never easy to draw.[45] That inherent difficulty—and the inherent arbitrariness that it would entail in close cases—did not traditionally, however, deter the courts from carrying out their critical screening function. Judges took very seriously their responsibility to ensure that

[42]Kemner v. Monsanto Corp., 576 N.E.2d 1146, 1154 (Ill. App.), *appeal denied*, 584 N.E.2d 130 (Ill. 1991). *See also* SUTHERLAND, *supra* note 10, § 403, at 1309 ("It is for the court to determine whether the evidence tends to show facts which warrant exemplary damages; the *sufficiency* of the facts is for the jury.") (emphasis added).

[43]The jury's discretion over punitive damages, of course, is asymmetrical: while juries have plenary discretion *not to award* punitive damages, their discretion *to award* punitive damages is limited. In most cases, the facts will not support punitive damages as a matter of law, and thus the jury cannot be given the option of awarding them. In contrast, there are *no* circumstances under which a defendant's conduct requires the jury to award punitive damages as a matter of law. As Sedgwick stated, "[i]t is error to instruct them to give exemplary damages." SEDGWICK, *supra* note 10, at 332 note; *see also* SEDGWICK, *supra* note 21, § 387, at 753.

[44]*See, e.g.*, BLI Constr. Co., Inc. v. Debari, 217 S.E.2d 426 (Ga. App. 1975); Christy v. Butcher, 134 S.W. 1058, 1059 (Mo. App. 1911).

[45]Indeed, it is for that very reason that courts determined that the former could not serve as a workable basis for awarding punitive damages:

> The term "gross negligence" is relative, and any rule stating where it begins must be an arbitrary one. Whether exemplary damages shall be given for gross

punitive damages were truly limited to the rare cases of extreme culpability.[46] They understood that punitive damages were very much the exception, not the rule, in our legal system, and routinely refused to send cases seeking such damages to the jury based on insufficient evidence of the requisite culpability. When a trial court erroneously did so, appellate courts did not hesitate to reverse, *even where a jury had in fact awarded punitive damages*.[47]

A classic example of the rigor with which the common law policed the state-of-mind issue is provided by the Supreme Court's decision in *Philadelphia, Wilmington & Baltimore Railroad Co. v. Quigley*.[48] The trial court there instructed jurors that they could "give such exemplary damages, if any, as in their opinion are called for and justified in view of all the circumstances of the case, to render reparation to plaintiff, and act as an adequate punishment to the defendant."[49] The Supreme Court, however, held that the court had failed in its antecedent duty to evaluate whether, as a matter of law, there was sufficient evidence of evil intent.

> In *Day v. Woodworth*, this court recognized the power of a jury in certain actions of tort to assess against the tort-feasor punitive or exemplary damages. . . . But the malice [necessary to sustain a punitive damages award] is not merely the doing of an unlawful or injurious act. The word implies that the act complained of was conceived in the spirit of mischief, or of criminal indifference to civil obligations. Nothing of this kind can be imputed to these defendants.[50]

---

> negligence or not, must, therefore, depend upon the definition to be given to the term. No precise definition has, however, become established, and the term "gross" is usually applied to any want of care exceeding that which is sufficient to establish a liability. This looseness of meaning seems to have been the consideration which has induced the courts to say that exemplary damages cannot be given for gross negligence.

SEDGWICK, *supra* note 10, at 328 note. *See also* Milwaukee & St. Paul R.R. v. Arms, 91 U.S. 489, 494 (1876) (because the case law "do[es] not define the term [gross negligence] with any accuracy . . . if it be made the criterion by which to determine the liability of the carrier beyond the limit of indemnity, it would seem that a precise meaning should be given to it").

[46]Common-law cases and commentators viewed the threshold question whether punitive damages were appropriate in a given case as more thoroughly a question of law than the distinct (and subsequent) question whether the *amount* of punitive damages set by a jury was appropriate. "[O]rdinarily, *if exemplary damages are authorized*, the amount is dependent on the enlightened conscience of impartial jurors." Jones v. Spindel, 177 S.E.2d 187, 191 (Ga. App. 1970) (emphasis added); *see also* Day v. Woodworth, 54 U.S. (13 How.) 363 (1851) ("the *degree* of punishment to be . . . inflicted [through an award of punitive damages] must depend on the peculiar circumstances of each case") (emphasis added). Thus, comments emphasizing jury discretion tend to arise in the context of judicial review of the *amount*—rather than the antecedent review regarding the availability—of punitive damages. *See generally infra* pp. 91-96.

[47]*See, e.g.*, Wolfsen v. Hathaway, 198 P.2d 1, 10-13 (Cal. 1948); Lexington Ry. v. Fain, 80 S.W. 463 (Ky. App. 1904).

[48]62 U.S. (21 How.) 202 (1859).

[49]*Id.* at 213.

[50]*Id.* at 213-14. (citation omitted).

Common-law judges, then, did not find the state of mind required to support an award of punitive damages particularly indeterminate, and certainly did not perceive it as a license for routinely sending punitive damages to the jury. Perhaps reflecting the traditional view of the law as a scientific and precise endeavor, they displayed little trouble drawing fine distinctions as a matter of law.

Recent decades, however, have witnessed a gradual transformation of the judicial attitude toward drawing the line on the spectrum of culpability between gross negligence and conscious indifference. The absence of any apparent bright line separating the categories has led modern courts too often to treat the distinction as no more than a matter of degree, and to toss the relevant line-drawing responsibility to the jury.

This judicial abdication of the preliminary state-of-mind determination, perhaps more than any other factor, has contributed to the progressive degeneration of the law of punitive damages. Given the amorphousness of the concepts involved, judges had always played a critical screening role by exercising their discretion, experience, and wisdom before the jury was allowed to exercise its own. The modern trend of characterizing the availability of punitive damages as a quintessential jury question is at war with the basic proposition that punitive damages are the limited exception, not the general rule, in our legal system.

Thus, while the law in this area has on a superficial level deviated surprisingly little from traditional common law—courts generally continue to recite the traditional "willful or wanton" formulation, or some variant thereof, and insist that punitive damages require some showing of culpability greater than gross negligence—its substantive content has changed dramatically. The rise of the product liability lawsuit in the 1960s and 1970s only exacerbated this unfortunate trend away from common-law strictures.[51] Product liability cases,

[51]The growth in the average tort award against manufacturers from the 1960s to the 1980s has been truly explosive, reflecting increases ranging from 200% to more than 1000%. MARK A. PETERSON ET AL., PUNITIVE DAMAGES—EMPIRICAL FINDINGS 14-15 (1987). Before 1970, for example, there was only one reported decision upholding an award of punitive damages in a product liability case, an award of $250,000. Toole v. Richardson-Merrell, Inc., 60 Cal. Rptr. 398 (1967). As of 1976, punitive verdicts had been approved on appeal in only *three* product liability cases. *See* David G. Owen, *Problems in Assessing Punitive Damages Against Manufacturers of Defective Products*, 49 U. CHI. L. REV. 1, 2-3 n.9 (1982). Now, of course, they are commonplace.

Indeed, the almost routine imposition of punitive damages in product liability cases may well raise serious questions under the federal Constitution as well as the common law. As Justice Kennedy noted in his *TXO* concurrence, 113 S. Ct. at 2726 (opinion concurring in part and concurring in judgment), punitive damages awards in cases involving "negligence, strict liability, or *respondeat superior*" present "different," and presumably more difficult, constitutional problems than cases involving intentional misconduct.

which typically involve corporate defendants and often novel causes of action and theories of causation, are a fertile field for jury parochialism. Yet judges have tended to allow juries to consider awarding punitive damages whenever a plaintiff alleges injury from an allegedly defective product—even where there is no evidence of any malicious intent (as opposed to some form of negligence) by the manufacturer, and indeed even when the manufacturer's conduct was approved or even required by federal regulatory agencies.[52]

Some courts have tried to restore some integrity to this corner of the law by insisting that punitive damages cannot be awarded on the basis of *implied* malice—a standard sufficiently meaningless as to support the imposition of punitive damages in virtually any product liability case. These courts have required a showing of *actual* malice, meaning in this context indifference to a known risk to safety.[53]

The proliferation of indiscriminate punitive damages awards is not only unfair in the short run, it is self-defeating in the long run:

> Punitive damages awards can only affect behavior if an actor is able to conform to *established standards* of conduct. If the standards are constantly changing, an actor may be unable to predict accurately the line that separates desirable from undesirable conduct. A potential defendant will either become too cautious, refusing to engage in socially beneficial behavior or will follow a course of behavior that imposes more harm on society than benefit.[54]

### *Amount*

Descriptions of a jury's discretion to calculate the appropriate amount of punitive damages are marked by a jarring inconsistency.

---

[52] *See, e.g.*, Wooderson v. Ortho Pharmaceutical Corp., 681 P.2d 1038 (Kan.), *cert. denied*, 469 U.S. 965 (1984); Dorsey v. Honda Motor Co., 655 F.2d 650, 656 (5th Cir. 1981).

[53] *See, e.g.*, Owens-Illinois v. Zenobia, 601 A.2d 633, 653 (Md. 1992) (emphasis added); Hodder v. Goodyear Tire & Rubber Co., 426 N.W.2d 826, 837 (Minn. 1988). Indeed, as the Texas Supreme Court recently explained, "[t]he requirement of conscious indifference, which our law requires, is superfluous unless it requires proof that the defendant had *actual subjective knowledge of an extreme risk of serious harm*." Transportation Ins. Co. v. Moriel, No. D-1507, 1994 Tex. LEXIS 23, *36 (Tex. Feb. 2, 1994) (emphasis added). The Texas court, moreover, stressed a point so obvious that it is often overlooked in evaluating allegations of malicious intent: "Determining whether an act or omission involves extreme risk or peril requires an examination of the events and circumstances from the viewpoint of the defendant at the time the events occurred, without viewing the matter in hindsight." *Id.* Because by definition a jury assessing damages will have determined that the plaintiff suffered some injury, and often very serious injury, it will invariably be tempting to punish the defendant for the injury, not for the wantonness of its behavior. "However, the magnitude of the injury may be entirely disproportionate to the riskiness of the behavior." *Id.*

[54] Owens-Illinois, Inc. v. Zenobia, 601 A.2d 633, 652 n.19 (Md. 1992) (emphasis added; internal quotation omitted).

Many cases and commentators begin by describing that discretion as absolute. As Sedgwick explained, "The amount of exemplary damages is generally said to be entirely within the discretion of the jury."[55] But those same cases and commentators invariably hasten to add significant qualifications. Sedgwick, for example, follows the sentence quoted above with this sentence: "But this discretion is subject to review by the court."[56] Indeed, he explains, the court's power is critical in "prevent[ing] the severe and arbitrary consequences that might otherwise result from the doctrine, and so to meet the principal objection to the allowance of exemplary damages: namely, that it gives the jury an arbitrary and unrestricted power over the property of defendants."[57]

Broad statements about a jury's discretion to assess punitive damages, then, cannot be taken at face value. The role of the jury in calculating damages is assuredly important, but so is that of the judge, who must review and ratify the amount awarded. To guide the judge, the common law in this area, as in so many others, developed not a mathematical formula, but rather a general standard. "The amount which may be recovered as punishment is for the jury [to decide] in the first instance, but subject to the power of the court to set aside the verdict if it is *so excessive that it is convinced that the jury have been influenced by passion or prejudice*."[58]

This standard is substantive, not merely procedural: "it is immaterial that exemplary damages were properly awarded if their amount indicates that it was fixed because of improper motives."[59] And no *actual* evidence of juror bias is necessary; the amount of damages awarded can give rise to a *presumption* of bias. Thus, "[a]n inordinately large deterrence award may be set aside as reflecting undue passion and prejudice rather than an enlightened conscience."[60]

---

[55]*See, e.g.*, SEDGWICK, *supra* note 21, § 388, at 755; Beggs v. Universal C.I.T. Credit Corp., 409 S.W.2d 719 (Mo. 1966) ("The amount to be awarded lies wholly within the sound discretion of the jury."); REDDEN, *supra* note 6, § 2.7, at 42 ("The amount of a punitive damage award is wholly within the discretion of the jury.").

[56]SEDGWICK, *supra* note 21, § 388, at 755; *see also id.* § 1344, at 2699 ("[T]he amount of [exemplary damages] is not entirely within the power of the jury."); *Beggs*, 409 S.W.2d, at 724 ("a court will not interfere with the jury's assessment of punitive damages unless there is an abuse of discretion"); REDDEN, *supra* note 6, § 2.7, at 42 ("Oftentimes, the courts have held that the award is purely a product of passion and prejudice and must therefore be set aside as unconscionable.").

[57]SEDGWICK, *supra* note 21, § 388, at 756.

[58]SUTHERLAND, *supra* note 10, § 403, at 1311 (emphasis added); *see generally Honda*, 114 S. Ct. at 2335–41.

[59]SUTHERLAND, *supra* note 10, § 459, at 1500.

[60]Hospital Auth. of Gwinnett County v. Jones, 386 S.E.2d 120, 123 n.9 (Ga. 1989), *vacated and remanded*, 499 U.S. 914 (1991); *cf.* Bryan v. Acee, 27 Ga. 87 (1859).

The presumption that a legally excessive award necessarily manifests "passion or prejudice" is, like all presumptions, at times a fiction. Recognizing this, an increasing number of courts in recent years have chosen to review jury verdicts not for evidence of "passion or prejudice," but rather expressly to ensure that they are substantively

Primary responsibility for careful scrutiny of punitive damages awards rests in the trial court, based largely on the court's traditional " 'broad discretionary powers' " to set aside improper verdicts.[61] Indeed, at common law the trial judge was regarded as "the thirteenth juror" who must confer his own "approval of the mind and conscience" upon a verdict before it became final.[62] "The law forbids a judge giving sanction to a verdict he deems unjust."[63]

As a corollary to its assignment of significant oversight responsibility to *trial* courts, the common law tended to limit the oversight responsibility of the *appellate* courts. Unlike the trial court judge who hears the witnesses and views the evidence firsthand, a panel of appellate judges examines a cold record. Thus, appellate courts traditionally displayed substantial deference where the trial court carefully reviewed the verdict;[64] the common-law standard of review of motions for remittitur or additur was abuse of discretion.[65] Even under this standard, appellate courts far from infrequently invalidated inordinately large awards. "We recognize that ordinarily, . . . an authorized verdict which has the approval of the trial judge should

---

"reasonable." *See, e.g.*, Angel v. Levittown Union Free Sch. Dist., 567 N.Y.S.2d 490 (N.Y. App. 1991); Republic Ins. Co. v. Hires, 810 P.2d 790 (Nev. 1991); State Farm Mut. Auto. Ins. Co. v. Zubiate, 808 S.W.2d 590 (Tex. App. 1991); Wollersheim v. Church of Scientology, 6 Cal. Rptr. 2d 532 (Cal. App. 1992); Manolas v. 303 West 42nd St. Enter., Inc., 569 N.Y.S.2d 701, *appeal denied*, 586 N.E.2d 62 (N.Y. 1991); Mason v. Texaco, Inc., 948 F.2d 1546 (10th Cir. 1991), *cert. denied*, 112 S. Ct. 1941 (1992).

[61]Smith v. Miliken, 276 S.E.2d 35 (Ga. 1981) (quoting Kiker v. Davis, 118 S.E.2d 861 (Ga. 1961)). *See* Fields v. Jackson, 115 S.E.2d 877 (Ga. App. 1960). *See also* Holland v. Williams, 60 S.E. 331, 332 (Ga. App. 1908) ("If the judge, had he been upon the jury, could not conscientiously have given acquiescence to the verdict rendered, he is not required to approve it, and we will not control him in refusing to do so.").

[62]Seaboard Air Line Ry. Co. v. Benton, 159 S.E. 717, 722 (Ga. 1931).

[63]SUTHERLAND, *supra* note 10, § 460, at 1513.

[64]*See, e.g.*, Smith v. Miliken, 276 S.E.2d 35, 38 (Ga. 1981); Romano v. Dibbs, 98 N.W.2d 146 (Minn. 1959); Holcroft v. Missouri-Kansas-Texas R. Co., 607 S.W.2d 158, 164 (Mo. App. 1980) ("[d]eference is due to this *considered action* of the trial court in denying remittitur") (emphasis added); Lang v. Hopkins, 10 Ga. 37, 46 (1851).

[65]*See, e.g.*, Texas Farmers Ins. Co. v. Soriano, 844 S.W.2d 808 (Tex. App. 1992); Burlington N.R. Co. v. Whitt, 575 So. 2d 1011 (Ala. 1990), *cert. denied*, 499 U.S. 948 (1991).

Unfortunately, the premise that the trial court has in fact carefully reviewed the jury's award is too often unjustified. Trial courts sometimes fail to articulate any explanation, written or otherwise, for refusing to disturb the award. Under these circumstances, appellate courts should not simply apply the deferential standard mechanically; the intensity of appellate scrutiny must vary inversely with the intensity of the trial court's original scrutiny.

*See, e.g.*, Crookston v. Fire Ins. Exchange, 817 P.2d 789, 808-13 (Utah 1991).

not be disturbed. Blind adherence to this rule, however, eliminates reason from the law."[66]

In reviewing a jury's award for excessiveness, common-law courts typically considered a number of factors. The factor cited most often is the relationship between the punitive award and the defendant's conduct, or the "nature of the offense." "Exemplary damages should . . . be commensurate to the nature of the offence, and when extravagant damages are allowed, they will be reduced to their proper standard."[67]

Another significant factor is the relationship between punitive and compensatory damages in a particular case.[68] "[T]he amount of [exemplary damages] is not entirely within the power of the jury, and the court will see to it that they bear some relation to the actual damages; if the amount is out of all proper proportion to the actual damages the verdict will be set aside as excessive."[69] Although courts typically refrain from setting any inflexible ratio of per se invalidity,[70] they have deemed skewed ratios persuasive evidence that "animosity was the deciding factor" behind the jury's decision.[71] Many courts, indeed, affirmatively insist on a "reasonable relationship" between compensatory and punitive damages,[72] and have reversed jury

[66]Jones v. Spindel, 177 S.E.2d 187, 191 (Ga. App. 1970), *cert. dismissed*, 180 S.E.2d 242 (Ga. 1971); *see also* McKinney & Co., Inc. v. Lawson, 357 S.E.2d 786, 787-88 (Ga. 1987); Gilman Paper Co. v. James, 219 S.E.2d 447, 450 (Ga. 1975).

[67]Burkett v. Lanata, 15 La. Ann. 337, 339 (1860). *See also, e.g.*, Texas Farmers Ins. Co. v. Soriano, 844 S.W.2d 808 (Tex. App. 1992); City Bank of Alabama v. Eskridge, 521 So. 2d 931 (Ala. 1988); Jordan v. General Growth Dev. Corp., 675 S.W.2d 901 (Mo. App. 1984); Adams v. Murakami, 268 Cal. Rptr. 467 (1990); Hardin, Rodriguez & Boivin Anesthesiologists, Ltd. v. Paradigm Ins. Co., 962 F.2d 628, 640 (7th Cir. 1992); Schneider v. Middleswart, 457 N.W.2d 33 (Iowa App. 1990); Parkin v. Cornell University, Inc., 581 N.Y.S.2d 914 (1992), *appeal dismissed*, 602 N.E.2d 229 (N.Y. 1992).

[68]Morrissey v. Welsh Co., 821 F.2d 1294, 1299 (8th Cir. 1987) (Missouri law); Brown v. Petrolite Corp., 965 F.2d 38 (5th Cir. 1992) (Texas law); Alaska Ins. Co. v. Movin' On Constr., Inc., 718 P.2d 472 (Alaska 1986); Mutual Life Ins. Co. of New York v. Estate of Wesson, 517 So. 2d 521 (Miss. 1987), *cert. denied*, 486 U.S. 1043 (1988).

[69]SEDGWICK, *supra* note 21, § 1344, at 2699 (giving examples).

[70]*See, e.g.*, Mailloux v. Bradley, 643 P.2d 797, 799 (Colo. App. 1982); *but cf.* Crookston v. Fire Ins. Exch., 817 P.2d 789, 808-11 (Utah 1991) (setting presumptive ratios).

[71]Rosener v. Sears Roebuck & Co., 168 Cal. Rptr. 237, 244 (1980), *appeal dismissed*, 450 U.S. 1051 (1981); *see also* Jones v. Spindel, 177 S.E.2d 187, 191 (Ga. App. 1970).

[72]*See, e.g.*, Missouri Pac. Ry. v. Tucker, 230 U.S. 340, 351 (1913) (striking down jury award as "grossly out of proportion to the possible actual damages"); Garnes v. Fleming Landfill, Inc., 413 S.E.2d 897, 909 (W. Va. 1991) ("As a matter of fundamental fairness, punitive damages should bear a reasonable relationship to compensatory damages."); Jacobsen v. Benson Motors, Inc., 216 N.W.2d 396 (Iowa 1974); Montgomery v. Tufford, 437 P.2d 36 (Colo. 1968); Beggs v. Universal C.I.T. Credit Corp., 409 S.W.2d 719 (Mo. 1966).

The Supreme Court has now elevated a variant of this common-law requirement into constitutional law. In order to be constitutionally "reasonable," punitive damages

awards where trial courts refused to inform the jury of such a requirement.[73] Other factors mentioned by common-law courts in evaluating jury awards of punitive damages include the impact on the defendant upon whom they are imposed,[74] the desirability of discouraging others from similar conduct (i.e., the award's impact on third parties),[75] and the size of awards given in analogous cases.[76]

With the rising concern about runaway punitive damages awards in recent years, some states have modified their common law to require trial courts to present some or all of these factors to the jury.[77] Other states, while not imposing such a requirement as an absolute rule, have encouraged trial courts to do so.[78] This development is sensible, as the rationality of the entire process is increased the more the jury's discretion is channeled. As Justice Scalia noted in *Haslip*, it is odd to assess the reasonableness of a jury's verdict by reference to factors unknown to the jury.[79]

---

must bear "some understandable relationship" to compensatory damages. *Haslip*, 499 U.S. at 22.

[73]Hall Oil Co. v. Barquin, 237 P. 255 (Wyo. 1925); Bangert v. Hubbard, 126 N.E.2d 778 (Ind. App. 1955) (actual damages $100; punitive damages $25,000).

Disproportionality between the compensatory and punitive awards is particularly serious when the trial court has refused to instruct the jury on the need for a reasonable relationship. "The likelihood that the instant award was the result of improper considerations is heightened by the trial court's failure to submit the proposed instruction on the reasonable relationship test to which appellant was entitled." *Rosener*, 168 Cal. Rptr. at 245.

[74]*City Bank of Alabama*, 521 So. 2d at 933; Petramale v. Local No. 17 of Laborers' Int'l Union, 847 F.2d 1009, 1013 (2d Cir. 1988); Fraidin v. Weitzmann, 611 A.2d 1046 (Md. App. 1992), *cert. denied*, 617 A.2d 1055 (Md. 1992); Walford v. Blinder, Robinson & Co., 793 P.2d 620, 627 (Colo. App.), *cert. dismissed*, 498 U.S. 977 (1990); *Adams*, 268 Cal. Rptr. at 473; *Rosener*, 168 Cal. Rptr. at 245; *Hardin*, 962 F.2d at 640; Vasbinder v. Scott, 976 F.2d 118 (2d Cir. 1992); S.J. Amoroso Constr. Co. v. Lazovich & Lazovich, 810 P.2d 775 (Nev. 1991).

A large net worth per se, of course, is not something to be deterred, and cannot serve as a license for awarding limitless punitive damages. *Estate of Wesson, supra* note 68; *cf.* Zazú Designs v. L'Oreal S.A., 979 F.2d 499, 507 (7th Cir. 1992).

[75]*City Bank of Alabama*, 521 So. 2d at 933; *Walford*, 793 P.2d at 627.

[76]Morgan v. Woessner, 975 F.2d 629 (9th Cir. 1992); General Motors Corp. v. Johnston, 592 So. 2d 1054 (Ala. 1992); Guy v. Commonwealth Life Ins. Co., 698 F. Supp. 1305, 1316 (N.D. Miss. 1988); Hilgedick v. Koehring Fin. Corp., 8 Cal. Rptr. 2d 76 (1992); Market Tavern, Inc. v. Bowen, 610 A.2d 295 (Md. App.), *cert. denied*, 614 A.2d 84 (Md. 1992). This approach, of course, is tricky, since every case will be different. Nonetheless, it provides some objective guideposts in this otherwise subjective area.

[77]*See, e.g.*, MGW, Inc. v. Fredericks Dev. Corp., 12 Cal. App. 4th 244, 254 & n.6 (1992); Oberg v. Honda Motor Co., 814 P.2d 517, 522 & n.10, 523-24 & nn. 13, 15 (Or. App. 1991), *aff'd*, 851 P.2d 1084 (Or. 1993), *rev'd and remanded*, 114 S. Ct. 2331 (1994); Hoff v. Bower, 492 N.W.2d 912, 914-15 (S.D. 1992); Hodges v. V.S.C. Toof & Co., 833 S.W.2d 896, 901-02 (Tenn. 1992).

[78]*See, e.g.*, Hospital Auth. of Gwinnett County v. Jones, 386 S.E.2d 120, 124 n.13 (Ga. 1989), *vacated and remanded*, 499 U.S. 914, *aff'd on remand*, 409 S.E.2d 501 (Ga. 1991), *cert. denied*, 112 S. Ct. 1175 (1992).

[79]"[I]t would surely not be considered 'fair' (or in accordance with due process) to . . . dispense with meaningful guidance concerning *compensatory* damages, so long

The common law, however, never developed a uniform rule as to what a reviewing court should do if it concludes that the size of a punitive damages award manifests passion or prejudice. In some states, the court is required to grant a new trial, at least on the issue of damages,[80] if not also liability.[81] This approach has much to commend it. "Where the erroneous part of the damages found by the jury cannot be ascertained and it is impossible to tell what the jury acted upon, or how they made up their verdict under the charge of the court, so as to correct the error and arrive at the amount they should have given, justice between the parties cannot be done by a *remittitur*."[82] In other states, in contrast, the court itself may simply remit the verdict,[83] a practice consonant with the historical flexibility afforded to trial courts. "The law . . . does not require that [the trial judge] refuse to add his judgment, soberness and experience to the decision of the jury, and, so doing, to award a result more equitable than either setting aside or wholly affirming a verdict."[84] And in yet other states, the court may remit the award only if the plaintiff agrees to waive his right to a new trial.[85]

## V. Conclusion

The past three decades have witnessed the transformation of punitive damages into a weapon often used in the service of parochial interests, a weapon particularly dangerous because of its arbitrariness. Unconstrained awards threaten the well-being of the Republic as much as the overt parochialism against which Story and Hamilton

as whatever number the jury picks out of the air can be reduced by the trial judge or on appeal." *Haslip*, 499 U.S. at 37 (opinion concurring in judgment).

[80]*See, e.g.*, Lightning Lube, Inc. v. Witco Corp., 802 F. Supp. 1180 (D.N.J. 1992), *aff'd*, 4 F.3d 1153 (3d Cir. 1993) (New Jersey law); State *ex rel.* Young v. Crookham, 618 P.2d 1268, 1272 (Or. 1980); Team Central, Inc. v. Teamco, Inc., 271 N.W.2d 914, 926 (Iowa 1978); Bower v. Hog Builders, Inc., 461 S.W.2d 784 (Mo. 1970); Louisville & N.R. Co. v. Complete Auto Transit, Inc., 259 S.W.2d 483, 484 (Ky. App. 1953).

[81]South Carolina has held that fundamental fairness requires a new trial on *both* the issues of liability and punitive damages, reasoning that a jury swayed by prejudice at the punitive damages stage is just as likely to have been swayed by such prejudice at the liability stage. Reid v. Harbison Dev. Corp., 345 S.E.2d 492, 493 (S.C. 1986).

[82]SUTHERLAND, *supra* note 10, § 459, at 1504-05. Indeed, some courts have held that awarding a new trial on the issue of damages in this situation is necessary to preserve the right to trial by jury. *See, e.g.*, Defender Indus., Inc. v. Northwestern Mut. Life Ins. Co., 938 F.2d 502 (4th Cir. 1991); Rommell v. U.S. Steel Corp., 168 A.2d 437 (N.J. Super.), *cert. denied*, 170 A.2d 544 (N.J. 1961).

[83]Ford Motor Credit Co. v. Washington, 420 So. 2d 14, 18 (Ala. 1982); Burnett v. National Enquirer, Inc., 193 Cal. Rptr. 206 (1983), *appeal dismissed*, 465 U.S. 1014 (1984).

[84]SUTHERLAND, *supra* note 10, § 460, at 1513-14.

[85]*See, e.g.*, Spence v. Hilliard, 389 S.E.2d 753, 754 (Ga. 1990); SUTHERLAND, *supra* note 10, § 460, at 1510.

warned so long ago, not only by the obvious costs imposed by runaway awards, but also by the less apparent costs of inflated settlement awards, decreased innovation, and diminished interstate commerce.

The legal transformation has been particularly insidious because it has been masked by semantic continuity. But while phrases such as "willful or wanton" and "passion or prejudice" survive, much of their substantive content has vanished.[86] This dramatic shift may also be less noticeable because it forms part of a larger shift in the overall legal culture. Since the 1950s, the law generally has come to be seen as an appropriate instrument for effecting social reform, and the prospect of bankrupting an entire industry through punitive damages no longer boggles the legal mind. To the contrary, every outrageous punitive damages award tends to legitimize the next one and to further numb the legal and popular consciousness to the ongoing decay. Deviancy now masquerades as normalcy.

Recent tort reform legislation in various states is, therefore, a healthy development. Such legislation has tended to restore, not undermine, common-law principles. Indeed, such legislation, in all probability, represents a backlash against the obvious unfairness and arbitrariness which has been allowed to creep into the law.[87]

Meanwhile, there is no reason why the courts should stay their own hand. The punitive damages explosion of recent decades cannot be attributed to American jurors suddenly going berserk; the courts surely share much of the blame for exalting the common law's forms over its substance. This crisis is a "self-inflicted wound,"[88] and to the extent courts refuse to minister to it, they necessarily undermine their own legitimacy and prestige. The more the public hears of multimillion dollar punitive damages claims filed over trifles,[89] the more our entire judicial system becomes a laughingstock.

[86]Professors Ghiardi and Kircher, in their comprehensive treatise on punitive damages, have put the point thus: "In the preparation of this work we gained the impression that some courts tended to repeat, as if by rote, old rules on the subject as one would intone an ancient ritual. Little consideration appears to be given to their substance. The rules of stare decisis should never be a commitment to intellectual stagnation." 1 JAMES D. GHIARDI & JOHN J. KIRCHER, PUNITIVE DAMAGES LAW AND PRACTICE § 2.13, at 28-29 (1985).

[87]One state's legislative solution is discussed in some detail in chapter 12.—Editor's note.

[88]Dunn v. Hovic, 1 F.3d 1371, 1399 (3d Cir.) (Weis, J., dissenting) (quoting Frilette v. Kimberlin, 508 F.2d 205, 212 (3d Cir. 1974)), *cert. denied*, 114 S. Ct. 650 (1993). That is not to say, of course, that a legislative solution to the tort crisis is undesirable, but merely that it should never have been necessary in the first place.

[89]Two recent examples of such claims include skater Tonya Harding's eleventh-hour lawsuit against the United States Olympic Committee, in which she sought $20 million in punitive damages, *see* Christine Brennan, *All Eyes Fixed on Ice for Harding-Kerrigan Show Today*, WASH. POST, Feb. 23, 1994, at B6, and a suit by singer Barry Manilow seeking $15 million in punitive damages against a radio station that openly refused to play his music, *see People*, DALLAS MORNING NEWS, Feb. 12, 1994, at 2A.

The common law, of course, is not rigid; in its flexibility lies its strength. State courts may well decide that the changes of recent decades in the common law of punitive damages are all for the best, and reaffirm those changes. But courts should not, at the very least, add insult to injury by asserting that the current judicial laissez-faire approach toward punitive damages is compelled by the common law, leaving little choice for them but to affirm awards by rote. Contemporary punitive damages simply are not "[c]lothed in common-law history and tradition."[90] It is time for courts and, failing that, legislatures to recognize that this emperor has no clothes.

[90]Hospital Auth. of Gwinnett County v. Jones, 409 S.E.2d 501, 504 (Ga. 1991), *cert. denied*, 112 S. Ct. 1175 (1992).

CHAPTER 6

# NONECONOMIC DAMAGES: THE NEED FOR REFORM

KEITH A. TEEL
JOSEPH K. DOSS

## I. Introduction

Damage awards in tort litigation often bear little relationship to the actual economic cost of the injuries suffered by the plaintiff. Perhaps the most frequently cited culprit is outlandish awards of punitive damages, discussed in the preceding chapter. But a far more common cause of this problem is large awards of noneconomic damages, which are intended to compensate plaintiffs for intangible injuries such as pain and suffering, grief, anxiety, humiliation, and loss of consortium.

Virtually everyone agrees that injured plaintiffs deserve to be justly compensated for their injuries. But there is a great dispute in the legal community over what "just compensation" should include. Most legal observers and practitioners agree that a successful plaintiff should be able to recover the economic costs associated with his or her injury. There is, however, a great deal of controversy concerning the awarding of noneconomic damages, which at present may be recovered in personal injury actions in every state.

Such awards are frequently based on highly subjective evidence, some of which is at best imagined or, sadly, fraudulent. Juries often receive minimal guidance from judges about the appropriate circumstances in which to make an award or the size of such awards. Without such guidance, juries frequently tend to act on emotion rather than fact or law.

There are widely differing views about noneconomic damages. Some observers believe that the current system provides juries the needed flexibility to make decisions on a case-by-case basis. Some believe that more guidance is needed, but that limits on awards of noneconomic damages are inappropriate. Others argue for absolute dollar limits on the size of noneconomic damages, and some call for the abandonment of noneconomic damages altogether.

This chapter first describes the current legal status of noneconomic damages in the United States, and highlights some of the empirical data that is available concerning such damages.[1] The chapter then discusses some of the proposals to change and reform this area of the law.[2]

## II. Current Abuses

*Defining "Noneconomic Damages"*

Compensatory damages awarded in personal injury actions are generally divided into two categories—economic and noneconomic.[3] Economic damages are intended to compensate an injured party for measurable losses such as lost wages, lost earning capacity, and medical expenses.[4] In contrast, noneconomic damages provide compensation for intangible injuries such as pain and suffering, humiliation, anxiety, fear, sadness, and loss of society, companionship, and consortium.[5]

Many courts use the term "pain and suffering" when referring to any type of noneconomic damage award, even though the compensation sometimes is for items such as fear or loss of society.[6] Moreover, when discussing pain and suffering, most courts do not draw distinctions between these two elements.[7] Those that do differentiate these concepts generally define pain as "an unpleasant sensation registered . . . in the brain as a result of the stimulation of pain fibers in the peripheral nerves."[8] Suffering is the recognition of the possible damages resulting from the pain sensation.[9]

Noneconomic damages were first awarded in England over two centuries ago.[10] In the United States, it appears that such damages were routinely awarded as early as the late nineteenth century.[11] In recent years, noneconomic damages have become part of almost every personal injury award. In fact, several courts have held that

---

[1]*Infra* Part II, pp. 100–06.

[2]*Infra* Part III, pp. 106–10.

[3]*See, e.g.*, Samsel v. Wheeler Transp. Servs. Inc., 789 P.2d 541, 552 (Kan. 1990).

[4]*Id.*

[5]*Id.*; CHARLES T. MCCORMICK, HANDBOOK ON THE LAW OF DAMAGES § 88, at 316–17 (1935).

[6]*See, e.g.*, Capelouto v. Kaiser Found. Hosp., 500 P.2d 880, 883 (Cal. 1972).

[7]*Id.*

[8]22 AM. JUR. 2D *Damages* § 240 (1988 & Supp. 1993); *accord* MCCORMICK, *supra* note 5, at 315.

[9]22 AM. JUR. 2D *Damages* § 240 (1988 & Supp. 1993).

[10]*See Samsel*, 789 P.2d at 551 (citing Scott v. Sheperd, 95 Eng. Rep. 1124 (K.B. 1773)).

[11]*Samsel*, 789 P.2d at 552 (citing Verril v. Minot, 31 Me. 299 (1850); Morse v. Auburn & Syracuse R.R., 10 Barb. 621 (N.Y. Sup. Ct. 1851); Ransom v. New York and E.R.R., 15 N.Y. 415 (1857)).

a pain and suffering award *must* be made whenever medical damages are incurred.[12]

*Calculating Noneconomic Damages*

In general, most states provide no substantive guidelines for a jury to use when deciding how much to award in noneconomic damages.[13] Consider the following example of a standard charge to a jury concerning damages:

> In determining the amount of plaintiff's damages, if any, you may take into consideration the following elements as shown by the evidence:
> 1. The [plaintiff's] pain and suffering, disabilities or disfigurement, and any accompanying mental anguish.
> 2. The reasonable and necessary medical expenses incurred or paid.
> 3. The loss of time or earnings.
>
> In arriving at the amount of your award, you will take into consideration the nature, extent, and duration of the plaintiff's injuries, if any, his age, and his general health and condition both before and after the occurrence of the injuries complained of.[14]

An instruction of this kind is used in virtually every state. It essentially permits the jury to weigh all relevant factors and to award an appropriate or reasonable amount of damages.[15] However, without any clear standards it is almost impossible for a jury to determine whether a particular award is "appropriate" or "reasonable." As a result, damage awards vary widely from case to case, even though the injuries are similar, with juries sometimes awarding staggering amounts to plaintiffs whose injuries are relatively minor. A brief examination of available empirical data highlights the problem.

A fair amount of empirical research has been conducted on awards of pain and suffering damages. An excellent summary of some of the evidence has been provided by Randall R. Bovbjerg, James F. Blumstein, and Frank A. Sloan.[16] Their article analyzes, in particular, jury awards of damages in Florida and Kansas City personal injury cases between 1973 and 1987.

The article concludes that, at least at a generalized level, juries award larger amounts of noneconomic damages as the severity of

---

[12] *See, e.g.*, 22 AM. JUR. 2D *Damages* § 242 (1988 & Supp. 1993); Odendahl v. Wild, 418 So. 2d 36, 37 (La. Ct. App. 1982); Wall v. Van Meter, 223 S.W.2d 734, 736 (Ky. Ct. App. 1949).

[13] *See, e.g.*, Hazelwood v. Beauchamp, 766 S.W.2d 439, 440 (Ky. Ct. App. 1989); Steinauer v. Sarpy County, 353 N.W.2d 715, 723 (Neb. 1984); Young v. Jack Boring's, Inc., 540 S.W.2d 887, 897 (Mo. Ct. App. 1976).

[14] 8 AM. JUR. PL. & PR. FORMS 274 (1982).

[15] *Id.*

[16] *Valuing Life and Limb in Tort: Scheduling "Pain and Suffering,"* 83 NW. U. L. REV. 908 (1989).

injury increases.[17] This is to be expected and is somewhat reassuring. More troubling, however, is the fact that otherwise the size distribution of pain and suffering awards was quite variable.

The authors grouped injuries by categories of severity, and while the average award in some categories does not seem overly excessive, the data identified excessive pain and suffering awards at the extreme levels in every category.[18] For instance, within the highest category of permanent grave injuries, such as quadriplegia or severe brain damage, pain and suffering awards ranged from zero to $14,207,000. The same pattern of variability was seen in virtually all categories of injury, with such awards ranging from five to nine times the mean. The discrepancy in the size of awards is even more striking when the extreme awards are compared with the median award for the category, which is the award of damages that is at the midpoint in terms of the number of all damage awards. The extreme award exceeded the median award by a factor of five to forty-five times.

The authors also note that the discrepancies in the size of awards across various jurisdictions will be significant. Thus, they cite an article which reported that in the aftermath of a 1979 airplane crash, one expert estimated that the likely awards for the deaths of people of identical age and background ranged from a low of $10,000 to a high of $2 million, depending on the varying legal rules in different states.[19]

These data suggest that some awards are simply too large, and that the variability in the size of awards is severe. Some would argue that the authority possessed by courts in most states to reduce an award can address the problems of excess and variability. But while some courts have the authority to reduce or overturn awards that

---

[17] *Id.* at 919–24, 936–38.

[18] Again, the study suggested that more severe injuries produced greater awards than did less severe injuries. Thus, awards for temporary insignificant injuries produced an average pain and suffering award of $10,000. Temporary major injuries, such as burns or drug side effects, resulted in average pain and suffering awards of $62,000. Permanent minor injuries, such as the loss of fingers or lost or damaged organs which are not disabling, produced average pain and suffering awards of $160,000, while permanent major injuries, such as paraplegia or blindness, resulted in average pain and suffering awards of $2,309,000. The average pain and suffering award for permanent grave injuries (quadriplegia, severe brain damage) was $4,252,000, and the average pain and suffering award in a wrongful death claim was $1,242,000. *Id.* at 937, Table 3. (The decrease of the average award in wrongful death actions is explained by the fact that a decedent's conscious pain and suffering is usually compensable under most state wrongful death statutes, but not the loss of enjoyment of life or the mental anguish of survivors.)

[19] *See id.* at 913 (citing James Warren, *How Much Is A Human Life Worth?*, CHICAGO SUN TIMES, May 25, 1980, at 5 (business section)).

"shock the conscience of the court,"[20] such findings are rare (in part because the rationale for the jury's action is rarely explained) and may not significantly reduce the original award.[21] Moreover, in some jurisdictions a jury determination concerning noneconomic damages may *not* be refuted or shown to be factually insufficient.[22]

The essentially unfettered discretion accorded to most juries when considering noneconomic damages can lead to unreasonable awards that are dictated more by passion than by reason.[23] Experienced plaintiffs' counsel are of course aware of this, and seek to play on these passions. They have a strong incentive to do so. Since most personal injury actions are handled on a contingency fee basis, very large noneconomic damages awards translate into correspondingly large attorney fees.[24] Just as with punitive damages, the possibility of huge noneconomic damage awards may encourage a "lottery" mentality among plaintiffs and their lawyers, who sue in hopes of hitting the "jackpot."

A review of just a few cases illustrates the problem of excessiveness. In *Treadway v. Uniroyal Tire Co.,*[25] the Oklahoma Supreme Court upheld a pain and suffering award of approximately $750,000 for a plaintiff whose wrist was fractured when a tire he was attempting to mount exploded. There was uncontroverted evidence that the plaintiff disregarded warnings provided by the manufacturer. In *Rattenborg v. Montgomery Elevator Co.,*[26] the plaintiff was awarded $505,000 in noneconomic damages for injuries to her finger that resulted when she tried to retrieve her shoe from an escalator.

The noneconomic damages awarded in these cases are plainly excessive given the nature of the injuries. In other cases, conversely, there may be instances in which the plaintiff's pain and suffering award is grossly undervalued by the jury. For example, in *Hazelwood v. Beauchamp,*[27] the jury awarded the plaintiff only $250 in pain and suffering damages for injuries caused when his hand was caught and crushed in a hay baler. Recognizing that the pain and suffering award was inadequate and contrary to the evidence, the Kentucky

[20]*See, e.g.,* Bingaman v. Grays Harbor Community Hosp., 699 P.2d 1230, 1233 (Wash. 1985).

[21]2 AMERICAN LAW INSTITUTE, ENTERPRISE RESPONSIBILITY FOR PERSONAL INJURY 202 (1991).

[22]*See, e.g.,* Skaggs Alpha Beta, Inc. v. Nabhan, 808 S.W.2d 198, 202 (Tex. App. 1991).

[23]Stanley Ingber, *Rethinking Intangible Injuries: A Focus on Remedy,* 73 CAL. L. REV. 772, 778–79 (1985).

[24]AMERICAN LAW INSTITUTE, *supra* note 21, at 215.

[25]766 P.2d 938 (Okla. 1988).

[26]438 N.W.2d 602 (Iowa App. 1989).

[27]766 S.W.2d 439 (Ky. Ct. App. 1989).

Supreme Court reversed and remanded the case. Such cases highlight the problem of the variability in the size of awards.

As noted at the outset of this section, the basic problem may be simply that juries are given inadequate guidance as to how to calculate an award. Typically, courts do not permit juries to be told of the size of awards in other, similar cases. Yet they often do allow highly suggestive or speculative argumentation about the size of an award. Plaintiffs' attorneys, recognizing the arbitrary nature of noneconomic damages, have developed various approaches that can "assist" juries in setting the amount of a noneconomic damage award. Using the so-called per diem argument, a plaintiff's attorney will ask the jury to reduce his client's pain and suffering into measurable units, such as years, days, hours, or minutes.[28] The attorney will then suggest a dollar amount for each such unit. The amount of damages can then be calculated by multiplying the number of units by the value of each unit. The value of each individual unit (e.g., minute or hour) may seem small, but when calculated over the plaintiff's lifetime the total amount can be considerable.

A variation of the "per diem" argument is the "job offer" approach.[29] When using this tactic, a plaintiff's attorney will offer the jurors a hypothetical job and set the compensation at a certain amount per day, typically a rather small sum. The jurors are then told that their job is to suffer the plaintiff's pain for the remainder of his or her expected lifetime.

Most courts allow the use of these tests.[30] Those that do not typically express concern about the lack of any evidentiary support for the suggested rule.[31] The widespread use of these tests suggests, in any event, the susceptibility that current procedures—and the lack of guidance to the jury—create for the imposition of extraordinary or unjustified awards.

### *The Special Problem of "Fear" Claims*

Traditional tort law demanded that the plaintiff prove actual physical harm before any damages could be awarded for any alleged intangible harm. This so-called injury requirement served as an effective check on baseless lawsuits. If a plaintiff could not establish physical harm of any type resulting from the allegedly tortious conduct, then common sense—and the injury requirement—dictated

[28] *See, e.g.*, Graeff v. Baptist Temple of Springfield, 576 S.W.2d 291, 302–03 (Mo. 1978).

[29] *Id.*

[30] *See* DAN B. DOBBS, HANDBOOK ON THE LAW OF REMEDIES 545–48 (1973).

[31] *Cf.* Ratner v. Arrington, 111 So. 2d 82, 88–89 (Fla. Dist. Ct. App. 1959) (explaining arguments for and against a per diem argument, and allowing its use).

that he should not be permitted to recover for noneconomic damages such as emotional distress and anxiety.

This principle was established very early on. For example, in *Lynch v. Knight,*[32] the court noted that "the law cannot value, and does not pretend to redress," mental pain or anxiety "when the unlawful act causes that alone." This equitable rule has been adopted by the American Law Institute in Section 436A of its 1965 *Restatement (Second) of Torts,* which states that recovery for emotional distress will not be permitted for negligent conduct without some proof of bodily harm.[33]

In recent years, however, the courts of many states have severely eroded the injury requirement,[34] and fourteen states[35] have abolished it. In these states, a plaintiff may recover damages for emotional distress without any showing that he was physically harmed by the defendant's conduct.

Courts have abolished the injury requirement in three ways. One influential court, in the context of a toxic exposure claim, held that physical injury is no longer a prerequisite for an award of damages for emotional distress, so long as there is proof that the fear stems from a knowledge, corroborated by reliable medical and scientific opinion, that it is more likely than not that the feared cancer will develop in the future due to a toxic exposure.[36] And, if the exposure resulted from conduct amounting to "oppression, fraud, or malice," then a plaintiff can recover merely by showing the fear is "serious, genuine, and reasonable."[37] A larger number of courts, though stopping short of formal rejection of the injury requirement, have held that mere exposure to a potentially harmful substance satisfies the injury requirement, even when that exposure has caused no discernible physical harm.[38] Finally, a few courts have suggested that the physical injury requirement can be satisfied by evidence of physical

[32]11 Eng. Rep. 854 (1861).

[33]*See also* RESTATEMENT (SECOND) OF TORTS §§ 313, 436 (1965). *But see id.* § 46, which allows recovery absent physical harm for *intentional* infliction of severe emotional injury when caused by "outrageous" conduct.

[34]*See generally* Scott D. Marrs, *Mind Over Body: Trends Regarding the Physical Injury Requirement in Negligent Infliction of Emotional Distress and "Fear of Disease" Cases,* 28 TORT & INS. L.J. 1 (1992); Merton E. Marks & James T. Acuff, Jr., *Legal Issues in Recovery for Fear of Future Disease Without Present Physical Injury,* 41 FED'N INS. & CORP. COUNS. Q. 235 (1991).

[35]Alabama, California, Connecticut, Hawaii, Maine, Missouri, Montana, Nebraska, New Jersey, North Carolina, Ohio, Oregon, Texas, and Washington. *See* Marrs, *supra* note 34, at 4.

[36]Potter v. Firestone Tire & Rubber Co., No. SO18831, 1993 Cal. LEXIS 6375 (Cal. Dec. 27, 1993).

[37]*Id.*

[38]*E.g.,* Plummer v. United States, 580 F.2d 72, 76 (3d Cir. 1978) (applying Pennsylvania law); Eagle-Picher Indus., Inc. v. Cox, 481 So. 2d 517, 526–27 (Fla. Dist. Ct. App. 1985); Laxton v. Orkin Exterminating Co., 639 S.W.2d 431, 434 (Tenn. 1982).

manifestations of emotional distress.[39] In each case, the effect of the courts' departure from the injury requirement is to permit plaintiffs to recover damages for emotional distress in the absence of any allegation or proof of traditional physical injury.

As the preceding paragraph indicates, a common application of the various liberalized forms of the injury requirement has been in the area of so-called toxic torts, or cases alleging harm caused by exposure to harmful substances. In many such cases, the plaintiff can establish that he was exposed to a hazardous substance, but cannot demonstrate that he was harmed by that exposure in any medically recognized sense. The erosion of the injury rule has permitted such plaintiffs to claim damages for their "fear" of developing a disease in the future as a result of the exposure.[40] A plaintiff successfully asserting a "fear of disease" claim may recover damages not only for this emotional distress, but also for the costs of medical monitoring far into the future aimed at discovering the advent of the feared illness.[41]

The disturbing trend of awarding noneconomic damages without proof of physical harm threatens to make this area of the law even more uncertain and unpredictable. By weakening the injury requirement, the courts are encouraging fraudulent and nonmeritorious lawsuits.[42]

## III. Efforts at Reform

### *Successes to Date*

Dissatisfaction with unpredictable and unreasonably high noneconomic damages awards has led many states to enact corrective legislation.[43] Most of these reform statutes place a limit or "cap" on the amount a plaintiff can recover.[44] These caps range from $150,000 to $1 million.[45] Instead of capping noneconomic damages, some states have abolished or limited the joint and several liability doctrine in claims for such awards.[46]

---

[39] *See, e.g.*, Poole v. Alpha Therapeutic Corp., 698 F. Supp. 1367, 1372 (N.D. Ill. 1988); Stites v. Sundstrand Heat Transfer, Inc., 660 F. Supp. 1516, 1526–27 (W.D. Mich. 1987).

[40] *E.g.*, Merry v. Westinghouse Elec. Corp., 684 F. Supp. 847, 848 (M.D. Pa. 1988); Wisner v. Illinois Cent. Gulf R.R., 537 So. 2d 740, 748 (La. App. 1988).

[41] *E.g.*, Ayers v. Jackson Township, 525 A.2d 287, 312 (N.J. 1987).

[42] *See* RESTATEMENT (SECOND) OF TORTS § 436A cmt. b (1965).

[43] AMERICAN LAW INSTITUTE, *supra* note 21, at 203.

[44] *Id.*

[45] *Id.*

[46] *See, e.g.*, CAL. CIV. CODE§ 1431.2 (Deering 1993); OHIO REV. CODE ANN. § 2315.19(D)(1)(b) (Baldwin 1993); FLA. STAT. ch. 768.81(3) (1992); OR. REV. STAT. § 18.485(2) (1991). [*See also* chapter 2.—Editor's note.]

A flurry of legislative activity took place in the mid-1970s and focused mostly upon limiting damages in medical malpractice actions. This was followed by other significant legislative enactments in the mid-1980s. According to the American Law Institute,[47] sixteen damage caps were enacted during the period 1975–77; fifteen were for malpractice actions only, of which four applied only to pain and suffering awards. In 1986–87, twenty-two states enacted such legislation; twelve were limited to malpractice actions, and nineteen applied only to pain and suffering damages.

Many of these statutes have been challenged on a variety of federal and state constitutional grounds,[48] including due process,[49] equal protection,[50] right of trial by jury,[51] and right of access to the courts.[52] While several of these statutes have been struck down by the courts, many others have been upheld.[53] Many of the earlier caps found to be constitutionally infirm applied to *all* damages and were therefore more vulnerable to a legal challenge, since a plaintiff could be barred from recovering actual medical expenses.[54]

To date, the United States Supreme Court has not ruled on the constitutionality of a state cap on noneconomic damages. In *Duke Power Co. v. Carolina Environmental Study Group Inc.*,[55] the Court upheld a federal damages cap for accidents involving nuclear power

---

[47]AMERICAN LAW INSTITUTE, *supra* note 21, at 203 n.10.

[48]A chart describing reported decisions on the constitutionality of medical malpractice and tort reform damages limits appears in Marci de Sa e Silva, Comment, *Constitutional Challenges To Washington's Limit on Noneconomic Damages in Cases of Personal Injury and Death,* 63 WASH. L. REV. 653, 675 (1988). Since the publication of this Comment, several other court decisions have been handed down. *See infra* note 53.

[49]*E.g.,* Etheridge v. Medical Ctr. Hosp., 376 S.E.2d 525 (Va. 1989).

[50]*E.g.,* Murphy v. Edmonds, 601 A.2d 102 (Md. 1992).

[51]Samsel v. Wheeler Transp. Servs., Inc., 789 P.2d 541 (Kan. 1990).

[52]*E.g.,* Adams v. Children's Mercy Hosp., 832 S.W.2d 898 (Mo. 1992), *cert. denied,* S. Ct. 511 (1992).

[53]Decisions upholding limits on noneconomic damages include: Scholz v. Metropolitan Pathologists, P.C., 851 P.2d 901 (Colo. 1993); University of Miami v. Echarte, 618 So. 2d 189 (Fla. 1993); Murphy v. Edmonds, 601 A.2d 102 (Md. 1992); Adams v. Children's Mercy Hosp., 832 S.W.2d 898 (Mo. 1992); Robinson v. Charleston Area Medical Ctr., Inc., 414 S.E.2d 877 (W. Va. 1991); Samsel v. Wheeler Transp. Servs., Inc., 771 P.2d 71 (Kan. 1989); Etheridge v. Medical Ctr. Hosp., 376 S.E.2d 525 (Va. 1989); Fein v. Permanente Medical Group, 695 P.2d 665 (Cal. 1985); Johnson v. St. Vincent Hosp., Inc., 404 N.E.2d 585 (Ind. 1980); Prendergast v. Nelson, 256 N.W.2d 657 (Neb. 1977).

Decisions finding statutes to be unconstitutional include: Moore v. Mobile Infirmary Ass'n, 592 So. 2d 156 (Ala. 1991); Brannigan v. Usitalo, 587 A.2d 1232 (N.H. 1991); Morris v. Savoy, 576 N.E.2d 765 (Ohio 1991); Sofie v. Fibreboard Corp., 771 P.2d 711 (Wash. 1989); Reynolds v. Porter, 760 P.2d 816 (Okla. 1988); Arneson v. Olson, 270 N.W.2d 125 (N.D. 1978); Wright v. Central Du Page Hosp. Ass'n, 347 N.E.2d 736 (Ill. 1976).

[54]*See Fein,* 695 P.2d at 682.

[55]438 U.S. 59 (1978).

plants. In doing so, however, the Court left undecided whether such a cap violates due process if injured parties are not provided a "quid pro quo" for a common-law right of recovery which is abrogated.[56]

In a later action, the Supreme Court dismissed an appeal in *Fein v. Permanente Medical Group*[57] for lack of a substantial federal question, leaving intact California's $250,000 cap on noneconomic damages for medical malpractice actions.[58] Justice White dissented and urged the Court to decide the question left unresolved in *Duke Power,* namely whether due process requires a "legislatively enacted compensation scheme to be a *quid pro quo* for the common-law or state-law remedy it replaces . . . ."[59] Several years later, the Supreme Court denied certiorari in a case challenging the constitutionality of Missouri's $350,000 cap on noneconomic damages in malpractice actions.[60] Justice White, demonstrating his continued interest in this issue, stated that he would have granted the petition.[61]

### *Alternative Systems for Awarding Noneconomic Damages*

When evaluating ways to improve the current system of awarding noneconomic damages, the rights of both plaintiffs and defendants must be considered. But while it is easy to say that a balance must be struck between adequately compensating plaintiffs and not subjecting defendants to unreasonable and unpredictable awards, in practice this balance is hard to achieve.

As we noted earlier,[62] some legal observers believe the current system for awarding noneconomic damages is working well and should not be changed. Others argue that noneconomic damages should be abolished completely. The empirical evidence suggests the first view is incorrect, and the second view is probably unfair and certainly politically infeasible. It should also be understood that any solution to the problem of "out of control" noneconomic damages will of necessity involve a certain degree of arbitrariness. The current system is totally arbitrary; our desired goal is to achieve more predictability, not absolute certainty.

#### Caps

Enacting legislation that adopts a flat cap on the dollar amount recoverable will reduce noneconomic damages awards. Such limits

[56] *Id.* at 87–88.
[57] 695 P.2d 665 (Cal. 1985).
[58] 474 U.S 892 (1985).
[59] *Id.* at 894.
[60] Adams v. Children's Mercy Hosp., 832 S.W.2d 898 (Mo. 1992), *cert. denied,* 113 S. Ct. 511 (1992).
[61] *Id.*
[62] *Supra* p. 99.

are, however, viewed by some as unduly harsh since they prevent some of the most seriously injured plaintiffs from being adequately compensated. One possible solution would be to allow the judge, under certain exceptional circumstances, to raise the cap and award the plaintiff additional damages. This would be similar to the additur procedure now used by the courts and would provide an extra safety net for the most severely injured plaintiffs.

Caps on noneconomic damages seem particularly appropriate in wrongful death actions. While an individual may have suffered before dying, it seems ludicrous to permit the decedent's estate to recover excessive amounts of money since the deceased will receive no benefit from the award. As noted above, in most states awards of noneconomic damages in wrongful death cases are already limited,[63] and in this special case flat caps also may be appropriate.

One problem with caps is that they typically do not take into account the effect inflation will have on future awards. As a result, the "real value" of the injury compensation available will decrease over time. Moreover, caps do nothing to prevent unreasonable noneconomic damage awards that fall below the statutory limit. To alleviate the first problem it is possible to include a provision that would adjust the cap upward if the rate of inflation increases. With regard to the latter problem, some have suggested placing a "floor" on noneconomic damages, requiring the plaintiff to demonstrate that his or her injuries exceeded a certain threshold (e.g., "serious" or permanent impairment of a bodily function) before noneconomic damages could be awarded at all.

### Schedules

Adopting a schedule would place limits on noneconomic damages based on the type of injury and/or the plaintiff's life expectancy.[64] For example, legislation could be adopted that would establish a fixed amount or a range of noneconomic damage award sizes for various categories of injury. Such a system would surely add certainty to the process of awarding noneconomic damages, but it fails to take into account the different reactions people may have to the same injury. For example, the emotional impact of losing a limb may be greater for a professional football player than for an attorney. And, while there is arbitrariness with every system of awarding noneconomic damages, the amounts awarded under a schedule seem particularly vulnerable to this criticism.

---

[63] *Supra* p. 102 n.18.

[64] AMERICAN LAW INSTITUTE, *supra* note 21, at 223–27.

Again, one possible solution to the problems inherent in a schedule system would be to grant the trial judge discretion to exceed the limits if there is compelling evidence that justice requires a higher award. Under such a system, independent appellate review of the facts should be permitted in order to prevent trial judges from routinely overriding the cap based solely on personal philosophical grounds.

In Washington, the state legislature enacted a statute that limited noneconomic damages by establishing a formula. Noneconomic damages could not exceed an amount determined by multiplying 0.43 by the average annual state wage and by the plaintiff's life expectancy. In a 1989 decision, however, the Washington Supreme Court held that this statute violated the plaintiff's constitutional right to a jury trial.[65]

### Evidentiary Changes

A third option for reform might be to change the rules of evidence that are applied in most states to noneconomic damage claims. Typically, juries are not given a great deal of guidance when determining the size of an award of compensatory damages. This could be changed, perhaps even by court rule. One possible change would be to permit juries to be told of noneconomic damage awards in similar cases. This approach might address the problem of variability, at least to a degree, but it may also introduce tangential issues in a case as to whether "similar" cases truly are comparable. This may be a matter the judge would have to consider outside the hearing of the jury prior to the presentation of such evidence. Of course, those who favor limiting noneconomic damage awards should keep in mind that the award in the comparable case may be one that is merely an "average" award or one that is at the upper end of awards in a particular type of case. Thus, allowing evidence of this kind may have only a minor effect on the variability of awards, and it is unclear in any event that it would result in lower awards.

### Special Verdicts

In the typical case a jury awards damages through a general verdict. This hinders the ability of the trial court or appellate courts to review a verdict, since they often do not know the basis for it. It would be possible to require the use of special verdicts in most cases, at least with regard to the issue of damages. The authors are unaware

[65] Sofie v. Fibreboard Corp., 771 P.2d 711 (Wash. 1989).

of empirical data that suggest whether this reform would be effective in limiting the excessive size or the great variability of awards.

## IV. Conclusion

It is clear that the current system for awarding noneconomic damages is highly subjective and often results in unreasonable and excessive awards. While plaintiffs with valid claims should be justly compensated, there should be meaningful standards to assist juries in making these determinations. In addition, reasonable limits are needed to bring greater certainty and predictability to this confusing and arbitrary area of the law.

Any attempt to craft a legislative solution to this problem must balance the needs of the injured claimants against the rights of the defendant. No statute can alleviate all the problems inherent in awarding noneconomic damages, and any attempted solution will involve a certain degree of arbitrariness, but failure to act will permit unreasonable and fraudulent awards to continue unabated.

# Court Procedures

CHAPTER 7

# DISCOVERY ABUSE AND REFORM

CLAUDIA WILSON FROST
MATTHEW P. EASTUS
DAVID HRICIK

## I. Introduction

Practitioners and commentators have charged for years that some attorneys view discovery as a war of attrition in which the goal is to harass an opponent until he capitulates because of cost, delay, or exasperation. Many states' current discovery systems contribute to this abuse, turning justice on its head by allowing the expense of unbridled discovery and its attendant disputes to supplant an examination of the merits of the parties' claims as the ultimate measure of a case's value. Nevertheless, some states have undertaken a variety of innovative reforms designed to check these abuses and return discovery to its proper role—that of a truth-seeking tool that is ancillary to the civil justice system's primary goal of just and fair adjudication.

The most ironic aspect of the discovery problem is that lawyers themselves clearly recognize its deleterious effects on the litigation process and the public's perception of the profession, as this editorial from the American Bar Association clearly shows:

> The journey from complaint to resolution is a slow trek across the badlands of discovery. The dominance of civil discovery has changed what it means to be a litigator. . . . The day is fast approaching—if it is not already here—when litigators will not try cases; they will just discover each other to death. . . .
>
> Discovery affects how the public, and clients, see trial lawyers. Few aspects of litigation are more criticized than foot-thick interrogatories and endless depositions. And who can doubt that discovery is a main cause of the escalating cost of lawsuits? The bill for a case not ended quickly will mostly cover discovery. What can be done? Probably very little. . . . There are abuses, but if all of them disappeared tomorrow, there would still be a lot of discovery. A radical cure might be worse than the disease.[1]

Few disagree with the symptoms described by the ABA, but the judges, bar associations, and legislatures of many states have differed with the ABA on the efficacy of a cure. They have instead

[1]*Discovery,* LITIG., Fall 1988, at 7.

concluded that steps can be taken to reform the current discovery system so that, instead of rewarding abuse, it provides incentives for a lawyer to consider carefully what information he actually needs, to try to obtain only that information, to use the most efficient means to obtain it, and to comply fully with all legitimate discovery requests.[2]

Over the past decade, several states have conducted experiments to find remedies for some of these ills. The most successful of these efforts, which involve clear-cut limitations on the amount of discovery permitted and comprehensive docket control management, have each improved the efficiency with which the courts and the litigants process cases and administer justice. This chapter describes the scope of the discovery problem and examines the states' experience with discovery reform.

## II. The Problem

### *The Impact of Discovery Costs*

The costs of litigation alone indicate that the need for reform is quite real. In a recent survey, some two hundred federal and eight hundred state judges rated abusive discovery as the chief reason for today's high litigation costs.[3] Similarly, inordinate discovery has been cited as a "primary reason" why litigation is unaffordable for low- and middle-income Americans and why courts are overburdened with discovery disputes.[4] Moreover, the costs of litigation have directly measurable consequences beyond direct legal fees and expenses. For example, many experts point out that

> the amount of money and other resources devoted to legal costs inevitably affects the bottom line of a balance sheet. If American businesses uniformly have higher legal costs than their international rivals, it gives these rivals a competitive advantage. It follows that the closer America moves toward a less costly civil justice system, perhaps more similar to the systems used abroad,

[2] Alfred W. Cortese, Jr. & Kathleen L. Blaner, *Civil Justice Reform in America: A Question of Parity With Our International Rivals,* 13 U. PA. J. INT'L BUS. LAW 1, 15 (1992).

[3] Maurice Rosenberg, *Federal Rules of Civil Procedure in Action: Assessing Their Impact,* 137 U. PA. L. REV. 2197, 2212 & n.26 (1989).

[4] Susan Keilitz et al., *Is Civil Discovery in State Trial Courts Out of Control?*, 17 STATE CT. J. 8, 8 (Spring 1993).

> the less likely it is that our legal system will be a factor negatively impacting American competitiveness in the international marketplace.[5]

Accordingly, states have acted under the premise that some reasonable limitations on discovery will reduce litigation costs, thereby encouraging business growth.

*Legitimate Discovery*

Any discussion of discovery abuse and reform must bear in mind the underlying purpose of discovery in civil cases. A key goal of discovery is to permit both sides to obtain the other's information so that each side can fully and knowledgeably evaluate a case, thereby fostering settlement. If both parties know the relevant facts and both parties are reasonable in their analyses and their evaluations of the likely result of trial or other ultimate resolution on the merits, then one normally expects settlement to result. Rational parties choose to litigate rather than settle a dispute only when their respective evaluations of the worth of a case do not coincide.[6] A primary purpose of discovery rules, then, focuses on forcing the exchange of relevant information to enable parties to evaluate the case completely and accurately.[7]

The second point that advocates of reform must remember is that not all discovery disputes and their attendant costs are avoidable. Run of the mill discovery disputes merely exemplify squabbles about the boundaries of what is or is not "discoverable" under the rules. Reformers can do little to eliminate such disputes because, absent bright-line rules circumscribing the limits of discoverable information or absolute limits on the time allowed or the number of discovery requests, disagreements about the precise boundaries of what is

[5]Cortese & Blaner, *supra* note 2, at 4. One need not assume that litigation does not result in *any* benefit to the parties, American business, or society for this conclusion to follow—just that we have reached the point where the marginal costs of, for instance, discovery are greater than its marginal benefits, a reasonable assumption. *See generally* A. Mitchell Polinsky & Daniel L. Rubinfeld, *The Welfare Implications of Costly Litigation for the Level of Liability,* 17 J. LEGAL STUD. 151 (1988); *see also* Richard C. Reuben, *Product Suits Help, Hurt Consumers,* 80 A.B.A. J. 24 (1994) (discussing study of effects of product liability suits on consumers, and concluding that although such suits succeed in removing some unsafe products from the market, they also deprive consumers of potentially beneficial products because of the threat of exposure).

[6]*See* Keith N. Hylton, *Asymmetric Information and the Selection of Disputes for Litigation,* 22 J. LEGAL STUD. 187 (1993); *see also* Keith N. Hylton, *Litigation Cost Allocation Rules and Compliance with the Negligence Standard,* 22 J. LEGAL STUD. 457 (1993).

[7]*See* Hall v. Clifton Precision, 150 F.R.D. 525, 528 (E.D. Pa. 1993) (discovery serves to (1) elicit facts before trial; (2) even the playing field by allowing access to the same information, thus preventing trial by surprise; and (3), especially with depositions, freeze testimony at an early stage).

discoverable in a particular case will inevitably arise. Common sense dictates and experience shows that the very nature of discovery slows the process and adds costs. The statistics bear this out: the mean time until disposition for cases in which no discovery occurs is less than half of the time for cases with discovery,[8] and the longer a case is on file, the greater the drain on judicial and other resources.[9] Furthermore, the parties do not abuse the discovery process in every case. Formal discovery actually takes place in only six out of ten civil cases, which means that no formal discovery takes place in the other forty percent, suggesting that a fairly low percentage of cases accounts for most of the discovery abuse and unnecessary costs.[10] Unless one disbelieves the fundamental value of the adversarial process, the cost of discovery is not an evil per se. The goal, then, is not simply to limit discovery, but to limit it when its costs begin to exceed its benefits.

In addition, reform advocates also must recognize that lawyers are pressured to examine every detail of every discovery request because of the ethical duties owed to their clients and the resultant potential liability for failure to fulfill those obligations. Any proposed reform must take into account the conflicting duties confronting an attorney seeking, or seeking to prevent, discovery. A lawyer has a legal and ethical duty to represent his client zealously[11] and yet a simultaneous duty to not abuse the judicial system by violating the rules.[12] Similarly, one cannot assume that there is an inherent advantage to making overly broad discovery requests, since a lawyer who requests millions of documents may actually receive them, making his effort to find the meaningful documents all the more difficult. Most lawyers take these practical considerations into account in framing their discovery strategies and truly believe they seek only relevant information that is necessary to represent their clients zealously.

---

[8] Keilitz et al., *supra* note 4, at 13.

[9] *Id.*

[10] *Id.* at 10.

[11] ABA MODEL RULES OF PROFESSIONAL CONDUCT Rule 3.1 (1983); MODEL CODE OF PROFESSIONAL RESPONSIBILITY EC 7-1 n.3 (1980). Indeed, a lawyer who fails to seek discovery vigorously on behalf of his client may face a malpractice suit. *See, e.g.*, McCann v. Pederson & Houpt, 621 N.E.2d 97 (Ill. Ct. App. 1993); Uhler v. Stix, 561 N.Y.S.2d 803 (N.Y. App. Div. 1990).

[12] Specifically, under the Model Code, an attorney should zealously represent his client "within the bounds of the law." MODEL CODE OF PROFESSIONAL RESPONSIBILITY Canon 7 (1980). Moreover, an attorney may not delay litigation or harass an opposing party or attorney through the legal process. *Id.* DR 7-102(A)(1); MODEL RULES OF PROFESSIONAL CONDUCT Rule 3.2 (1983). Finally, state analogs to the Federal Rules of Civil Procedure subject an attorney who abuses the legal process to discipline or monetary sanctions by the court. *See* FED. R. CIV. P. 11.

*Discovery Abuse*

True discovery abuse is designed not to discover information necessary to appraise a case accurately but instead to increase the value of a case apart from its merits by increasing the costs of litigation, or to deny an opponent access to information necessary to make that evaluation. Discovery abuse quite often takes the form of burdensome requests served to increase settlement costs through the exorbitant cost of compliance. For example, by sending an enormously onerous request for production of documents—knowing that the opponent will have to have lawyers review each document to determine its content and to ensure that no privileged information is inadvertently revealed—a party can greatly increase the potential cost of litigation, and thus the settlement value of the case.[13]

More subtle forms of abuse can also effectively inflate costs and harass an opponent. One familiar and particularly disruptive tactic centers on attempting to depose the defendant's chief executive officer or other high corporate official. Courts from jurisdictions as disparate as Texas,[14] Connecticut,[15] and Delaware[16] have ordered such depositions even though a lower-ranking officer usually has access to the same or better information, the CEO has no relevant personal knowledge, and the CEO has been targeted for no apparent reason other than to harass the corporate party and increase the discovering party's settlement leverage.

Another common kind of discovery abuse that has inspired the drive for reform involves obstructing access to information that is

[13]Litigants too often drive up costs, both on their opponent and the system, by seeking patently overbroad discovery. *See, e.g.,* State *ex rel.* Kawasaki Motors Corp. v. Ryan, 777 S.W.2d 247 (Mo. Ct. App. 1989) (request for production in product liability suit seeking "all documents relating in any way to the assembly or adjustment of all Kawasaki ATVs" held overbroad and unduly burdensome); Lilling v. Syracuse Bros. Dev. Corp., 495 N.Y.S.2d 206 (N.Y. App. Div. 1985) (request for copies of any and all bills rendered to purchaser regarding any work performed on or at certain premises held unduly burdensome); Boykin v. Preferred Risk Ins. Co., 297 S.E.2d 496 (Ga. Ct. App. 1982) (request for production that would require turning over 1,500 insurance policies written over 2½-year period held overly burdensome); *cf.* State Farm Mut. Auto. Ins. Co. v. Stephens, 425 S.W.2d 577 (W. Va. 1992) (request for information through interrogatory on all bad faith, unfair trade or settlement practices, and excess verdict claims filed nationwide against insurer over last 10 years was overbroad and oppressive).

[14]Wal-Mart Stores, Inc. v. Street, 761 S.W.2d 587 (Tex. Ct. App. 1988) (ordering Wal-Mart CEO Sam Walton to appear for the taking of his deposition in a slip-and-fall case).

[15]Lougee v. Grinnell, 582 A.2d 456 (Conn. 1990) (ordering former CEO of tobacco company to appear for deposition even though other sources of information may have been available).

[16]*In re* Siegman, Civ. A. No. 11152, 1992 WL 133068 (Del. Ch. Apr. 14, 1993) (ordering further deposition of CEO and other corporate officials).

clearly discoverable, resulting in unnecessary delay, increased attorney's fees, and motion practice.[17] This kind of discovery abuse typically results from perfectly understandable strategic behavior. Where one side has discoverable information which would greatly increase the value of the case once that information is disclosed, that party has a clear incentive to obstruct discovery.[18]

In sum, burdensome and dilatory discovery tactics may be used to affect settlement by unnecessarily dragging out the preliminaries to a trial. The harm to the system and to American business is that discovery abuse permits the value of cases to be skewed by conduct wholly divorced from the merits.[19] When an opponent or his counsel lacks the resolve or financial resources to continue fighting in the face of such intransigence, or when it simply makes no economic sense to do so, then the tools of discovery are perverted into means for obviating the "ultimate purpose of discovery," which is "to seek the truth, so that disputes may be decided by what the facts reveal, not by what facts are concealed."[20] Thus, the need for reform is patent.

## III. The States' Efforts to Reform

Today, state courts and legislatures are debating less *whether* discovery reform is needed than *how much* and *how soon*. Throughout the past decade, various states and localities have experimented with techniques aimed at reducing the costs and burdens of discovery.[21] These efforts fall into several broad categories: limiting the time allowed for discovery; limiting the permitted number of interrogatories, the most widely abused discovery tool, and restrictions

[17]*See, e.g.,* District of Columbia v. Greene, 539 A.2d 1082, 1083–84 (D.C. 1988).

[18]Delay also occurs for reasons other than strategic behavior, such as neglect, which are best addressed by means other than discovery reform. *See* Azer v. Courthouse Racquetball Corp., 852 P.2d 75, 81–86 (Haw. Ct. App. 1993) (distinguishing negligent and willful discovery abuse). Such cases may indicate that sanctions for violating discovery rules should be increased, but they do not demonstrate flaws in the rules themselves.

[19]*See generally* Bradford Cornell, *The Incentive to Sue: An Option-Pricing Approach,* 19 J. LEGAL STUD. 173 (1990).

[20]Jampole v. Touchy, 673 S.W.2d 569, 573 (Tex. 1984).

[21]Interestingly, "California is the only state in which the legislature has mandated a delay reduction program." Genevra Kay Loveland & Alexander B. Aikman, *California's Efforts to Reduce Delay in Civil Litigation,* 15 STATE CT. J. 4, 5 n.6 (Summer 1991). The other successful reforms generally involved the close cooperation of an enthusiastic bench and a generally accommodating bar. In particular, a chief judge with vision, leadership skills, persistence, and political acumen was a common denominator in the successful reform efforts. Additionally, a cooperative trial court administrator or clerk played a key role in any measurable improvement in the pace and cost of civil discovery. BARRY MAHONEY ET AL., CHANGING TIMES IN TRIAL COURTS 198–99 (1988).

on other discovery devices; limiting the use of expert testimony; an emphasis on early judicial intervention by discovery conferences; case differentiation; and mandatory disclosure. Finally, and perhaps more important than using any of these techniques, was a shift in attitude: discovery was presumed to be limited, and exceptions were made harder to come by. Most fundamentally, discovery must be accepted as a means, not an end, in a litigation process aimed at fair resolution on each case's merits.

As will be seen, most of these reforms create disincentives for discovery gamesmanship or serve to set absolute restrictions on discovery, thus capping costs and effectively constraining the ability of one or both parties to use high discovery costs or burdensomeness as a means to affect the value of the case. (It should be noted that most, if not all, of the states that have reformed their civil discovery practices have done so as part of an integrated civil justice overhaul.) Each type of reform has its own benefits, costs, and limitations.

*Time Limits*

Perhaps the key reform has been time limits on various phases of the lifetime of a case, including discovery, as measured by a presumptive (or mandatory) number of days until disposition. The theory seems to be that, with only so many hours in a day and so many days until disposition, any limit will necessarily cap discovery costs and so prevent excessive costs from driving the litigation.[22]

As of 1985, eighteen states had adopted some form of time limit on processing civil cases.[23] The number of days allowed to complete discovery usually depends on the type of case, which is part of the overall technique known as "differential case management" that most successful reforms have embraced.[24] For example, in Kansas the guideline for disposition of limited civil cases is 60 days and for major civil cases is 180 days.[25] Discovery, of course, must be completed even more quickly, which aids in reducing discovery requests and disputes and also arguably encourages early disposition through settlement.

[22]While "time standards are not a panacea, 'they can be an important part of a comprehensive program to reduce or prevent delays.' " Robert E. Litan, *Speeding Up Civil Justice,* 73 JUDICATURE 162, 165 (1989). *See also* MAHONEY, *supra* note 21, at 209.

[23]Larry L. Sipes, *Reducing Delay in State Courts—A March Against Folly,* 37 RUTGERS L. REV. 299, 312 (1985).

[24]*See infra* pp. 128–33. *See generally* Holly Bakke & Maureen Solomon, *Case Differentiation: An Approach to Individual Case Management,* 37 RUTGERS L. REV. 299, 312 (1985).

[25]Sipes, *supra* note 23, at 313.

Apparently, several courts have had success with this approach. For instance, under the system adopted by the Dayton, Ohio, court of common pleas, parties face maximum time-to-trial periods ranging from 60 days to 360 days, depending on the complexity of the case.[26] In personal injury and medical malpractice cases, which the judges considered the most complex, the Dayton guidelines required the parties to complete discovery by the end of the established time frame, and medical malpractice cases were further subject to nonbinding arbitration at the close of discovery.[27] The time to disposition dropped significantly.[28]

As one of the nation's largest counties, Wayne County, Michigan, presented a somewhat different problem than Dayton. Wayne County faced almost unbearable delays: the time to reach trial had grown to fifty months.[29] Wayne County responded with a management system that allowed a case to proceed rather independently for twenty-six months, during which time discovery was to be completed.[30] During the twenty-seventh month, a "mediation" hearing was scheduled. These hearings essentially constituted nonbinding arbitrations consisting of a short oral argument and a written summary of the case.[31] Nearly two-thirds of Wayne County's civil cases settled through this mediation process.[32] Still, Wayne County has had to institute further reforms because the case management system itself still took too long to process the majority of civil cases, which were not complex disputes.[33]

Finally, prior to statewide reforms in 1992, Phoenix civil courts used a case management program in which the parties had nine months from the time of filing to prepare their cases for trial.[34] In this period, the parties had to file a certificate of readiness and a motion to set for trial, indicating that discovery would be completed within sixty days of the motion's filing and that the parties had exchanged exhibit and witness lists.[35] Failure to comply subjected the case to dismissal with prejudice.[36] The results were dramatic.

---

[26] MAHONEY, *supra* note 21, at 110, 117.
[27] *Id.*
[28] *Id.* at 120–21.
[29] *Id.* at 155–56.
[30] *Id.*
[31] *Id.*
[32] *Id.* at 157.
[33] *Id.*
[34] Bonnie C. Dicus, *Phoenix Revisited,* STATE CT. J., Winter 1986, at 24. The goal for the Phoenix plan was to reduce the filing-to-trial time from well over two years to one year. Howard Schwartz & Robert C. Broomfield, *Delay: How Kansas and Phoenix Are Making It Disappear,* JUDGES' J., Winter 1984, at 22, 25.
[35] Dicus, *supra* note 34, at 24.
[36] *Id.* at 24–25.

Despite Phoenix's rapid growth in the 1980s, the median case-processing time fell to eight months, with trials occurring at fifteen months.[37] Similarly, the plan caused a drop in the average number of trial-ready cases pending per judge from 357 to about 100.[38] Close cooperation among the judges, clerks, and litigants, as well as rigorous enforcement of the case management plan, all contributed to Phoenix's success.

### *Absolute Limits on Interrogatories and Other Discovery*

Numerical, absolute limits on discovery have two clear benefits. First, they operate as cost reduction devices, preventing a party from using sheer volume to increase costs unnecessarily, and, second, they are relatively easy to enforce. For these reasons, they have been a very popular reform mechanism. Limits have been placed on written discovery as well as on the number and length of depositions.

Perhaps the most important of these restrictions are those that apply to interrogatories, because eighty-eight percent of the cases in which the parties engage in discovery involve the use of interrogatories.[39] The perceived need for limits on the number of interrogatories arises from their overuse. Interrogatories, although "the most efficient of discovery tools,"[40] have been used by "[m]any litigators . . . for purely tactical purposes if doing so might promote their client's interest and generate greater fees for themselves."[41] Interrogatories pose such a problem because they require the responding party to give more detailed and well-considered responses than do inquiries by way of other discovery devices, such as deposition upon either written or oral questions; and the considerable time required to provide these complete answers imposes significant costs upon a responding party. This difference between the time and expense incurred by the proponent and by the respondent makes interrogatories a particularly attractive method for inflicting abuse upon an adversary.[42]

Parties have used interrogatories, not as a legitimate information-gathering devices, but rather to "intimidate an opponent into settlement by overwhelming him with questions that are irrelevant,

[37]Schwartz & Broomfield, *supra* note 34, at 25.

[38]Dicus, *supra* note 34, at 24.

[39]Keilitz et al., *supra* note 4, at 16.

[40]Werner v. Miller, 579 S.W.2d 455, 459 (Tex. 1979) (McGee, J., dissenting).

[41]Wayne D. Brazil, *The Adversary Character of Civil Discovery: A Critique and Proposals for Change,* 41 VAND. L. REV. 1295, 1321 (1978).

[42]Robert Sacks, Note, *Coping with the Jekyll-Hyde Nature of Interrogatories by Imposing a Numerical Limitation: The Uses and Abuses of Discovery Procedures as Exemplified by Texas Rule of Civil Procedure 168,* 2 REV. LITIG. 95, 100 (1981).

unnecessarily invade business or personal privacy, and require vast quantities of time, personnel and money to answer."[43] One example, while extreme, proves the point. A party served a two-inch thick, 381-page set of 2,736 interrogatories on his opponent.[44] In striking down this set of oppressive interrogatories, the court noted that a "conservative estimate of the total cost of answering is $24,000."[45] Such a request hardly represents a fast and reasonable use of the discovery system.

Not surprisingly, some states limit this most popular form of discovery by capping the number of interrogatories. Texas, for example, limits parties to no more than two sets of thirty questions,[46] and New Jersey allows each party to interpose only fifty interrogatories without subpoenas.[47] Other states and many federal district courts impose limits from twenty to fifty.[48] California's experimental Economical Litigation Program (ELP) took the more radical step of eliminating interrogatories altogether.[49]

To be sure, such restrictions are not uniformly favored. Critics charge that limits are unfair because of their "unnatural, restrictive nature" and object that "a limit flies in the face of the philosophy that has long governed pretrial discovery."[50] But proposals to limit interrogatories simply recognize that an adversarial confrontation at the discovery stage should not be allowed to become the primary contest in the lawsuit. In short, jurisdictions adopting this approach obviously have concluded that limiting interrogatories is a reasonable and justifiable method for taming discovery abuse, particularly if there are exceptions for good cause shown, while still permitting

---

[43]James L. Underwood, *The New Amendments to the Federal Discovery Rules,* 26 PRAC. LAW. 23, 29 (June 1, 1980).

[44]*In re* United States Fin. Sec. Litig., 74 F.R.D. 497, 497–98 (S.D. Cal. 1975).

[45]*Id.*

[46]*See* TEX. R. CIV. P. 168(5).

[47]*See* Bakke & Solomon, *supra* note 24, at 20.

[48]*See, e.g.,* S.D. CAL. R. 230–1; S.D. FLA. R. 10(I)(1); N.D. ILL. R. 9(g); S.D. TEX. R. 10(c)(4); GA. CODE 81 A-133(a); IDAHO R. CIV. P. 33(a)(3); IOWA R. CIV. P. 126(a); KAN. S. CT. R. 135(b); ME. R. CIV. P. 33; MO. R. CIV. P. 417(a)(2); MA. R. CIV. P. 33; MINN. R. CIV. P. 33.01; R.I. R. CIV. P. 33(b); S.C. R. CIR. CT. PRAC. 90 (allowing only six interrogatories); *cf.* OR. R. CIV. P. 36(A) (disallowing interrogatories). *See generally* Sacks, *supra* note 42, at 95–96 & n.3; Stephen N. Subrin, *Federal Rules, Local Rules, and State Rules: Uniformity, Divergence, and Emerging Procedural Patterns,* 137 U. PA. L. REV. 1999, 2031–32 & n.171 (1989).

[49]The ELP, as it began in 1978, applied to small and intermediate civil litigation and combined severe limits on discovery (no interrogatories, and depositions generally limited to parties) as well as a form of disclosure of evidence if either party requested it. Although problems with the ELP led to major revisions, its effects were generally positive, resulting in "some reduction" in attorney preparation time, costs, and fees, as well as shorter case-processing time. Steven Weller et al., *ELP Revisited: What Happened When Interrogatories Were Eliminated,* 21 JUDGES' J. 8, 10 (Summer 1982).

[50]Sacks, *supra* note 42, at 104.

lawyers to obtain important information about their opponents' claims or defenses.

While interrogatories may remain the discovery device most susceptible to abuse, reforms have focused on other discovery tools as well. Some states have advocated limiting the number of requests for production, as well as presumptively limiting the number of requests for admissions that a party may serve. For example, Arizona now limits requests for production to ten[51] and one federal court has a local rule limiting such requests to thirty,[52] but the appropriate limit may lie somewhere in between. Likewise, the limitations on requests for admissions, as measured by the local rules in several federal district courts, range between ten and forty.[53] These limits might not produce a significant change in attorney behavior or litigation costs, however, since in the average case in which parties use formal discovery the mean number of requests for production is 2.3 and the mean number of requests for admissions is 1.6.[54]

Some states have also limited the number and length of depositions. A Kentucky program, for instance, prohibited the deposition of nonparty witnesses without leave of court.[55] Similarly, Arizona's 1992 rules limit depositions to parties, custodians of records, and expert witnesses,[56] and also presumptively limit the length of a deposition to four hours.[57] Both lawyers and judges generally have approved of these changes. As one Arizona practitioner noted, " 'In 99 cases out of 100, you can get whatever you want in four hours. . . . If you look at really long deposition transcripts, . . . much of it is taken up by attorneys casting aspersions at one another.' "[58] Likewise, another prominent Arizona lawyer notes that as a result of the new deposition limitations, "deposition practice has improved immensely."[59]

---

[51]ARIZ. R. CIV. P. 34(d).

[52]*See* COMMITTEE ON RULES OF PRACTICE AND PROCEDURE, JUDICIAL CONFERENCE OF THE UNITED STATES, LOCAL RULES PROJECT pt. II, at 111 (Tentative Draft Dec. 31, 1988) [hereinafter 1988 LOCAL RULES PROJECT].

[53]*Id.* at 116; ARIZ. R. CIV. P. 36(b) (providing that a party may not, without leave of court, submit more than 25 requests for admissions).

[54]Keilitz et al., *supra* note 4, at 4.

[55]Paul R. J. Connolly & Michael P. Planet, *Controlling the Case Flow—Kentucky Style,* JUDGES' J., Fall 1982, at 8, 9.

[56]ARIZ. R. CIV. P. 30(a).

[57]ARIZ. R. CIV. P. 30(d). Similarly, some federal courts have experimented with limiting the length and number of depositions. 1988 LOCAL RULES PROJECT, *supra* note 52, at 112; *see also* Subrin, *supra* note 48, at 2025; J. Stratton Shartel, *After One Year, Arizona Bar Cautiously Supports State's April 7, 1994 Discovery Reforms,* INSIDE LITIG., Sept. 1993, at 1, 6.

[58]Shartel, *supra* note 57, at 6.

[59]*Id.*

Thus, to address the problem of overuse of expensive and unnecessary depositions,[60] an effective solution may be to adopt presumptive limits on the number of depositions and their length. Because depositions are taken in only six of ten cases in which discovery takes place, and the average number of depositions taken for all cases is only 3.5, limiting depositions might produce less dramatic cost reductions than would curtailing interrogatories.[61] Still, the cost of a single deposition can easily exceed even a complicated set of interrogatories.

While the Arizona rules offer one option, states must consider what limitations on depositions would best meet the practices of its own attorneys. For example, under California's ELP experiment, discovery in superior court cases was prohibited altogether except for requests for admissions; inspections and copying; physical examinations; depositions of parties or persons likely to be unavailable for trial, or to perpetuate testimony; and certain other limited discovery.[62] Although this drastic plan worked well in some instances, one wonders how well limited discovery would fare, for example, in a complex securities or patent infringement case.

Still, the experiences in Arizona and elsewhere represent a dramatic shift away from the current system of "over-discovery"[63] as exemplified by the Federal Rules of Civil Procedure, which require the party or person desiring to *limit* discovery to show good cause therefor.[64] Instead, the states are moving toward presumptively limited discovery, with the burden of proving the necessity of exceeding the limit placed on the party seeking additional discovery. Generally, a party may override the presumption of "absolute curtailment" of discovery only by "proof that persuades a judge that the party seeking more discovery is entitled to it."[65]

The benefits of numerical limits are apparent: they are easy to understand, easy to enforce, and offer bright-line rules for compliance. But limited discovery also increases the ability of an obstructive party to prevent the disclosure of damaging information. This has prompted some jurisdictions to provide for mandatory sanctions for noncompliance.[66]

---

[60]ARIZ. R. CIV. P. 30(a) comm. cmt. to 1991 amend.

[61]Keilitz et al., *supra* note 4, at 11, 15.

[62]Weller et al., *supra* note 49, at 10–12.

[63]Sacks, *supra* note 42, at 98.

[64]FED. R. CIV. P. 26(c); *see also* Subrin, *supra* note 48, at 2024–25.

[65]Subrin, *supra* note 48, at 2024–25.

[66]In Arizona, for example, the failure to disclose potentially discoverable information results in a mandatory sanction unless "good cause" is shown. ARIZ. R. CIV. P. 26.1(e); *see also id.* 16(f).

### *Limiting the Number of Experts and Their Opinions*

Discovery costs have also inspired limitations in an area which overlaps discovery and trial—expert witnesses. Many trials have devolved into little more than shouting matches between experts. Overly permissive rules regarding the admissibility of expert testimony on areas of "expertise" which are dubious at best have fostered the use of experts with questionable credentials and novel theories. Perhaps the most significant explanation

> for the expert witness explosion was the liberalization of the Federal Rules of Evidence in 1975. Expert witnesses no longer need to possess academic degrees in areas in which they are called to testify. Witnesses may testify to their opinions if it will assist the trier of fact. Experts may now give testimony based on no more than their familiarity with the subject matter.[67]

Many states followed suit, thus expanding the possible uses of experts, and thus the need to depose them.[68] The only currently effective ways to combat expert witnesses at trial are through effective trial cross-examination, which requires a lengthy and expensive pretrial deposition,[69] and contrary testimony by one's own expert, also a costly exercise.

One method for deemphasizing the importance and cost of such expert testimony is to limit each party to one expert per issue. Not only do such limits save time and reduce expenses, circumscribing the number of experts that may testify in a case will likely have the salubrious effect of shifting the focus of a trial away from the plausibility of an expert's theory toward the actual facts of the case. Arizona adopted this approach in 1992,[70] and it has generally been praised by Arizona's practicing attorneys. One noted, "Instead of having three experts say the same thing . . . now you pick one. The limitation works fine, cuts expenses and time, and doesn't adversely affect justice."[71]

Other commentators suggest that the abuse of expert testimony be limited by banning "professional experts" (those who earn more than twenty percent of their income from testifying), by requiring peer review, by permitting only prescreened or court-appointed experts (as provided for in Rule 706 of the Federal Rules of Evidence,

[67]Carol Henderson Garcia, *Expert Witness Malpractice: A Solution to the Problem of the Negligent Expert Witness,* 42 DEF. L. J. 195, 199–200 (1993).

[68]*See id.* at 201 & n.33.

[69]*See id.* at 218–20.

[70]*See* ARIZ. R. CIV. P. 26(b)(4)(D). Arizona's goal in enacting this limit was "to cut down on the 'battles of experts' and the cost associated with hiring and deposing experts." Robert D. Myers, *MAD Track: An Experiment in Terror,* 25 ARIZ. ST. L. J. 11, 17 (1993).

[71]Shartel, *supra* note 57, at 6.

for example), or by using sanctions.[72] In all events, limiting the number of experts reduces the number of depositions and also eliminates the need to have another expert ready in rebuttal. That is why many states have sought to reduce expert testimony.

*Discovery Conferences: Early Judicial Intervention*

Early intervention by the judge can set the tone of case management. By involving a judge with the parties and the merits of their dispute early on, if a discovery dispute arises later, the judge will not have to resolve it based solely on the short arguments of anonymous counsel. Instead, he will have some understanding of the case, and the parties will have some early impression of his view of their dispute.

For example, under the Dayton, Ohio, system, the judges review a complaint within two months of filing, and hold scheduling conferences to set deadlines and a tentative trial date.[73] The court's management system also uses an automated civil case information system, nonbinding arbitration for small claims, extensive use of visiting judges, and monitoring of case loads. The plan has demonstratively increased the efficiency of Dayton's civil courts. For example, the median time for disposition of tort claims decreased by twenty percent.[74]

Kansas also adopted a rule requiring district judges to become more actively involved in case management[75] as well as time guidelines (not enforceable limits) to complete discovery and to reach trial and a statistical reporting system. An important part of the reform process was to require a discovery conference within sixty days of filing.[76] Overall, the Kansas program was quite successful,[77] and the median time for disposition dropped by almost half.[78]

*Case Differentiation*

Differential case management (DCM) is a popular form of discovery reform.[79] DCM accords different treatment to cases, including differences in the timing of discovery, depending on their complexity. For example, a simple two-party intersection collision case will

[72] *See* Garcia, *supra* note 67, at 220–24.
[73] MAHONEY ET AL., *supra* note 21, at 119.
[74] *Id.* at 120–21.
[75] *Id.* at 172–74.
[76] *Id.* at 173–74.
[77] *Id.* at 174.
[78] *Id.*
[79] Thomas A. Henderson & Janice T. Munsterman, *Differentiated Case Management: A Report From the Field,* STATE CT. J., Spring 1991, at 25, 26.

be put on one track while a complex multiparty business dispute is put on another. DCM relies on two important assumptions: first, that cases are readily susceptible to categorization based on their perceived management requirements, and, second, that rules for particular types of cases can expedite their processing to disposition.[80] The experiences of the five jurisdictions discussed below demonstrate that DCM can reduce delay and lower costs, as least in part because of restrictions on discovery.

### New Jersey

New Jersey has developed the "fullest development of the case-differentiation concept to date."[81] The New Jersey approach is simple: assigning cases to an appropriate track for processing, rigorously using deadlines to complete major elements in a case, and close court scrutiny.[82] Cases are assigned to either the expedited, standard, or complex track, each of which has its own deadlines.[83] No case is presumptively complex, and an attorney must justify designating a case as complex.[84] Except for complex cases, a track coordinator monitors each case and reviews compliance with the deadlines.[85] Complex cases are handled by a judge and his staff, and these cases necessarily vary in the time permitted for discovery and resolution.[86] In expedited cases, which are relatively simple ones often requiring little or no discovery, the rules allow 100 days to complete discovery.[87] Discovery in standard cases must be completed in no more than 200 days.[88]

### District of Columbia

In 1978, the District of Columbia Superior Court began a screening and tracking program designed to reduce the delay and disorientation caused by increasingly complex cases on the court's civil

---

[80] *Id.*
[81] Bakke & Solomon, *supra* note 24, at 18.
[82] *Id.*
[83] *Id.* at 19.
[84] *Id.*
[85] *Id.* at 19–20.
[86] *Id.* at 20.
[87] *Id.*
[88] *Id.* The New Jersey plan also includes specific limitations on discovery. For example, in expedited and standard track cases, each party may ask only 50 questions (without subparts). *Id.* Moreover, on the expedited track, a party may take a deposition only with leave of court, while in a standard track case, depositions of parties, experts, treating physicians, and nonparty witnesses may be taken.

docket.[89] Cases are assigned to either the complex or routine civil case management track.[90] While cases are not assigned solely by subject matter or any other single criterion, the extent to which discovery might require supervision by the court is an important factor in the assignment process.[91]

Pretrial and discovery procedures used in the two tracks also differ. For example, in complex cases the court schedules a "status and scheduling" conference within thirty days after assignment to the track.[92] At this meeting, the judge discusses potential problems that may arise with discovery—e.g., scheduling experts, privilege and work product disputes—as well as the amount and type of discovery anticipated by each side.[93] The court then issues a discovery schedule, which may merely set a discovery cutoff or may contain specific directions, such as setting dates for particular depositions or indicating when objections or responses are due.[94] Additionally, the court schedules a pretrial conference, which signals the close of discovery and is set as close to trial as possible.[95]

By comparison, the routine case track follows a much more standardized pretrial and discovery schedule, which is set by the court's rules.[96] In particular, in routine jury cases, the parties must complete discovery within 180 days of joinder.[97] As with complex cases, however, the court arranges for a pretrial conference, followed closely by trial.[98] Experience has revealed that the 120 or 180 days of discovery in routine cases is enough to complete the two to three discovery events which normally occur in routine cases.[99]

### Kentucky

In 1980, the Kentucky Supreme Court established an experimental discovery and case management system (the "special rules") designed to reduce delay and costs.[100] In this experiment, a random group of cases from a circuit court was assigned to one of five

[89]Michael D. Planet et al., *Screening and Tracking Civil Cases: Managing Diverse Caseloads in the District of Columbia,* 8 JUST. SYS. J. 338, 339 (1983).

[90]*Id.* at 338–40.

[91]*Id.* at 341.

[92]*Id.* at 345.

[93]*Id.*

[94]*Id.*

[95]*Id.* at 345–46.

[96]*Id.* at 346.

[97]*Id.*

[98]*Id.*

[99]*Id.* at 348.

[100]Maurice Rosenberg, *The Impact of Procedure-Impact Studies in the Administration of Justice,* 51 LAW & CONTEMP. PROBS. 13, 22 (1988); *see also* Connolly & Planet, *supra* note 55, at 9.

dockets: contract, personal injury, property damage, property rights, and termination of parental rights.[101] Cases selected for the experiment were subject to the special rules, which had been drafted by the local bar and bench and approved by the Kentucky Supreme Court.[102] The special rules required a continuous calendar control, clear deadlines for major procedural stages, a discovery conference, restricted discovery, and a pretrial conference.[103]

The Kentucky program attacks discovery abuse through a tight discovery schedule and fairly rigid limits on the amount of the discovery permitted. Each side may serve no more than twenty interrogatories, and depositions of nonparty witnesses are not permitted without court approval.[104] Moreover, the defendant must take the plaintiff's deposition before any other discovery.[105] The special rules also provide for a mandatory discovery conference two weeks after the filing of the defendant's answer.[106] The special rules provide that discovery should end within fifty days of the discovery conference. While, upon a showing of good cause, the judge may extend this deadline,[107] counsel have rarely requested an extension.[108]

At the close of the discovery period (normally fifty days), the special rules mandate an exchange of information.[109] Specifically, the parties must exchange exhibits, the identity of witnesses and their expected testimony, the identity of experts and their qualifications and a summary of their expected testimony, and a summary of each party's legal and factual contentions.[110] Ten days later, the parties are required to attend a pretrial conference to discuss expected trial problems and settlement.[111] While the rules call for trial to begin no more than thirty days after the pretrial conference, in practice it took about sixty days.[112]

Overall, the Kentucky program has resulted in significant reductions in delay and litigation costs.[113] For example, the average length of time for disposition of a case in the experimental program was five months, dramatically less than the sixteen-month average

[101]Rosenberg, *supra* note 100, at 22.
[102]Connolly & Planet, *supra* note 55, at 11.
[103]Rosenberg, *supra* note 100, at 23.
[104]Connolly & Planet, *supra* note 55, at 11–12.
[105]*Id.* at 13.
[106]*Id.*
[107]*Id.*
[108]*Id.* at 11.
[109]*Id.* at 12–13.
[110]*Id.* at 13.
[111]*Id.*
[112]*Id.*
[113]*Id.* at 54–55.

for regular cases.[114] Additionally, in the experimental cases, discovery was completed approximately ten months earlier than in regular cases.[115] Moreover, the tight schedule tends to deter over-discovery and to reduce the number of contested discovery motions, because there simply is not enough time for discovery disputes. Half of the attorneys reported that they spent less time overall on cases subject to the special rules.[116] In addition, attorneys passed on their savings to their clients in the form of reduced billings.[117] Because of these favorable results, Kentucky implemented a modified version of the experiment statewide.[118]

### Washington

A large backlog of cases for trial prompted the King County, Washington, Superior Court to implement a plan that, in two years, disposed of the backlog and reduced the average time to trial for a civil case from three years to eighteen months.[119] The King County plan established two timeliness criteria. For domestic cases, ninety percent were to be disposed of within nine months, ninety-eight percent within twelve months, and all within eighteen months. For civil cases, ninety percent were to be disposed of within twelve months, ninety-eight percent within eighteen months, and all cases within twenty-four months.[120] To reach these targets, upon the filing of a complaint the court enters a "case scheduling order," which sets firm deadlines for eleven separate events.[121] The King County program worked principally because of close court monitoring of these eleven events, which the court accomplished largely through the aid of a computerized reminder system.[122]

While the King County project achieved its goals of eliminating case backlog and reducing delays in the administration of new cases, the reforms did disrupt the local legal culture.[123] The family law attorneys, who were required to proceed on an even faster course than attorneys litigating civil cases, had difficulty meeting the "extremely demanding" schedule.[124] In response, the court modified

---

[114] *Id.* at 54; Rosenberg, *supra* note 100, at 23.
[115] Connolly & Planet, *supra* note 55, at 54.
[116] *Id.* at 55.
[117] *Id.* at 55.
[118] *Id.* at 9.
[119] M. Janice Michels, *Management Note: Transition to Court Management of Cases from Filing to Disposition,* 16 JUST. SYS. J. 89, 90–94 (1992).
[120] *Id.* at 93.
[121] *Id.*
[122] *Id.* at 94.
[123] *Id.*
[124] *Id.*

a few of the deadlines on the general domestic case scheduling order, allaying these concerns. In addition, some attorneys objected on the general ground that they opposed vigorous court management of a case, which had previously been left up largely to the attorneys.[125] Still, because the local bar association was a codrafter of the reforms, there was actually little resistance. Moreover, the forum through which attorneys could communicate with the court and numerous attempts by the court to inform local attorneys of the progress of the reforms, including updates through the local bar newsletter, probably helped the system to gain acceptance.[126]

### New York

Finally, in what is perhaps the ultimate in DCM, New York has recently established a special group of judges in the Manhattan trial court division who hear only commercial cases.[127] These judges are empowered to set strict time limits and enact other controls to speed their processing. New York's reform apparently is based on the view that judges expert in a particular area of law can most effectively and efficiently deal with disputes in that specialty.

Case management, then, offers another method for reducing overall delay and costs. In conjunction with time limits and restrictions on the total amount of discovery, DCM has demonstrated its effectiveness at improving the pace of justice in those jurisdictions which have tried it.

## *Mandatory Disclosure*

One of the most controversial state and federal reforms is mandatory disclosure, which requires parties simultaneously to disclose specified information shortly after the defendant files its answer. According to its proponents, early disclosure of information eliminates the need to request much information and stops the game of "hide the ball,"[128] avoiding significant costs.

For example, under the Arizona system, within forty days of the defendant's answer, the parties must reveal nine specific types of information, which essentially requires giving one's opponent all the known facts and legal theories on which a party intends to rely.[129]

---

[125]*Id.*
[126]*Id.*
[127]Ira Pilchen, *Court Reform Watch: New York Tries Commercial Cases Separately,* 76 JUDICATURE 266 (1993); REVIEW COMM. ON THE INDIVIDUAL ASSIGNMENT SYSTEM, REPORT TO THE CHIEF JUDGE AND CHIEF ADMINISTRATOR 14–15 (1992).
[128]Myers, *supra* note 70, at 25.
[129]*Id.*; *see also id.* at 16.

Moreover, the rules demand supplementation of the disclosure statements and provide preclusionary remedies, including *mandatory* sanctions, for failure to comply absent good cause.[130] The disclosure provision thus seeks to "expedite the exchange of information" and reduce gamesmanship in the discovery process,[131] and the presiding judge of Phoenix's civil superior courts reports that, as a result of the disclosure rules, "the discovery process is much less burdensome and hostile."[132]

Not everyone agrees, though, and some commentators warned that Arizona's new system runs counter to a lawyer's ethical duties and eviscerates the attorney-client privilege.[133] Some clients have objected strenuously when their attorneys advised them about what would have to be turned over to opposing counsel.[134] The resultant "erosion of attorney-client confidence" is a problem that may take time, or revision, to overcome, or may prove insurmountable.[135] Moreover, some see an initial informational advantage for plaintiffs, who can spend months or years gathering information before filing a complaint, while a defendant must prepare his disclosure statement forty days after answering.[136] Nonetheless, the Arizona disclosure provision thus far appears to have more supporters than detractors, perhaps largely because, as one practitioner observes, "Either we have full disclosures or attorneys will continue playing games."[137]

The Arizona system, which also includes other limits on discovery, assumes that restricted discovery increases the potential for obstructive conduct—and this in part can explain Arizona's provisions for mandatory sanctions and exclusion of improperly withheld evidence. In addition, mandatory disclosure provisions which do not carefully balance the lawyer's duties to his client may risk exposing attorneys to increased liability and conflicting duties. Mandatory disclosure remains controversial, and the experiences of the federal courts under the recent amendment to Federal Rule of Civil Procedure 26 may largely determine whether more states follow the federal lead.

---

[130] ARIZ. R. CIV. P. 26.1(e), (f).

[131] Myers, *supra* note 70, at 16.

[132] *Id.*

[133] Robert J. Bruno, *The Disclosure Rule Is a Mistake,* MARICOPA LAW., Aug. 1992, at 1, 15; *cf.* Griffin B. Bell et al., *Automatic Disclosure in Discovery—The Rush to Reform,* 27 GA. L. REV. 1 (1992) (criticizing recently enacted federal mandatory disclosure rule on this and other grounds).

[134] Shartel, *supra* note 57, at 4.

[135] *Id.*

[136] *Id.*

[137] *Id.*

*A Shift in Attitudes*

The reaction of the bar to reform teaches that changes in the discovery system can succeed only by a change in focus. Proponents of reform contend that lawyers have come to believe that a bad case can be made better by denying the other side access to important information or by seeking to bury the other side with requests for production and other discovery requests designed to increase costs and thus make settlement at a higher level than the merits would indicate a more palatable result. Proponents of discovery reform believe that the focus needs to return to the merits of the case, not the production of reams of documents and volumes of depositions. Discovery should be the means, not the end, of the litigation process. With this premise, it becomes easier to accept the notion that discovery is presumptively limited, with only carefully crafted exceptions to those limitations. Redirecting the energies of the bench and bar to trying cases on the merits, rather than emphasizing discovery gamesmanship, must be a goal of any reform effort.

## IV. Conclusion

Not all discovery is bad, but the reported cases reveal that trial judges across the country must every day face severe discovery abuse as both sides of the bar resort to obstructionist tactics, hoping that the costs they impose on their opponents and the system will benefit their clients. Unfortunately, this is more than a hope, as the current process leaves open the possibility of achieving success through abuse of discovery that may not be possible on the merits. The costs of excessive discovery to the litigants, the judicial system, and American competitiveness can no longer be tolerated.

*Editor's Note*

In addition to the basic discovery reform measures discussed in this chapter, more far-reaching reforms are advocated by some—reforms that challenge the basic premises upon which present procedural rules are based.[138] These advocates reason as follows: Current

[138]*See, e.g.*, Alfred W. Cortese, Jr. & Kathleen A. Blaner, Comments of the United States Chamber of Commerce on Proposed Amendments to Federal Rules of Civil Procedure 11, 26, and 56 (submitted to the U.S. Judicial Conference Comm. on Rules of Practice and Procedure on Feb. 12, 1993); Phillip A. Lacovera, Comments on Proposed Amendments to the Federal Rules of Civil Procedure (Disclosure and Discovery) (submitted to the U.S. Judicial Conference Comm. on Rules of Practice and Procedure on Jan. 17, 1992); Loran Kieve, *Discovery Reform: Maybe the Best Solution Is No Discovery At All,* A.B.A. J., Dec. 1991, at 79–81.

rules attempt to promote access to the courts by allowing civil claims to be filed based on meager information. They then authorize extensive opportunities to increase the specificity of the claims and to uncover evidence to support them during the discovery process. The underlying belief that informs current rules is that litigation should be encouraged. But the premise ought to be that litigants need to assume greater responsibility for investigating and assessing the legitimacy of their claims *before* they are filed. Marginal claims should be barred at the courthouse door, before they can impose significant costs on other parties and the court system itself. In sum, litigation should be discouraged.

One of the more striking reform proposals being considered as part of this new philosophy would require more specific pleadings in all civil cases.[139] Under the "liberal ethos" behind current rules of civil procedure, a litigant need do little more than give an opponent notice that he has been named as a party in a lawsuit. In fact, notice pleading was considered the centerpiece of the Federal Rules of Civil Procedure when they were adopted in 1938. The proponents of increased pleading specificity, however, question the utility of notice pleading in today's litigation environment, and they challenge its goal of facilitating undifferentiated access to the courts. In an already overcrowded civil justice system, exacerbated by an increasingly litigious society, reformers argue that the rules should help control overcrowding—and certainly should not encourage it.

Another reform under consideration would restrict the scope of discovery.[140] Under current rules, the parties are permitted discovery of much more information than the evidence relevant to their claims. The current scope of discovery permits access even to tangential information, as long as it pertains to the "subject matter" of the lawsuit. The theories behind such a standard are that broad discovery rights provide the only means of overcoming the information "imbalance" between the parties, and that broad discovery is more certain to allow the truth ultimately to surface. The reformers believe that this broad standard is intrusive and fosters far-reaching discovery requests made for purely tactical purposes, which in turn drives litigation costs even higher—for the court system as well as the opponent. The reformers advocate a closer nexus between the parties' claims and the discovery that they are permitted.

---

[139]*See* Richard L. Marcus, *The Revival of Fact Pleading Under the Federal Rules of Civil Procedure,* 86 COLUM. L. REV. 433 (1986).

[140]*See, e.g.,* Cortese & Blaner, *supra* note 138; PRESIDENT'S COUNCIL ON COMPETITIVENESS, AGENDA FOR CIVIL JUSTICE REFORM IN AMERICA (1991); New York State Bar Ass'n, Comm. on Discovery, *Report on Discovery Under Rule 26(b)(1), reprinted in* 127 F.R.D. 625 (1990).

The justification for the reformers' philosophy toward litigation stems from a belief that certain aspects of the civil justice system are dysfunctional and exceedingly prone to abuse. Further, there is recognition that the world and, more importantly, litigation are very different today from what they were in 1938. The present rules no longer "fit."

The reformers point to several specific developments to support these claims. For example, Congress has enacted many statutes creating substantial new causes of action. The courts themselves encouraged dramatic changes in civil litigation by interpreting laws to create private rights of action, by defining broad due process rights, and by granting remedies that require long-term judicial oversight. Societal changes also have dramatically affected the civil courts. Advanced communications technology has made information available immediately, in large quantities, without regard for geography or time. Pervasive media advertising of legal services and a higher tolerance for litigation have caused more people to consider litigation as a viable solution to many of life's problems. Given these dramatic changes since 1938, the reformers argue that the time to rethink many of the fundamental premises behind the civil rules of procedure has arrived. The proposals discussed herein are only the beginning of what could be a dramatic new direction for the American system of civil justice.

CHAPTER 8

# BASICS OF ALTERNATIVE DISPUTE RESOLUTION

JOHN L. HOWARD*

## I. Introduction

It cannot be credibly denied that there is a great deal of absurd litigation in America. The multimillion dollar awards in many individual cases, and what the public rightly perceives as simply ridiculous results in others, might be "merely anecdotal" evidence, but it is no less real for that. Reports that a person was awarded one million dollars because some product destroyed her psychic powers, a robber who fell through a roof skylight was awarded one-half million dollars in damages, and a person hit by a careless driver while in a phone booth was allowed to sue the phone company, legitimize the perception that, in America today, people can and do sue for anything—and win.[1]

Yet, it also cannot be credibly denied that there are situations where resort to the courts is both appropriate and required. At the same time, legal services appear to be beyond the financial reach of many—perhaps most—Americans. Even those who believe that the litigation explosion has been exaggerated acknowledge that lawsuits often cost too much and take too long to resolve. And the most ardent supporters of the status quo acknowledge that unless some reform occurs, problems will only worsen.[2] A recent American Bar Association survey found that almost forty percent of low- and moderate-income households each year confront a legal problem but do not turn to the court system to solve it.[3] If you remove the moderate-income families from the survey, the discrepancy is even greater. And one in seven low-income families specified cost as the reason they did not seek legal help.[4] While many politicians, consumer activists, legal scholars, economists, and untold others

*The author would like to thank Dirk Haire of the National Legal Center for his research and assistance in drafting this chapter.

[1]Stephen D. Sugarman, *Taking Advantage of the Torts Crisis*, 48 OHIO ST. L.J. 329, 336-37 (1987).

[2]Robert N. Sayler, *Tigers at the Gates—The Justice System Approaches Melt-Down*, LITIG., Fall 1993, at 1.

[3]INSTITUTE FOR SURVEY RESEARCH, REPORT ON THE LEGAL NEEDS OF THE LOW- AND MODERATE-INCOME PUBLIC (report released Feb. 5, 1994, by the ABA Consortium on Legal Services and the Public).

[4]*Id.*

continue their rancorous exchange over sweeping issues of policy and procedures, many individuals are left waiting for their day in court. Quite frequently, the litigant's distress while waiting for the conclusion of a protracted court proceeding is compounded by the economic stress of hefty legal fees.

Cases that drone on interminably, clogged courts, and the high costs of legal systems are not recent phenomena. One of the earliest agendas for legal reform was proposed by Emperor Kanghsi, one of the greatest Manchu emperors. Faced with a complaint about corruption and tyranny in the courts, the emperor took a novel if drastic approach—concluding that his subjects ought to find going to court a frightful experience:

> As a man is apt to delude himself concerning his own interests, contests would then be interminable . . . . [T]herefore, those who have recourse to the courts should be treated without any pity and in such a manner that they shall be disgusted with the law and tremble to appear before a magistrate. In this manner the evil will be cut up by its roots; the good citizens who may have difficulties among themselves will settle them like brothers by referring to the arbitration of some old man or the mayor of the commune. As for those who are troublesome, obstinate and quarrelsome, let them be ruined in the law courts; that is the justice that is due them.[5]

Americans, on the other hand, have always embraced the ideal that resort to the courts will result in a fair and impartial resolution, and so did not hesitate to bring their disputes there. Alexis de Tocqueville, one of the earliest and most quoted observers of American life, noted that "scarcely any political question arises in the United States that is not resolved, sooner or later, into a judicial question."[6] Accordingly, our legal system has almost always had to contend with issues of overcrowded dockets. One example can be found in the impeachment of Justice Samuel Chase, where one of the charges was that he "did, in his judicial capacity, conduct himself in a manner highly arbitrary, oppressive and unjust" in limiting oral argument of counsel in a case set for retrial. While the historical practice was that counsel had virtually unlimited time for oral argument, Justice Chase refused to hear argument on an issue of law he considered decided—more than 100 civil cases were pending before the trial court at that time, and observers note that Chase thought it imperative not to spend the court's time on arguments "regarded as all but useless."[7] Chase's action, while a departure from then-current practices, subsequently has been justified as prudent court management.

---

[5]Frank Johnson Goodnow, *The Geography of China*, NAT'L GEOGRAPHIC, June 1927, at 651, 661-62.

[6]ALEXIS DE TOCQUEVILLE, DEMOCRACY IN AMERICA 290 (P. Bradley ed. 1954).

[7]WILLIAM H. REHNQUIST, GRAND INQUESTS 72 (1992).

Resort to the legal system continues to present a mounting problem. Of course, a "crisis" in which people are overconfident about the ability of their legal system to resolve disputes is far better than the fear and distrust encouraged by Emperor Kanghsi. Perhaps the greatest tribute paid to our courts in recent times is the ever expanding reliance placed upon them by all segments of society—rich and poor, corporation and individual, and representatives of virtually every imaginable political point of view. But this broad acclaim has significant costs to the legal system and, ultimately, its users.

Perhaps today, therefore, the problem is more accurately defined by its magnitude, rather than its newness. Every year, our legislatures produce thousands of additional statutes which create complex new rights and remedies. Our administrative agencies issue reams of new regulations to "explain" these new statutes, or to alter their previous guidance. Consequently, our judges, even those beset with the task of stretching scarce resources over burgeoning demands, must continue to publish manifold decisions. The "law explosion" has created challenges for the American system of justice unlike any before.

Given the expanding role of the judicial system in enforcing a wide array of new rights, it is not surprising that the costs and delay of litigation, and the dissatisfaction with our legal system, are growing. But addressing the mounting challenges of overcrowded dockets, excessive costs, and unacceptable delays does not lend itself to a single stroke remedy. Restoring the system, so that it delivers justice to all, will require concerted efforts to change legal procedures, attorney culture, and societal expectations. And it will require potential litigants to consider methods of dispute resolution besides the traditional trial. It is these alternatives which are the subject of this chapter.

## II. Origins and Growth of Alternative Dispute Resolution

Judge Irving Kaufman observed that meaningful judicial reform in the next century requires an eagerness to pursue new avenues, instead of mere willingness to retrace timeworn paths.[8] Many states and the federal government are taking a newer, different route called Alternative Dispute Resolution (ADR). While ADR is not a completely new approach to resolving controversies, it presents enormous potential for providing litigants with faster and fairer resolutions of their disputes through a variety of techniques.

[8] Irving R. Kaufman, *New Remedies for the Next Century of Judicial Reform: Time as the Greatest Innovator*, 57 FORDHAM L. REV. 253 (1988).

The civil justice system should provide litigants with a cafeteria-style variety of options for resolving their disputes. This "multidoor courthouse" concept was first introduced less than twenty years ago as an alternative legal environment where individuals would have access to the proper "door" for resolving their disputes.[9] As envisioned by its primary architect, Professor Frank Sander, the multidoor courthouse expands the services and options available to litigants. Rather than setting every size and type of case on the same course, the multidoor courthouse provides a variety of opportunities to resolve disputes using methods other than traditional litigation.

Indeed, as ADR becomes an integral part of the litigation process, it is important to realize that there are many different ADR techniques. If ADR is to fulfill its promise of promoting access and choice, care must be taken to match parties and their disputes with the appropriate ADR mechanism. Lawyers must understand the full range of ADR techniques in order to provide their clients with sound, and effective, legal guidance.

Of course, one door in the multidoor courthouse that will remain open is to a traditional trial, since ADR might not be appropriate for every dispute.[10] For instance, ADR is unlikely to offer a satisfactory resolution for cases involving complex constitutional issues. Nor is ADR well suited to cases where vindication of a reputation or a principle is at stake. Unfortunately, some cases reach such a level of intractability or mental anguish that they can be resolved only by the formal litigation process. In other instances it is impossible to resolve matters on terms favorable to all parties, and it may be in their best interest to go forward with the litigation.[11]

ADR combines old techniques with new. For years, many judges have conducted mandatory, but informal, settlement conferences. These conferences have varied considerably with the personality of

---

[9]Frank E.A. Sander, Address Delivered at the National Conference on the Causes of Popular Dissatisfaction with the Administration of Justice (Apr. 7-9, 1976), *reprinted in Varieties of Dispute Processing*, 70 F.R.D. 79, 111 (1976).

[10]Some have argued against *any* type of alternative dispute resolution or, for that matter, any settlement, suggesting that when parties settle on their own, they leave justice undone. Owen Fiss, Comment, *Against Settlement*, 93 YALE L.J. 1073, 1085 (1984). To these commentators, settlement means a private act that requires parties to accept less than some "ideal" and, accordingly, denies the public justice. It follows from this ideal that parties would abdicate all control over their legal or contractual rights once a lawsuit was filed, and only a judge would be empowered to end the dispute. This is insupportable. Eliminating the parties' ability to determine their own best accommodations would not only remove litigant choice, but also produce a caseload avalanche that could only lengthen current delays. The result likely would be systemwide turmoil not unlike Emperor Kanghsi's design.

[11]Christian Doherty & Christopher Moeller, Note, *Before the First Shot Is Fired: Hypothetical Use of Alternative Dispute Resolution to Avoid a Re-enactment of the Hatfields and the McCoys*, 1990 J. DISP. RESOL. 455, 456.

the judge, but often involve a combination of jawboning, veiled threats, and reality testing of law and facts, all designed to move the parties toward settlement.[12] The ADR movement has introduced a new range of pretrial settlement procedures outside the traditional judge-conducted settlement conference.[13] Many do not involve a judge, and most effective ADR programs are designed to work much farther in advance of trial than the traditional judicial settlement conference. Accordingly, most ADR procedures are far less costly than litigation. This is not just a savings of direct costs, such as lawyers' fees, but a savings of indirect costs, such as diverting personnel from more productive activities.

Perhaps even more significantly, ADR advances the important public policy of meaningful access to the court system. Any alternative to traditional litigation must be gauged by this criterion and a variety of other measures, including the monetary and emotional costs for the parties; the interests of the parties in achieving results that suit their needs and fix their legal rights; the need to have courts function efficiently and effectively; the importance of the public's trust in the justice system; the importance of the courts' development of legal precedent; and the general interest in maximizing party choice.[14] In all respects, ADR has been successful. Moreover, ADR does not eliminate the underlying premise of our legal system. Parties utilizing ADR remain just that—parties to a controversy. The fact that some method other than a trial is used to decide a dispute does not alter the fundamental concept that the dispute is a contest, and that the parties to the contest will be vigorous in their attempts to prevail. First and foremost, the lawyer acts as an advocate for his or her client. Well-prepared presentations will continue to affect the decisionmaking process. No matter which ADR mechanism is used, throughout the process the attorney acts as an advisor to the client, assessing risks and supplying legal analysis.[15] These reasons, coupled with real savings in both time and costs, are beginning to erode lawyer resistance to ADR.

In a relatively short period, the multidoor courthouse is proceeding well beyond the theoretical stage. ADR methods and procedures have been debated—and attempted—for many years, but the discussion often reverts to skepticism about effectiveness and practicality.

[12]Dudley Odlham & Robert N. Sayler, Reaching Common Ground: A Summit on Civil Justice System Improvements; Civil Justice Improvements Proposals 12 (Nov. 1993) (unpublished discussion draft, on file with author).

[13]*Id.*

[14]LAW & PUB. POLICY COMM. OF THE SOC'Y OF PROFESSIONALS IN DISPUTE RESOLUTION, MANDATED PARTICIPATION AND SETTLEMENT COERCION: DISPUTE RESOLUTION AS IT RELATES TO THE COURTS 1-2 (Jan. 1991).

[15]Daniel Noonan, *Mediation: Answering your questions*, WIS. LAW., July 1990, at 17.

These doubts finally seem to be diminishing as actual experience with dispute resolution techniques increases.[16] After a period of infancy and toddlerhood that lasted about a decade, the business of alternative dispute resolution has entered a growth spurt.[17] In the years since Professor Sander unveiled his plan, numerous courts implemented procedures giving litigants some form of choice in determining how their dispute is resolved, and whether trial is necessary. A recent survey of in-house counsels and law firm attorneys, conducted by Deloitte & Touche's Litigation Services Group, found that eighty-three percent of the in-house counsels responding, and seventy-five percent of the law firm attorneys responding, expect to increase their use of ADR in the future. When asked about the actual cost savings that occurred when ADR was used, more than two-thirds indicated such savings typically ranging between eleven and fifty percent of the costs of litigation.[18]

Thus, the trend toward greater use of ADR is clear. The Civil Justice Reform Act of 1990 requires that each of the ninety-four federal district courts implement a plan to reduce the costs and delays in civil litigation.[19] The Act requires that each pilot program include "authorization to refer appropriate cases to alternative dispute resolution programs." State courts are also increasingly likely to view practical and effective ADR techniques not only as alternatives to trial, but also as integral parts of judicial procedures.

## III. Kinds of ADR

This section will discuss the general attributes of the more common ADR mechanisms, explain their relative benefits, and provide representative examples of how the state courts and legislatures have used them.

### *Early Neutral Evaluation*

Early Neutral Evaluation (ENE) offers a confidential, nonbinding conference where the parties present the factual and legal bases for their cases to one another and to an impartial third party. The heart of ENE is an early, frank, and thoughtful assessment of the parties'

[16]Rob McManamy, *Quiet Revolution Brews for Settling Disputes*, ENGINEERING NEWS-RECORD, Aug. 26, 1991, at 21.

[17]Debbie Levy, *Great Work If You Can Get It*, LEGAL TIMES, May 9, 1994, at S30.

[18]*Lack of Control Over Judicial Process Drives ADR*, CORP. LEGAL TIMES, Sept. 1993, at 14.

[19]Civil Justice Reform Act of 1990, Pub. L. No. 101-650 (Dec. 1, 1990) (codified at 28 U.S.C. §§ 471-482).

relative positions and the overall value of the case. Ideally, an evaluation is given by a neutral, experienced, and respected private attorney. This confidential evaluation, based on the neutral's reaction to the parties' written statements and subsequent oral presentations, is presented to the parties and their attorneys. The evaluation forces the parties to confront the relative merits of their positions.[20]

The evaluator's assessment can serve as a reality check for parties or lawyers, bringing some frivolous matters to an abrupt halt or, short of that, fundamentally altering some parties' expectations. The mere prospect of a neutral and frank evaluation could induce some parties to dismiss their claims, or make the type of offer that could result in prompt settlement.[21]

One of the most successful ENE programs is in the Northern District of California. In a two-hour informal session held within 150 days after the complaint is filed, the neutral evaluator hears both sides. The evaluator then identifies the primary issues in dispute, as well as areas of agreement, and explores the possibility of settlement. If the parties desire, he assists the parties in devising a discovery or motion plan, and discusses whether a follow-up session would be fruitful. This program has proved effective because it provides an *early* assessment. The parties communicate and learn more directly and productively about their case than they would in formal litigation. The evaluator's objective assessment frequently results in settlement and significant costs savings.[22]

Several other states have also found that ENE is effective. Colorado law provides specifically for this type of ADR mechanism. Any court of record in that state may, in its discretion, refer most civil cases to a court-appointed evaluator in an attempt to facilitate early settlement.[23] Utah also has a comprehensive ADR statute that provides for court appointment of "neutrals" early in the litigation process to facilitate settlement. Utah's law allows for "neutral expert fact-finding" in an effort to provide objective analysis to the parties.[24]

### *Mediation*

Mediation may be the most widely utilized ADR technique. Until recently, mediation was used primarily for contractual and labor

---

[20]David I. Levine, *Northern District of California adopts Early Neutral Evaluation to expedite dispute resolution*, 72 JUDICATURE 235 (1988-89).

[21]Wayne D. Brazil et al., *Early neutral evaluation: an experimental effort to expedite dispute resolution*, 69 JUDICATURE 279, 283 (1986).

[22]U.S. DIST. CT., N.D. CAL., DISPUTE RESOLUTION PROCEDURES IN THE NORTHERN DISTRICT OF CALIFORNIA 3-4 (undated).

[23]COLO. REV. STAT. ANN. §§ 13-22-302 to -311 (Supp. 1993).

[24]UTAH CODE ANN. § 58-39a-2 (1994).

disputes, but it is now being used in many other contexts as well. This informal process provides for a neutral third party—a mediator—to assist in negotiating an agreement. The mediator does not render a decision in the matter. Any settlement reached through mediation must be achieved by the parties themselves. Successful mediation depends, in large part, on the mediator's skill in defining the issues, encouraging communication between the parties, and offering realistic options for settlement.[25]

Mediation is essentially an extension of the negotiation process, initiated by the parties, that does not bind the parties beyond their own agreements. As in direct negotiations, the parties continue to control the substance of the discussions and any agreement reached.[26] In most cases, neither side has anything to lose in mediation. Lawyers and their clients reveal as much or as little as they like, and they can control the outcome through effective negotiation. If, however, it does not work, it is a walk-away situation—everyone simply returns to litigation.[27]

The popularity of mediation is reflected in the number of states that include this ADR technique in their statutes. One state with an expansive approach to mediation is Oklahoma. Oklahoma has a statewide mediation program that encourages any county, municipality, law school, or state agency to establish a dispute resolution program that will provide mediation services. The Oklahoma statute outlines general procedural and liability issues but leaves broad discretion to the individual programs. The program is funded through a two-dollar surcharge assessed on all civil filings.[28]

Other states have followed suit. In 1990, for example, Florida passed a law allowing courts to refer all or any part of a civil suit to mediation.[29] Texas also has a statute that encourages its judges to refer most civil suits to mediation.[30] In 1987, in fact, Texas lawmakers inserted a policy section into their ADR law that specifically states: "It is the policy of this state to encourage the peaceable resolution of disputes, with special consideration given to disputes involving the parent-child relationship, including the mediation of

---

[25]*See* DANIEL LEVINSON ET AL., HOW ADR IS USED IN THE FEDERAL GOVERNMENT 12 (1993).

[26]CIVIL DIV., U.S. DEP'T OF JUSTICE, GUIDANCE ON THE USE OF ALTERNATIVE DISPUTE RESOLUTION FOR LITIGATION IN THE FEDERAL COURTS 5 (undated).

[27]Noonan, *supra* note 15.

[28]OKLA. STAT. ANN. tit. 12, §§ 1801-1813 (1993).

[29]FLA. STAT. ANN. §§ 44.1011 to .103 (Supp. 1994). Cases where there is a history of domestic abuse are not referred to mediation.

[30]TEX. CODE ANN. CIV. PRAC. & REM. § 154.024 (West Supp. 1994).

issues involving conservatorship, possession, and support of children, and the early settlement of pending litigation through voluntary settlement procedures."[31] Thus, it appears that Texas views the less confrontational dispute resolution process of mediation as the best process to follow when attempting to settle particularly difficult and sensitive disputes, especially those involving minors.

The Michigan courts have produced a new type of ADR, commonly referred to as "Michigan mediation." It is a hybrid of mediation and arbitration that uses financial incentives to encourage early settlement of disputes. Under Michigan court rules, a court may submit almost any civil dispute over money damages to mediation. The unique feature of the Michigan procedure is that if the parties reject the mediator's evaluation and choose to go to trial, they will be penalized if the results of trial are not significantly more favorable to them. Similar to fee-shifting provisions found in some court-annexed arbitration statutes, the penalty consists of payment of costs and attorney fees.[32]

In order to avoid these penalties, a plaintiff who rejects the evaluation must obtain a verdict at trial that is at least ten percent greater than the mediator's assessment. Conversely, a defendant who rejects the evaluation must obtain a verdict of less than ninety percent of the original evaluation.[33] By implementing a stringent fee-shifting provision, Michigan encourages parties to engage in forthright and serious negotiations during the mediation process.

### *Minitrial*

The minitrial is an ADR technique involving a structured method of mediation. Minitrials permit the parties to present their cases—or an agreed-upon portion of them—to a neutral third party who renders a nonbinding decision. The presentation itself may be a summary or an abbreviated hearing, with testimony and cross-examination as the parties agree. Following their presentations, the parties may reinstitute negotiations, possibly with the aid of the third-party neutral.[34]

Although the parameters of the minitrial can be set by the parties, most minitrials share common features. The minitrial procedure is an early intervention technique that ideally should occur well before the court date. Although the minitrial is a "litigation-type" process, it is a voluntary, confidential, nonbinding, consensual

[31]*Id.* § 154.002.
[32]MICH. CT. R. PRAC. 2.403 (Supp. 1993).
[33]*Id.*
[34]CIVIL DIV., U.S. DEP'T OF JUST., *supra* note 26, at 9.

undertaking, and the parties usually agree that the formal, court-imposed rules are suspended. At the same time, the minitrial gives the parties a taste of litigation that provides an objective view of the merits.[35]

In general, minitrials are appropriate in cases involving only a small number of parties, and are most useful where significant legal or factual issues exist that would benefit from a face-to-face presentation to a "decisionmaker"—as opposed to an evaluator or mediator. The "decision" is nonbinding, but is useful in narrowing the issues.[36] Minitrials work best if they are observed by the high-ranking disputants, the better to show them the strengths and especially the weaknesses of their respective positions.

Some states with comprehensive ADR statutes now include the minitrial as an available option. For example, both Texas[37] and Utah[38] give parties the opportunity to use the minitrial process. It is likely that as the various forms of ADR become more widely utilized, and states continue to codify broad-based ADR programs, the minitrial technique will grow in popularity.

*Summary Jury Trial*

The summary jury trial is an ADR technique that recognizes one reason that litigants are often unable to settle their disputes quickly is the huge gap in their respective beliefs of how a jury will view their claims. The summary jury trial gives disputants a nonbinding indication of how their claims actually might be received.[39]

A jury is selected from the regular jury pool, and the parties present opening and closing statements and summarize the evidence. Following limited deliberations, the jury delivers a nonbinding advisory verdict on liability and damages.[40] The jury's reasoning and advisory verdict can spur the settlement process by giving both parties a new perspective on the strengths and weaknesses of their case. Because the summary jury trial involves a jury similar to one that would actually decide the case, the decision is viewed as an objective assessment. Summary jury trials are especially well suited for complex business disputes, where they serve as a surrogate for an actual jury's decisionmaking process.

---

[35]Lawrence J. Fox, *Mini-Trials*, LITIG., Summer 1993, at 36.

[36]CIVIL DIV., U.S. DEP'T OF JUST., *supra* note 26, at 9, 11.

[37]TEX. CODE ANN., *supra* note 30, § 154.025.

[38]UTAH CODE ANN., *supra* note 24, § 58-39a-1.

[39]John R. Allison, *Five Ways to Keep Disputes Out of Court*, HARV. BUS. REV., Jan.-Feb. 1990, at 166, 172.

[40]Stephanie B. Goldberg, *Free to Choose*, A.B.A. J., Dec. 1993, at 77.

A growing number of states include summary jury trials among their available ADR mechanisms. Of particular note is Colorado. In 1992, the legislature enacted a statute including the summary jury trial as a specific ADR technique that may be invoked at the court's discretion. The language of the Colorado law is interesting, since it states that the findings of the jury "may or may not be binding" on the parties.[41] As most ADR techniques do not bind the parties, it seems that Colorado encourages its courts to consider the possibility of having the summary jury trial take the place of a formal court hearing.

*Arbitration*

Arbitration can be chosen before a dispute through an agreement between the parties, or it can be chosen after a cause of action has arisen. After a claim is filed, one or more arbitrators are selected and the opposing party files a response. Formal discovery generally is not available, but the parties often voluntarily exchange some information. Depositions may be taken to replace witnesses' appearances. Unlike the less formal ADR procedures, the rules of evidence apply, albeit in a slightly relaxed manner. The arbitrator's award may be written or oral, and is considered an enforceable judgment. In short, arbitration is much like a trial.[42]

Arbitration is widely used to decide business disputes. Parties are usually represented by lawyers who present evidence and arguments supporting their client's position. Arbitrators are expected to base their decisions on applicable legal doctrines and the facts of the case to reach a fair decision. Arbitrators are selected for their expertise in a particular field, unlike the public judge or a member of a jury. Therefore, one of the advantages of arbitration is that the parties usually present their case to arbitrators who are experienced in the subject.[43] Nevertheless, arbitration is not without its critics. Because arbitration often requires formal processes, and its procedures sometimes come to resemble litigation (with a multiplication of briefs and motions), it costs more and is less accessible.[44]

Despite these criticisms, many states are adopting arbitration as a broad-based ADR measure. Arizona has a good model "court-annexed"—i.e., mandatory—arbitration statute, requiring that all

[41]COLO. REV. STAT. ANN., *supra* note 23, § 13-22-302.
[42]*See* Louise A. LaMothe, *Thinking About Mediation*, LITIG., Summer 1993, at 1, 2.
[43]*Steps in Persuasion*, N.Y. L.J., Aug. 1, 1991, at 3.
[44]This criticism has been made in particular of current arbitration of securities class actions. *See* C. Evan Stewart, *Arbitrary Securities Law Claims: Can the Failed Promise Be Redeemed?*, *in* SECURITIES CLASS ACTIONS: ABUSES AND REMEDIES (Edward J. Yodowitz et al. eds., 1994) (monograph of the National Legal Center for the Public Interest).—Editor's note.

civil actions involving $50,000 or less be referred to arbitration.[45] The arbitration ruling is binding, although it may be appealed by filing a demand for a trial de novo. If the subsequent judgment award is not at least ten percent more favorable to the moving party than the initial arbitration award, that party is responsible for the arbitrator's compensation and the additional attorney fees incurred by the nonmoving party.[46] In practical terms, requiring the loser to pay the winner's attorney fees should cause parties to be more careful in determining whether to pursue an appeal. Florida has a similar arbitration statute that also includes attorney fee-shifting. In contrast to the Arizona approach, however, arbitration in Florida is imposed at the court's discretion.[47]

## IV. Second-Level Issues

In addition to the fundamental questions of whether and what variety of ADR to use, there are three important second-level issues as well: whether the use of ADR should be voluntary or mandatory, the qualifications for "third-party neutrals," and expanding ADR to consensual "pre-arrangements" (e.g., ADR contractual agreements and liquidated damages).

### *Voluntary Versus Mandatory ADR*

As the ADR procedures discussed above, and others, demonstrate satisfactory results, many trial courts welcome multiple forms of ADR as a complement to formal litigation. While ADR began as a voluntary process independent of the courts, many courts now view ADR as a mandatory part of judicial procedure that is a prerequisite to trial. This annexation of ADR by courts raises questions as to both the wisdom of court-mandated ADR and as to what form of participation should be required in the ADR proceeding.[48]

Proponents of voluntary ADR argue that the parties should be able to select any dispute resolution technique of their choosing,

[45]ARIZ. REV. STAT. ANN. § 12-133 (Supp. 1993). A 1992 amendment to this section also allows the Arizona supreme court, in its discretion, to submit civil claims *exceeding* $50,000 to arbitration.

[46]*Id.* Arizona's approach to arbitration typifies the mandatory approach to ADR. There is substantial debate whether mandatory ADR is as effective as voluntary dispute resolution methods. *See* discussion *infra* at 150–51.

The 1992 amendment to this section adding the 10% requirement follows an incentive-based, fee-shifting approach first established in Michigan. *See* discussion *supra* at 147.

[47]FLA. STAT. ANN., *supra* note 29.

[48]Edward F. Sherman, *Court-Mandated Alternative Dispute Resolution: What Form of Participation Should be Required?* 46 SMU L. REV. 1001 (1993).

and that the decision to use ADR should itself be completely the decision of the parties, not the court. For disputes which are not appropriate for ADR, of course, they would point out that requiring the parties to pursue an ADR measure simply adds another costly and time-consuming barrier to trial. But, more fundamentally, their views are based on the argument that mandatory ADR implicates the Constitution's Seventh Amendment by conditioning the right to a jury trial on participation in a court-annexed program. As one federal judge explained: "Some of these voluntary ADR programs may offer opportunities to settle controversies. Wonderful! But if the parties have decided to file suit and go to trial, they should not be forced to go through one of these ADR procedures as a condition precedent to their right to a trial before a jury or a judge."[49]

In answering the constitutional argument, proponents of mandatory ADR programs note that many ADR techniques are nonbinding and, if the parties are unable or unwilling to resolve their dispute, they can proceed to litigate the case as they would any other case. As a practical matter, proponents of court-mandated ADR point out that the costs of a court-ordered ADR proceeding are minimal compared with other costs of litigation.[50]

While it is beyond the scope of this chapter to resolve this debate, it should be borne in mind that more durable results are achieved if the parties have willingly embraced the ADR process. Resolutions achieved by consensus are obviously less likely to be challenged than resolutions imposed by third parties.[51]

### *Qualifications for Third-Party Neutrals*

Effective ADR programs rely upon third parties who have experience, expertise, and independence. The formal requirements for "third-party neutrals" vary, however, from jurisdiction to jurisdiction.

Many individuals who serve as third parties are volunteers operating within the auspices of the court system. For example, the D.C. Superior Court operates its Multi-door Dispute Resolution Division—which handles 8,000 small claims, domestic relations, and probate and tax assessment matters a year—through the efforts of a volunteer corps of about 600 mediators and other neutrals. To join

[49]G. Thomas Eisele, *No to Mandatory Court-Annexed ADR*, LITIG., Fall 1991, at 3.

[50]Joshua D. Rosenberg, *Court Studies Confirm That Mandatory Mediation Works*, NAT'L L.J., Apr. 11, 1994, at C7.

[51]Harry N. Mazadoorian, *Practice Experience Is Solid Evidence of ADR's Effectiveness*, NAT'L L.J., Apr. 11, 1994, at C10.

this corps, applicants must complete one of the court's training sessions.[52]

A number of states have legislated more extensive requirements for the qualification and training of third-party neutrals. Utah adopted a statutory approach that requires procedures for licensing "certified dispute resolution provider[s]."[53] Under this certification scheme, individuals must fill out an application to the Division of Occupational and Professional Licensing, pay a fee, be of good moral character, and either complete a program of dispute resolution training (although the statute does not provide specific training requirements) or demonstrate sufficient experience in the area.[54] Only those individuals who have met the above certification requirements are allowed to mediate or assist in other dispute resolution proceedings.

Other states have legislated even more specific requirements. For example, Texas has established statutory guidelines calling for uniform qualifications for all dispute resolution providers, regardless of the ADR technique employed.[55] Under the Texas statute, third-party neutrals must complete at least forty hours of training in dispute resolution techniques from an approved source, or receive approval from a court based on prior professional training or experience. Nebraska has a similar statute, requiring that mediators have a minimum of thirty hours of training from an approved source and serve as an apprentice for three sessions before being allowed to mediate.[56] Given the increased demand for ADR services, it is likely that other states will adopt training requirements or impose some form of accreditation for third-party neutrals.

While, as noted, many court systems rely upon volunteers to facilitate the ADR process, there are a growing number of both for-profit and nonprofit organizations which act as hired third-party neutrals, or "rent-a-judges." Providing dispute resolution services is a multimillion dollar industry for many lawyers and retired judges.[57] By using these independent contractors, parties are able to select a third party with the experience and expertise most likely to result in a balanced proceeding. Typically, the parties split the expense. As should be apparent, the chief appeal of this process is speed, especially in jurisdictions where dockets are clogged. Parties

---

[52]Debbie Levy, *ADR in D.C.: They're Giving It Away*, LEGAL TIMES, May 9, 1994, at S31.

[53]UTAH CODE ANN., *supra* note 24, §§ 58-39a-2 to -5.

[54]*Id.* § 58-39a-5.

[55]TEX. CODE ANN., *supra* note 30, § 154.052.

[56]NEB. REV. STAT. § 25-2901 (Supp. 1992). Nebraska imposes a minimum of 60 hours of training for third parties who mediate domestic relations matters.

[57]Karen Donovan, *Searching for ADR Stars*, NAT'L L.J., Mar. 14, 1994, at 1.

who rent a judge want the equivalent of court litigation, but are willing to pay rather than wait.[58] These contract ADR services are most likely to be used in cases involving both large sums of money and a complex set of facts and issues.

*Consensual "Pre-Arrangements" for Dispute Settlement*

The evolution to more formal "settlement procedures" often results in parties agreeing ahead of time not to seek remediation in the courts. These voluntary methods of dispute resolution are therefore contract-based methods.[59] Parties involved in such a transaction are limited only by their imagination in fashioning procedures to resolve conflicts. For instance, parties can contract to decide their case according to the rule of some private association—commercial, religious, or otherwise—and will be bound by the results because they agreed to be bound.[60]

A contract clause in which the parties agree to use ADR in the event of a future dispute is more easily negotiated before rather than after the dispute, and so they allow one to overcome the single greatest obstacle to the use of ADR—the task of convincing a reluctant adversary to engage in ADR after the filing of a complaint.[61] The fact that the parties to a contract in good faith include an ADR clause demonstrates a mutual commitment to avoiding litigation and maintaining a continuing business relationship.

One of the most widely used contractual ADR provisions is the Center for Public Resources (CPR) Corporate Policy Statement on Alternatives to Litigation.[62] The Corporate Policy Statement provides in part:

> In the event of a business dispute between our company and another company which has made or will then make a similar statement (adopting ADR as their corporate policy), we are prepared to explore with that other party resolution of the dispute through negotiation or ADR techniques before pursuing full-scale litigation. If either party believes that the dispute is not suitable for ADR techniques, or if such techniques do not produce results satisfactory to the disputants, either party may proceed with litigation.

By signing this statement, companies in effect pledge that they will try ADR before going to trial. The pledge is becoming increasingly

[58]Arthur H. Aufses III, *Thinking About ADR*, LITIG., Spring 1990, at 33.

[59]*Greenebaum calls for alternatives to litigation*, BILL OF PARTICULARS, Fall 1993, at 43.

[60]*Id.*

[61]John Wilkinson, *Assessing the Odds of Settling Disputes With ADR*, NAT'L L.J., Apr. 11, 1994, at C4.

[62]A copy of the statement may be obtained by contacting the Center for Public Resources. CPR reports that as of May 1994, 743 major companies have signed the CPR Corporate Policy Statement on behalf of themselves and 2,667 subsidiaries.

popular as businesses look for less costly ways to settle disputes. In fact, the signatories to the pledge represent a cross-section of American business that accounts for about one-half of the gross national product.[63]

In addition, many industries have reached industry agreements that are ancillary to, or an elaboration of, the CPR pledge. Detailed, industry-specific dispute resolution procedures are being developed for recurring types of disputes involving antitrust, construction, employment, franchise and dealer, insurance, oil and gas, product liability, securities, Superfund, technology, and toxic torts issues.[64] Although the relevant industries benefit from having developed specific ADR procedures, member companies report that the biggest advantage is not the customized or more specialized rules per se, but the fact that there has been a focus on how to resolve disputes within the industry.[65]

It is a small step from parties agreeing in advance how to resolve potential disputes to parties contracting for damages in advance. Consensual arrangements, which allow contractual specification of damage payments for injuries, may become an increasingly effective method to help reduce litigation—especially since a liquidated damages clause is a fairly common contract provision. One of the leading proponents of this approach suggests that courts should allow parties to specify by contract the allowable damage payments even for an accident, and parties should specify damage payments in contracts.[66]

A predictable objection to this approach is that the parties may lack the equal "bargaining power" required for a voluntary transaction. Assuming arguendo that this objection has political if not economic validity, contractual limitations can nonetheless still prove effective. Contract provisions could be enforceable at least where they were the result of a bargained-for exchange, the most likely form being a pricing differential. If such contract provisions were allowed, then parties may choose to limit possible damages payments. Some parties might choose to contract for actual monetary losses, including medical expenses and lost earnings, but decide not to contract for some types of nonpecuniary losses, such as pain and suffering, emotional distress, or lost pleasure of life.[67] Rather than limiting damage payments to fixed amounts determined by legislators, payments could

---

[63] *Id.*

[64] Harry Mazadoorian, *Widespread Disgust with Civil Justice Is Boon to ADR*, CORP. LEGAL TIMES, Apr. 1994, at 17, 18.

[65] *ADR Is More Than a Means of Resolving Disputes*, CORP. LEGAL TIMES, May 1994, at 36, 42 (text of roundtable discussion, Mark Haller, moderator).

[66] PAUL H. RUBIN, TORT REFORM BY CONTRACT 3 (1993).

[67] *Id.* at 9.

be set at whatever level to which the parties had agreed before the event. And because this approach is based on contract, the process is self-correcting. If one party does not desire to limit the types of damages recoverable, it need not enter the contract.[68]

Determining resolution processes in advance, and bargaining for remedies, will take ADR to even more effective levels.

## V. Conclusion

The costs and delays in modern litigation have convinced many lawyers and litigants that, so long as judicial precedent is not needed and there is no other need for a formal judgment, an ADR mechanism is often the better process. There are many benefits. A true multidoor approach offers multiple options for dispute resolution, and allows the parties to choose the most appropriate one. While selected ADR vehicles are available in most jurisdictions, only a few states have actually implemented a comprehensive approach.[69] As more people gain familiarity and experience with the advantages ADR provides, however, it will become increasingly a part of our civil justice system. Variations and hybrids of the ADR methods outlined here can take an infinite variety of forms, depending only on the ingenuity of disputants, attorneys, and judges.[70]

[68] *Id.*

[69] James Podgers, *Maine Route: Multidoor proposal reflects growing role of ADR*, A.B.A. J., Sept. 1993, at 118.

[70] Allison, *supra* note 39, at 173.

# PART II

# STRATEGY AND TACTICS

CHAPTER 9

# THE POLITICS OF STATE CIVIL JUSTICE REFORM

SAMUEL A. BRUNELLI

Our American republic is founded on the principles of individual liberty, representative government, and the rule of law, each of which is critical to our way of life. The rule of law creates the social contract through which individuals can conduct transactions in which both parties better their situation. With the exception of language, the rule of law is arguably the most basic component essential to the establishment and maintenance of a civil society. The goal of civil justice reform is to preserve our nation's legal system and ensure its status as an institution for the public good. For too long, some in the legal profession have viewed the courts not as forums in which fairness and justice prevail but rather as their personal lottery system in which they seek benefit from tragedy and society's sympathy.

That this has happened has been clear to many legal scholars and to those who face firsthand the consequences of the litigation explosion. What is now also becoming clear is that the American public is increasingly of the opinion that our civil justice system is badly broken and needs to be reformed. This public consensus is a critical component of the reform efforts underway throughout the nation. Not only is the public willing to support reform efforts, but they are increasingly becoming active at the grass roots level on the issue. This popular support has provided a window of opportunity for meaningful reforms crafted to bring about a return to a traditional fault-based civil justice system that assigns liability and provides for damages awards in a fair and objective manner.

How has the public's perception changed? In the past, most voters saw the tort system as resembling a lottery. When they read in the newspaper of enormous awards bestowed to plaintiffs on speculative grounds, they noted the recipients' good fortune and wondered whether they might someday be the lucky party enriched at the expense of some nameless corporation, faceless public institution, or otherwise hapless deep-pocket defendant. This perception was compounded by the fact that the public felt the awards wouldn't actually impose any cost on the defendants, as their insurance would cover it.

Now, however, the public sees the tort system as raising the cost of living, reducing innovation and economic competitiveness, and lowering their standard of living. Our system of tort law is seen as making products more expensive, causing manufacturers to withdraw new products, and raising taxes. The public's view of the tort system has changed from a lottery with no losers, to a crisis having a direct impact on everyone's pocketbook and well-being. "The problem of frivolous lawsuits is so serious that nearly one out of four residents say they are either extremely or very concerned that they will be sued in the near future," noted David J. Sackett, senior vice president of The Tarrance Group, a polling organization, at a December 2, 1993, press conference. Lawsuit abuse and the resulting "tort tax" have caused the public to call for a return to personal responsibility, in which liability requires proof of actual fault by the defendant and awards are related to and proportional to the damages suffered.

An anecdote helps show this shift in public mood. NBC's *Saturday Night Live* has featured a pair of commercial parodies based on a fictitious law firm, Green & Fazio. One features actor Phil Hartman asking if the viewer has ever witnessed an accident or had an accident described to them. Mr. Hartman proceeds to debunk certain litigation myths. The myths include the belief that you actually need to be involved in an accident in order to sue. Green & Fazio have pioneered new areas of litigation, he says, replete with new causes of action such as "phantom whiplash," "bystander trauma," and "near-collision stress disorder." A similar skit explains that litigation may be the viewer's means to financial security. Featuring a series of successful litigants, reminiscent of a Publishers' Clearinghouse sweepstakes commercial, the sketch includes actor Chris Farley noting that while there was a warning sign at the construction site, what's a warning sign to someone as drunk as he was? While the commercials are parodies, they strike a cord with people because behind the humor is the recognition that we live in a litigation-happy society. Having seen so many actual commercials in which real lawyers urge the viewer to sue as a first rather than as a last recourse, the public has grown weary of the marketing of litigation.

Not only do such anecdotes reflect a widely held perception that the civil justice system is not serving the public good and is in need of reform, there is now hard empirical data to indicate the strength of that feeling. One of the most striking developments to come out of the civil justice reform effort has been polling which shows the tremendous dissatisfaction with the status quo and equally strong desire to see something done about it. The polling data summarized below have provided encouragement, support, and leverage to legislators pushing reform legislation.

## Alabama[1]

75% think they would be better off if liability reforms were enacted by the legislature.

88% favor limits on attorney fees.

80% favor proposals to prevent trial lawyers from contributing to judicial campaigns.

60% favor changes in punitive damages laws.

80% would vote against a candidate for the legislature or the court who took large contributions from trial lawyers.

70% would be more likely to vote against a candidate if he or she were endorsed by plaintiffs' trial lawyers.

## California[2]

82% of voters believe that the current contingency fee level of thirty to forty percent of an award encourages too many frivolous and fraudulent lawsuits.

71% of voters believe that the current contingency fee level of thirty to forty percent should be reduced.

85% of voters believe that injured persons who are interested in suing for damages are entitled to know how many hours a contingency fee lawyer is planning to work on the case, what the lawyer's hourly rate is, and how much time the lawyer actually worked on the case after it is tried or settled.

62% of voters believe that state bar fines—$5,000 for each violation, up to a maximum of $25,000—should be increased to punish lawyers who violate laws and state bar rules.

## Louisiana[3]

59% are dissatisfied with the state's liability lawsuit system.

84% believe that frivolous lawsuits have increased health care costs.

81% favor limiting trial lawyers' fees.

[1]Polling conducted in March 1993 by Marketing Research Institute, Pensacola, Florida.

[2]Polling conducted August 26 through September 2, 1993, by Market Strategies, Inc., Southfield, Michigan.

[3]Polling conducted in April 1993 by Marketing Research Institute, Pensacola, Florida.

86% believe that there are too many frivolous lawsuits in Louisiana.

75% agree that the liability lawsuit problem is caused by greedy lawyers.

71% would vote against a candidate endorsed by trial lawyers.

80% would vote against a candidate receiving trial lawyer contributions.

## Mississippi[4]

68% believe they would be better off if there were reform of the lawsuit system.

87% believe that liability lawsuits have increased the cost of medical care.

74% say the liability lawsuit problem in Mississippi is due mainly to trial lawyers who will take any case to make money.

59% are likely to vote against a candidate for the state legislature who received an endorsement from personal injury lawyers.

74% are likely to vote against a candidate for the state legislature who receives large campaign contributions from personal injury lawyers.

70% think it is unfair for trial lawyers who serve on the state legislature to vote on bills that affect their practice.

## New Jersey[5]

79% agree that the present liability lawsuit system has problems and should be improved.[6]

70% consider frivolous lawsuits to be an "extremely important" or "very important" problem.[7]

---

[4]Polling conducted in January 1993 by Marketing Research Institute, Pensacola, Florida.

[5]Polling conducted on August 24–26, 1993, by The Tarrance Group, Alexandria, Virginia.

[6]Those employed in manufacturing (84%) and small business (86%) are especially likely to think that the present system has problems and needs to be changed.

[7]42% consider frivolous lawsuits to be an extremely important problem, while 28% considered them to be very important. Only 21% regard frivolous lawsuits as only somewhat important, and a mere 3% rate them as not important at all.

66% believe that they would be "better off" if the sorts of tort reform discussed in the survey were enacted by the state legislature.[8]

70% favor legislation that would place tighter restrictions and limits on an individual's right to sue another person or company.[9]

81% favor a law that would require proof that something is wrong with the way that a product was designed, manufactured, or marketed before the manufacturer could be held liable.

71% favor a law that would require proof that a product is more dangerous than most people think before a manufacturer may be held liable.[10]

*Most to Blame for Frivolous Lawsuits*

| | First Choice | Second Choice | Combined |
|---|---|---|---|
| Personal injury lawyers | 41% | 17% | 58% |
| Juries giving too much money | 15% | 23% | 38% |
| Insurance companies | 9% | 9% | 18% |
| State law regarding lawsuits | 7% | 8% | 15% |
| Judges | 4% | 8% | 12% |
| State legislature | 3% | 8% | 11% |
| Business cutting corners on manufacture of products | 3% | 4% | 7% |

*Impact of Frivolous Lawsuits*

| | Have impact | No Impact |
|---|---|---|
| Caused higher insurance premiums | 95% | 2% |
| Increased the cost of medical care | 88% | 8% |
| Increased prices of goods and services | 84% | 8% |
| Increased cost of drugs and medical equipment, thereby hurting health care system | 75% | 17% |
| Led to higher taxes | 69% | 19% |
| Cost jobs by forcing businesses to leave NJ | 66% | 22% |
| Increased prices for products we buy | 65% | 25% |

[8]This opinion was held by 72% of Republicans, 64% of Independents, and 59% of Democrats. In addition, 51% of respondents who had originally indicated that the issue of frivolous lawsuits was not important to them still felt that they would be better off as a result of legislative reforms.

[9]51% indicate that they would "strongly" favor this legislation. Only 18% would oppose efforts to place tighter restrictions on lawsuits. 67% of both Democrats and Independents indicate that they would favor restrictions, as do 76% of Republican voters.

[10]Only 19% indicate they would oppose such a law.

## Texas[11]

62% disapprove of lawyers advertising.

88% believe that frivolous lawsuits are a serious problem.

73% favor limits on contingency fees.

71% believe that there should be limits on the size of awards for medical malpractice.

69% would be more likely to vote against a candidate if he or she were endorsed by personal injury lawyers.

80% would be more likely to vote against a candidate if he or she received campaign contributions from personal injury lawyers.

## West Virginia[12]

71% believe that the current liability lawsuit system has problems and should be changed.

80% believe that there are too many "frivolous lawsuits" in West Virginia.

79% feel statutes should be enacted to limit the size of damage awards for pain and suffering.

73% support limits on the size of punitive damages awards.

70% would vote against a candidate endorsed by trial lawyers.

83% would vote against a candidate who received large campaign contributions from personal injury trial lawyers.

That the public supports meaningful reform of our tort system, with a return to a more traditional fault-based standard, is clear. The interesting development of the past year has been the means by which legislators and their allies transformed that popular mandate into legislative action. While the specifics of the reform campaigns vary from state to state, as the following chapters by the state legislators indicate, there were some common themes that present themselves.

[11]Polling conducted in October 1992 in State Senate District 3 (east Texas) by Voter/Consumer Research, Bethesda, Maryland. Additional surveys were taken in Texas with similar results.

[12]Polling conducted in February 1993 by Marketing Research Institute, Pensacola, Florida.

One of the most important features of the successful campaigns was the development of coalitions. As with most campaigns, a coalition effort can produce success by both marshalling resources and providing specific provisions which attract disparate legislators to the entire package. Those efforts which saw success were supported by broad-based coalitions that included small businesses, manufacturers' associations, chambers of commerce, medical providers, professionals (especially accountants, engineers, and architects), and municipalities.

While it may not be surprising that organizations such as these would support an effort to reform the civil justice system, what *is* surprising is the final component to these coalitions. These coalitions received a great deal of support and gained a great deal of credibility with legislators by enlisting the *grass roots support* of ordinary citizens throughout the state. The ordinary voters gave financial help, advanced public education, and provided logistical support.

The coalitions undertook a number of efforts on behalf of tort reform, including public information campaigns featuring commercials, informational mailings, and even bumper stickers. The campaigns got the message out that the malfunctioning civil justice system hits people's pocketbooks and helped recruit new supporters to the cause.

Of course, popular support does not always translate into statutory change. In many states, the trial bar continues to exercise significant political clout. For example, Alabama's punitive damages cap enacted in 1987 has been eroded through a series of court decisions. An effort to enact legislation that would reassert fair and coherent punitive damages as the public policy of Alabama was defeated last spring.

But the trial bars' victories may prove to be pyrrhic. In Texas, opponents of tort reform suceeded in keeping a product liability bill bottled up in a committee of the state senate, but in the 1992 elections, four members who had opposed the bill were defeated. In one instance, a trial lawyer was defeated by a rancher by a margin of more than thirty points in a campaign that centered on tort reform. Both candidates were incumbent Democrats in a new district with the redistricting favoring the personal injury lawyer. Similarly, in Mississippi, a corporate lawyer defeated an incumbent trial lawyer who served as chairman of the Senate Appropriations Committee in an election where, again, the large contributions the incumbent received from the trial lawyers were an issue.

The strong public sentiment in favor of tort reform has not escaped the notice of the legal profession. The American Bar Association recently undertook a project culminating in a meeting in Washington, D.C. entitled, "Reaching Common Ground: A Summit on Civil

Justice Improvements." The project was limited to developing a consensus on case management, early settlement offers, and discovery reforms. Predictably, participation by organizations representing the plaintiffs' bar and allied consumer groups effectively eliminated any prospect of reaching a consensus on product liability, punitive damages, or contingency fees, despite broad public support for these measures.

The ABA's efforts were, of course, in response to concerns over the growing public disaffection with the American legal process and, in particular, the civil justice system. At the meeting, it was noted that the ABA has done polling to assess the public mood relative to the civil justice system. The results were startling. Not only did respondents have a poor opinion of lawyers in general, but they did not even hold their own lawyers in high esteem. So disappointing were the poll results that the ABA declined to make them public. Nonetheless, the results emphasize the public support for tort reform legislation demonstrated in the state polling detailed above.

The message is clear. A functioning civil justice system based on traditional principles of accountability, objectivity, and fairness is central to our way of life. Accordingly, the American public is not willing to tolerate a narrow interest group enriching itself at the expense of economic growth, the rule of law, and people's faith in the legal system to serve the public interest. State legislators, operating with a mandate to restore the tort system to an institution for the public good, have enacted and will continue to champion reform legislation. Legislative battles like those detailed in the following five chapters will continue until the legal system is rejuvenated and public confidence returns.

CHAPTER 10

# ARIZONA: WINNING BUT NOT YET WON

SENATOR JOHN GREENE
SUSAN CHARLTON

On April 19, 1993, Governor Fife Symington signed into law Arizona Senate Bill 1055. "S.B. 1055" contained thirteen sweeping civil justice reform measures. This chapter will describe how they came to be enacted.

## I. Background

*The Arizona Landscape*

We use the phrase "sweeping civil justice reform measures" in the context of Arizona law, for Arizona is one of five states with severe constitutional impediments to tort reform.[1] Under Arizona's constitution, the legislature may not abrogate any cause of action[2] or limit the amount of damages a person may recover[3] in a personal injury case. Thus, for example, capping noneconomic damages is not a reform option available in Arizona because of constitutional restraints.

Moreover, it is safe to say that Arizona's appellate courts tend to construe these constitutional provisions liberally. Indeed, on October 21, 1993, the Arizona Supreme Court handed down a decision which overturned years of case law.[4] In a shocking decision, the court held that the constitutional protection against the abrogation of causes of action applies to all causes of action, even those created by the courts *after the constitution was enacted*.[5] The impact of this decision on future tort reform efforts in Arizona, as well as the legal fate of S.B. 1055 itself, remains to be seen. In yet another case pending

[1]In addition to Arizona, the states of Arkansas, Kentucky, Pennsylvania, and Wyoming have constitutional prohibitions against limiting damages. ARK. CONST. art. V, § 32; KY. CONST. art. 54; PA. CONST. art. III, § 18; WYO. CONST. art. X, § 4.

[2]ARIZ. CONST. art. 18, § 6.

[3]*Id.* art. 2, § 31; art. 18, § 6.

[4]Hazine v. Montgomery Elevator Co., No. CV-92-0295-PR, 150 Ariz. Adv. Rep. 14 (Oct. 21, 1993).

[5]*Id.*

before the Arizona Supreme Court, the constitutionality of the Periodic Payments Act of 1989, applicable only to medical malpractice cases in Arizona, is being challenged.[6]

*History of Tort Reform in Arizona*

Twenty years prior to S.B. 1055, a few dedicated people led by attorney William "Bill" Jones[7] began the long and arduous task of bringing some rationality and fairness back to Arizona's civil justice system.

The first success was the passage of the Medical Malpractice Reform Act in 1976.[8] In 1978, the Product Liability Act was passed into law.[9] It is still regarded as one of the best statutes of its kind in America. After several attempts in the mid-1980s to pass the Uniform Contribution Among Tortfeasors Act, the Arizona legislature passed a pure comparative fault statute in 1984.[10] In 1987, the legislature abolished joint liability.[11] In 1989, the Periodic Payments Act was passed, under which parties may elect to receive or pay future damages for economic losses in periodic installments.[12]

The Zlaket Committee, named after the then-president of the state bar, was also formed in 1989 by the Arizona Supreme Court

---

[6]Smith v. Superior Ct., 831 P.2d 1279 (Ariz. App. 1991) (supreme court decision pending). *See infra* note 12 and accompanying text.

[7]Our success in Arizona was helped greatly by the technical expertise we had. S.B. 1055's primary draftsman was Bill Jones, senior partner of the law firm Jones, Skelton & Hochuli, in Phoenix, Arizona. Mr. Jones is a legal scholar who has been the driving force behind all significant civil justice reform measures passed in Arizona over the last 20 years. As a practicing attorney for over 30 years, Mr. Jones has tried more than 250 cases before Arizona juries, more than any other practitioner in Arizona history.

[8]The Medical Malpractice Reform Act, ARIZ. REV. STAT. ANN. §§ 12-561 to 12-571 (1976), was enacted to relieve some of the burden of medical malpractice cases. The act allows the introduction of evidence of payments from collateral sources in medical malpractice actions; provides for the review of attorney fees in health care actions at the request of any party; prohibits the introduction of certain types of evidence relating to professional liability insurance; requires that a malpractice claim report be filed with the appropriate regulatory board; and establishes a qualified immunity for health professionals who provide services to nonprofit clinics.

[9]The Product Liability Act, ARIZ. REV. STAT. ANN. §§ 12-681 to 12-686 (1978), provides several affirmative defenses to product liability actions, including the "state of the art" defense; addresses the issues of indemnification and satisfaction of judgments; prohibits a dollar amount from being included in the complaint; and prohibits the introduction of evidence of subsequent remedial modifications.

In Hazine v. Montgomery Elevator Co., No. CV-92-0295-PR, 150 Ariz. Adv. Rep. 14 (Oct. 21, 1993), the Arizona Supreme Court struck down another provision in the act, namely the 12-year statute of repose applicable to product liability actions. According to the court, this was an unconstitutional "abrogation" of the plaintiff's right of action to recover damages for injuries.

[10]ARIZ. REV. STAT. ANN. § 12-2505 (1984).

[11]*Id.* § 12-2506 (1987).

[12]*Id.* §§ 12-581 to 12-594 (1989).

to address the state's ailing civil justice system. As a result of the committee's recommendations, sweeping and sometimes controversial changes were made to Arizona's arbitration system and discovery process.[13]

In January 1992, after many months of working with the American Legislative Exchange Council, I introduced several tort reform measures in the Arizona senate. Identical measures were introduced in the house of representatives by Lisa Graham.[14] Representative Graham was successful in having some of these bills heard in the house. Unfortunately, these measures were killed in the senate. Nonetheless, the seeds of a new crop of tort reform had been planted in the Arizona legislature.

## II. The Passage of S.B. 1055

### *The Political Struggle*

The 1992 election brought control of the Arizona senate back to the Republicans, who retained control of the house. In addition to having the luxury of one-party control, leadership in both houses was committed to making tort reform a priority issue. Governor Symington's support for tort reform confirmed that we were, indeed, faced with a window of opportunity to enact meaningful civil justice reform.[15] In fact, no one who would be in a blocking position in the

[13]For instance, in ARIZ. REV. STAT. ANN. §§ 12-1501 to 12-1518 (1962), Arizona adopts UNIF. R. ARB. § 1(b), which requires arbitration of all cases under the following conditions: (1) no party seeks affirmative relief other than a money judgment; and (2) no party seeks an award in excess of $50,000.

ARIZ. R. CIV. P. 26.1 replaced the costly and adversarial system of discovery with a more efficient and forthright system of disclosure. This system of disclosure has since been included in the recommendations regarding changes to the Federal Rules of Civil Procedure submitted to Congress by the Federal Judicial Center in Washington, D.C.

[14]S.B. 1221, H.B. 2343 comparative fault; S.B. 1257, H.B. 2345 assumption of the risk; S.C.M. ("Senate Concurrent Memorial") 1002, H.C.M. ("House Concurrent Memorial") 2006 product liability resolution; S.B. 1223, H.B. 2339 drug and alcohol defense act; S.B. 1268, H.B. 2448 landowner's liability; educational, recreational purposes; S.B. 1267, H.B. 2341 punitive damages; limitations; S.B. 1266, H.B. 2338 damages; personal injury; wrongful death; S.B. 1252, H.B. 2335, eliminating double recovery; collateral source; S.B. 1262, H.B. 2336 periodic payments; S.B. 1224, H.B. 2337 volunteer immunity; S.B. 1222, H.B. 2340 limitation of wrongful termination; S.B. 1215, H.B. 2344 recovery of attorney fees; S.B. 1219, H.B. 2342 expert witness fees; S.B. 1269, H.B. 2346 privileged communications; S.B. 1220, H.B. 2447 liability for damages; felony acts; S.B. 1231, H.B. 2334 subrogation of medical expense claims.

[15]We have not always been so fortunate to have the support of our governor. On May 6, 1982, Governor Bruce Babbitt vetoed S.B. 1011 uniform contribution among tortfeasors act.

legislature opposed reform.[16] The judiciary chairs in the senate and house, Patti Noland and attorney Ernie Baird, respectively, are strong supporters of civil justice reform. As a result, we acted swiftly in communicating our commitment and cultivating the support needed.

S.B. 1055, introduced in January 1993, was the culmination of many prior efforts. Developed by a group of individuals committed to reform, the bill was designed to make sweeping changes to Arizona's civil justice system, within Arizona's severe constitutional restraints. In addition to the support of the elected officials just discussed, attorney Bill Jones, the primary scrivener of this legislation, led the charge from the private sector.[17]

Two other major civil justice reform measures of note were also introduced in the first session of the forty-first legislature. One was successful, the other was not. A major rewrite of Arizona's draconian civil RICO statute was successful despite much resistance from the plaintiffs' bar.[18] The other measure was intended to eliminate the court-created tort of wrongful termination in Arizona and reassert the doctrine of employment at will.[19]

---

[16]While this is true, the house ran S.B. 1055 through their commerce committee, chaired by Representative Gary Richardson. The commerce committee's makeup was more friendly to tort reform during the early stages of the session.

[17]The Arizona Chamber of Commerce was an immense help in the effort. Chamber members such as The Dial Corp., under the leadership of Vice President and General Counsel Gene Lemon and Associate General Counsel Bob Wilmoth, helped breathe life into the effort. Chamber members such as Michael Preston Green, Chuck Shipley, Don Isaacson, Phil MacDonnell, Ed Wren, Allan Stanton, John Mangum, Russell Smolden, and Pete Dunn provided an invaluable lobbying effort.

In addition, the support and counsel of Rodger Bailey of the nationally recognized political consulting firm of Bailey Consulting of Salt Lake City, Utah, gave us important insights on how to approach the issues. For example, we learned early that being right was not enough, and that to gain public support it is sometimes more important *how* you say things. Thus, we learned to speak of "lawsuit" reform as opposed to "tort" reform.

[18]S.B. 1197 (Laws 1993, ch. 257) restricts the use of Arizona Racketeer Influenced and Corrupt Organization (RICO) statutes by private litigants in civil actions. Substantial changes to the prior law include requiring private litigants to establish a "pattern of racketeering," raising the burden of proof to "clear and convincing," and making treble damages discretionary.

[19]S.B. 1315 wrongful termination; prohibited personnel practice attempted to narrow the court-created exceptions to the "at will" doctrine of employment, as well as to prevent further erosion of the doctrine. Specifically, the bill would have overruled Wagonseller v. Scottsdale Memorial Hosp., 710 P.2d 1025 (Ariz. 1985), which held that an employer may discharge an employee for "good cause" or for "no cause" but may not discharge an employee for "bad cause"—that which violates "public policy." Under *Wagonseller,* what constitutes "bad cause" or what violates "public policy" is determined by the courts. According to the court, an explicit statutory expression of public policy is no longer required. *Id.* at 378. "Reliance on prior judicial decisions as part of the body of applicable common law, is appropriate . . . [and] we will look to the pronouncement of our founders, our legislature, and our courts to discern the public policy of this state." *Id.* at 379. Needless to say, this holding has wreaked havoc in the employment law field. Employers now live in constant fear that anyone

As in earlier reform efforts, several of the provisions of S.B. 1055 were inspired by the American Legislative Exchange Council model acts which were expertly fashioned by ALEC's civil justice task force. Indeed, the technical resources provided by ALEC in our fight for reform were invaluable.[20]

Unlike some earlier reform efforts, a strategic decision was made *not* to include provisions in S.B. 1055 that would require a constitutional amendment. We believed that the timing was not right for such an amendment and that substantial reform could be enacted without one. We also decided to include certain provisions which were considered politically appealing, such as the provision prohibiting a felon from suing his victim. Not surprisingly, the most politically appealing provisions were usually not the most important in terms of real reform. The provisions dealing with periodic payments and subrogation were considered the "meat" of the bill yet drew relatively little attention from the public.

During the early stages of drafting the bill, another strategic decision was made to put all of the reform provisions in one bill instead of introducing thirteen separate bills. We believed that this would make it more difficult for the plaintiffs' bar to "pick off" some of the better provisions. We essentially put all our eggs into one basket. It was a gamble, but we did not want to give lawmakers the opportunity to justify "no" votes on some reform measures based on their "yes" votes on other reform measures. More importantly, it allowed legislators and others who would shepherd the bill through the process to unify the effort at every stage. Unfortunately, the down side to running a single bill was that the job of the plaintiffs' bar was simplified. If it could convince enough soft votes that one small piece of the bill was bad, all of the rest might go down, too.

The last strategic decision made was to solicit broad-based support for the bill. We knew from the start that this bill would not be successful if it was viewed as an "insurance company" bill or a "doctors" bill. The truth is that it was not, but the plaintiffs' bar would inevitably try to portray it as such. We would therefore have to garner support from the "average" citizen if it was to be successful. Garnering that support meant waging an education campaign on

they discharge, for whatever reason, will bring or threaten a wrongful termination suit based on "bad cause." S.B. 1315 sought to bring some consistency and rationality back into employer-employee relations.

[20]AMERICAN LEGISLATIVE EXCHANGE COUNCIL, THE SOURCE BOOK OF AMERICAN STATE LEGISLATION (1987–88 ed. and 1991–92 ed., vol. 5). The reform effort was helped enormously by the ALEC legislative chairs for Arizona who also happen to be the house and senate majority leaders, Representative Brenda Burns and Senator Tom Patterson. On the business side, Russell Smolden, the ALEC business chair from Arizona, also made a difference by helping to coordinate the business lobbying effort through the Arizona Chamber of Commerce.

the community level. This involved a great deal of leg work, and much of the credit goes to Rodger Bailey of Bailey Consulting for organizing the effort. Mr. Bailey and his staff went out into our communities and spoke to groups and individuals about how those groups and individuals would benefit as a result of the reforms contained in S.B. 1055. They then encouraged those groups and individuals to call or write their legislators and voice their support. Their efforts proved successful. In both the senate and house committees, parent-teacher groups, cities and towns, volunteers, environmental groups, and other laypersons testified for some or all of the bill.[21]

Once these early strategic decisions were made, we began the long, arduous task of shepherding the bill through the legislature. Needless to say, none of the aforementioned positive conditions deterred the plaintiffs' bar from putting up a fight. As a result of our decision to run with one "omnibus" bill, the plaintiffs' bar was relentless in its misinformation on many details of the legislation. They chose portions of the bill which would be ripe for controversy, particularly if such portions could be misinterpreted or confused. The primary weapon of the plaintiffs' bar was misinformation, followed closely by exaggeration, scare tactics, and misplaced sympathies.

For example, one provision in the bill would allow "interested parties" to interview a willing doctor regarding the basic details of an injury alleged to have been caused by a defendant without having to go through an expensive deposition. This informal procedure has been used in the worker's compensation area in Arizona without any known problems since 1969.[22] The plaintiffs' bar, however, claimed that the bill would waive the plaintiff's doctor-patient privilege, that *any* party or person who was simply "interested" in learning about the medical secrets of the plaintiff could have the information, and that insurance companies and people off the street would use the law to learn about a plaintiff's most intimate sexual disorders, regardless of the nature of the alleged injury. The truth, of course, is that "interested parties" is a term of art limited to the parties to

[21]Over 42 individuals testified in support of S.B. 1055 in the senate judiciary committee hearing, including volunteers and representatives from Arizona cities and counties, the Arizona Chamber of Commerce, Arizona Rural Water Association, Arizona Farm Bureau, United Dairymen of Arizona, Salt River Project, Retail Grocers, Arizona PTA, and the Canal Users Association.

[22]This section of S.B. 1055 is essentially identical to ARIZ. REV. STAT. ANN. § 23-908(C) (1978) (the Arizona Worker's Compensation Act), which became effective in 1969. In a speech to the Arizona Independent Agents and Brokers at their annual convention on August 26, 1993, attorney Bill Jones related that in 30-plus years of practice in the area, he has never heard of one complaint against this system of informal discovery.

the suit and their representatives, the privilege is waived under existing law already by the institution of the suit, and the bill makes it clear that, as under current law, only information directly relevant to the lawsuit is available. All the bill would do is overrule existing case law to allow a party to ask basic questions of the treating physician, outside a formal deposition, upon notice to all parties, and with the physician's permission.

To counteract the misinformation being conveyed by the plaintiffs' bar, an all-out education effort was commenced by legislative leadership. The minute a concern was expressed by a member, key legislators and staffers would move in, usually to dispel misinformation. We repeatedly extended invitations to legislators to communicate their concerns and questions to us so that we could work with them in addressing their problems. Because the characterization of a provision in the bill by the plaintiffs' bar was rarely what was intended by the bill, often a slight clarifying change, while perhaps not needed for technical purposes, would give a worried legislator some comfort.[23]

We responded to the plaintiffs' bar's daily attacks by continuing and strengthening our education campaign and expanding it to the press. We made countless speeches to various groups urging their support for S.B. 1055. We met with editorial boards to urge their support. Finally, we met with reporters covering the legislation and meticulously explained every provision in the bill so that they would not be misled by the plaintiffs' bar's misinformation. When the true facts of the bill were made known, most supported it. Thus, we made great efforts to ensure that *everyone* knew exactly what the bill did and did not do.

As the bill progressed through the legislature, it became clear that the only chinks in our political armor were some soft votes in the house majority caucus. Aware of these soft votes, the plaintiffs' bar naturally targeted the house to defeat the bill. When they failed to kill the bill in committee or caucus, despite extensive theatrics, the plaintiffs' bar directed all of their efforts to defeating the bill in the House Committee of the Whole.

While debate in Committee of the Whole is not generally known to sway members' votes, the fate of S.B. 1055 was by no means certain when debate started at approximately 10:00 p.m. on April

---

[23]For example, due to misinformation being circulated by the plaintiffs' bar, the statute of repose section of the bill had to be amended to address specifically the issue of when a cause of action "accrues," despite the fact that this point is already well established in case law. We credit Bill Jones' great knowledge and perseverance for our ultimate success. Rather than lose patience every time some less than necessary amendment was offered by a well-meaning legislator, he found a way to accommodate these ideas and concerns without defeating the purpose of the bill.

8, 1993. Armed with questions and purported "facts" about the bill by the plaintiffs' bar, many minority members barraged proponents of the bill. Fortunately, house leadership was ready for the challenge. Bill Jones had warned leadership about the kinds of questions and misinformation the bill's opponents would likely use in floor debate on S.B. 1055. As a result, a legislative "tag team" of well-informed house members was created to address the arguments against S.B. 1055 and help keep the soft votes in the "aye" column.[24] This approach was considered necessary due to the length and complexity of the bill.

Each member of the tag team chose a few sections of the bill on which to become expert. A great deal of time and energy was subsequently spent by these members learning the bill's technical nuances, the relevant case law, and the arguments both pro and con surrounding their issues. During floor debate, questions on a certain section would be referred to the tag team expert on that issue. This approach proved highly successful. The tag team members were able to respond effectively to every question and criticism thrown at them by the opponents. The debate went on for over seven hours and into the wee hours of the morning but, despite the efforts of the plaintiffs' bar, every member of the majority caucus voted "aye" on S.B. 1055 when the final vote was taken.

S.B. 1055 was subsequently passed by the entire legislature and signed into law by the governor. Unfortunately, that is not the end of the story. Unable to defeat the bill in the legislature, the plaintiffs' bar has referred most of S.B. 1055 to the ballot. They collected—using dubious tactics—enough signatures to put several of the provisions of S.B. 1055 on hold until the voters agree or disagree with such provisions in the 1994 general election.[25] Thus, while we rejoice in the success of S.B. 1055, the battle is not yet won.

### *Summary of S.B. 1055*

*Emergency medical service.* Section 1 of S.B. 1055 amends current law[26] and expands the limited immunity currently available to fire and ambulance companies for providing emergency care to instances

[24]Representatives Gary Richardson, Ernie Baird, John Kaites, Lisa Graham, and Laurie Daniels were S.B. 1055's house tag team.

[25]The plaintiffs' bar submitted 106,000 signatures to the Arizona secretary of state, most of which were gathered by paid petition circulators. Unfortunately, the actions of several petition circulators reflect the continuing campaign of misinformation waged by the plaintiffs' bar. Petition circulators were heard to have made such outrageous statements as "Sign this and restore your civil rights!" or "Sign this and your insurance rates will go down!" in an effort to collect signatures.

[26]ARIZ. REV. STAT. ANN. § 9-500.02 (1983).

in which those services are contracted for by private individuals.[27] Under the bill, the emergency medical technician would be held to a gross negligence or intentional misconduct standard. The bill also clarifies that the immunity stops at the hospital door. This section of S.B. 1055 is not subject to the referendum.

*Statute of repose*. Section 2 of the bill also amends current law.[28] Heretofore, minors and individuals who are mentally incapacitated are legally incapable of maintaining a lawsuit on their own behalf. In those instances, the general two-year statute of limitations on personal injury actions is tolled; that is, the statute is effectively stopped until the person is no longer a minor or incapacitated. For example, a baby who is injured at birth currently has twenty years to bring a suit; eighteen years while the statute is "tolled" and two years after that for the generally applicable statute of limitations. S.B. 1055 provides that "notwithstanding any provision for tolling of a statute of limitations, except in cases of fraud by the defendant which prevented discovery of a cause of action within the applicable limitations period, no action may be commenced more than twelve years after the cause of action accrues." Therefore, in the example given above, the baby, or more realistically his parents or guardians, would have twelve years to bring a suit for injuries incurred at birth.

Under the bill, a cause of action accrues when the injured party realizes he or she has been injured and knows or reasonably should know the cause of the injury. In the case of an incapacitated person or a minor, the cause of action accrues when an adult person, who has legal custody of the incapacitated person or minor, knows that the incapacitated person or minor has been injured and knows or reasonably should know the cause of the injury.

Admittedly, this provision carries with it some emotional baggage in the case of minors. It was decided, however, that the better public policy is to bring finality to lingering potential liability. Needless to say, the plaintiffs' bar included this provision in its referendum drive.

*Privileged communications*. Part of section 5 of the bill is intended to reverse the holding in the Arizona court of appeals case *Duquette v. Superior Court*,[29] where the court held that once a party puts his medical condition at issue, the physician-patient privilege is waived. The court also held, however, that discovery of that pertinent medical

[27]In 1992, the legislature passed a similar law which provided partial immunity to emergency medical technicians and paramedics under contract with a governmental entity. It was considered a partial victory by both the plaintiffs' bar and proponents of the bill.

[28]ARIZ. REV. STAT. ANN. § 12-550.

[29]778 P.2d 634 (Ariz. App. 1989).

information must be made through formal methods such as depositions and interrogatories.

Section 5 of the bill merely allows access to this nonprivileged medical information without going through the long and expensive process of formal discovery. Specifically, the bill allows the defendant, his agent, or attorney to confer directly with the health care provider, with or without the consent of the party seeking damages or his counsel, instead of having to hold a formal deposition. The doctor may always refuse to talk to the defendant. Moreover, while consent is not required, the defendant, his agent, or attorney must notify the party seeking damages or his counsel that they intend to confer with the doctor. Finally, the bill clarifies that the information available is that which is "for purposes of properly understanding the case and determining the rights involved."

One of the policies upon which this provision is based is that in cases where the doctor is not himself a party, he should be a neutral, unbiased witness. He should not be an advocate for the plaintiff, but rather should just report to both sides on the injured party's condition. Therefore, both sides should have equal access to the doctor.

This provision is subject to the referendum and is expected to be the basis of the scare tactics used by the plaintiffs' bar in its media blitz. They have used, as an example, the claim of a neck injury to a young woman who now will face revelation of intimate gynecological records which, it is said, will be used by insurance companies to expose her sexual activity.[30]

*Drug and alcohol defense*. Section 3 of the bill establishes a new affirmative defense in all personal injury actions which can be invoked if a claimant, as a result of the influence of alcohol or drugs, is determined to be more than fifty percent at fault for the accident or event which resulted in his or her own harm. In such cases, the jury is given the *discretion* to bar recovery by the plaintiff. This approach was necessary to meet Arizona's constitutional requirements against abrogating a cause of action.[31] This provision is not subject to the plaintiffs' bar's referendum.

*Liability for damages; felony acts*. Section 3 of the bill also provides that a defendant is not liable for damages that the plaintiff incurred if the plaintiff was harmed while attempting to commit, committing,

[30]This was an example given by a member of the plaintiffs' bar and panelist in a program on S.B. 1055 hosted by the Arizona Independent Agents and Brokers at their annual meeting in Phoenix, Arizona, on August 26, 1993.

[31]ARIZ. CONST. art. 18, § 6.

or fleeing from a felony criminal act.[32] This provision is not subject to the plaintiffs' bar's referendum.

*Eliminating double recovery; collateral source.* In order to eliminate double and triple recoveries, section 4 of S.B. 1055 allows the jury to learn whether a plaintiff has been compensated for the injury by another source. The jury is not required to deduct the amount previously received by the plaintiff, but is allowed to consider it when determining what the plaintiff's actual damages are.

Section 4 would also extend "collateral source" to all personal injury cases. This provision has worked very well in the area of medical malpractice in Arizona for seventeen years, but it is nonetheless subject to the plaintiffs' bar's referendum and is expected to be a key issue in the bar's media plan. The bar claims that it is only fair that the defendant reveal its liability insurance coverage if the plaintiff has to disclose to the jury its insurance or other collateral sources of economic protection. This conveniently ignores, however, the fact that the defendant's ability to pay (e.g., the depth of his or her pocket) is irrelevant in an injury suit. On the other hand, the plaintiffs' real loss or damages (taking into account all sources of compensation) *is* relevant.

*Suits against the state.*[33] Section 6 of the bill expands the state's qualified immunity to injuries arising out of the maintenance or operation of highways, roads, streets, bridges, and rights-of-way. Under the bill, the state will be held to a "gross negligence" standard for maintenance- or operation-related injuries. (What constitutes "gross negligence" is a question of fact to be determined by the jury based on the particular set of circumstances.) For injuries arising out of the construction or design of the highway, the state will continue to be held to an ordinary negligence standard. The bill also provides for a one-year statute of limitation for suits against the state.

The bill clarifies that this immunity does not extend to injuries arising out of the operation of a motor vehicle by a state employee. Therefore, if a street sweeper hits someone crossing the street, the public entity could be held liable under an ordinary negligence theory.

[32]This provision is a strong statement of public policy by the legislature. As a matter of public policy, the legislature will not tolerate a felon reaping benefits from his own wrongdoing. Whether the courts will invalidate this policy based on the constitutional provisions remains to be seen.

[33]Despite Arizona's relatively small population, it ranks as one of the top five states for the amount paid on tort claims against the state. The Arizona Department of Administration reports that, in 1991 alone, Arizona paid out $28 million on tort claims filed against the state.

This section of the bill also expands the state's qualified immunity to injuries incurred by a driver which are directly attributable to that driver's violation of a drunk driving statute. Again, in these instances the state would be held to a gross negligence standard. Of course, the drunk driver himself remains fully liable to civil suit (and criminal prosecution).

This provision is subject to the plaintiffs' bar's referendum.[34]

*Volunteer immunity*. Section 10 of the bill added two new sections to the Arizona code.[35] The first provides that a volunteer is not liable for acts and omissions that result in damage or injury if: (i) the volunteer acted in good faith and within the scope of the volunteer's official duties for a nonprofit corporation or organization, hospital, or governmental entity and (ii) the damage or injury was not caused by willful or wanton misconduct on the part of the volunteer. The injured party still will be able to sue the organization for which the volunteer works under an ordinary negligence standard. The second part of section 10 requires all automobile insurance policies to provide coverage when the insured is acting as a volunteer for a nonprofit organization. In such a case, the policy is secondary to the insurance of the organization involved. Principally because of its widespread public appeal, the plaintiffs' bar left section 10 out of its referendum.

*Comparative fault*. Sections 11 and 12 of S.B. 1055 provide a modified comparative fault system allowing the finder of fact to bar recovery by the plaintiff if the plaintiff is over fifty percent at fault.[36] Arizona is currently a "pure" comparative negligence state which would, in theory, allow a plaintiff who is ninety-nine per cent at fault to recover one percent of his or her damages. This provision is subject to the plaintiffs' bar's referendum.

*Assumption of the risk*. The bill codifies the common-law assumption-of-the-risk doctrine. Under it, the plaintiff may be barred by

[34]As a result of the plaintiffs' bar's selective referral of S.B. 1055, certain provisions became effective on July 17, 1993, while others were put on hold until the 1994 general election. Unfortunately, this discrepancy created an unforeseen crisis for the state.

S.B. 1055 repealed the existing affirmative defenses for the state in highway accident cases and replaced them with the new, tougher gross negligence standard. The plaintiffs' bar referred the new gross negligence standard but did not refer the repeal of the existing affirmative defenses. Consequently, the state was left with no statutory protection for highway accident cases for the period between July 17, 1993, and the 1994 general election. In order to avert a possible fiscal crisis, the governor convened a special session of the legislature on September 2, 1993, to reenact the affirmative defenses which had been repealed by S.B. 1055.

[35]ARIZ. REV. STAT. ANN. §§ 12-981, 12-982 (1993).

[36]The Arizona constitution provides that "the defense of contributory negligence or of assumption of risk shall, in all cases whatsoever, be a question of fact and shall, at all times, be left to the jury." ARIZ. CONST. art. 18, § 5.

the finder of fact from recovering damages if the person suffering the injury was aware or should have been aware that there was a risk of death or injury to the person and proceeded voluntarily to expose himself or herself to the risk. This provision is subject to the referendum.

*Periodic payments*. Current Arizona law allows periodic payments in the area of medical malpractice.[37] S.B. 1055 amends current law by allowing for periodic payments of future economic damages in all personal injury cases. Under the bill, instead of receiving a lump sum award, the plaintiff may receive his future economic damages through an annuity purchased by the defendant. All damages incurred prior to the trial or settlement plus any award for noneconomic damages (i.e., pain and suffering) must still be paid in a lump sum up front, at the time of trial or settlement. Only future economic damages are included in the annuity.

Upon the plaintiffs' death, future medical expenses will be cut off since they are no longer needed. All other future economic damages, such as lost income, will be paid to the decedent's beneficiaries.

This provision is subject to the plaintiffs' bar's referendum.

*Subrogation*. Section 5 of the bill created a new section in the Arizona code[38] and is designed to overrule common law.[39] This provision allows insurance policies to contain a provision giving the insurer a lien against any proceeds collected in a claim for injuries against a third party by the insured to the extent of the actual costs of services provided by the insurer. For example, if the insurer pays out $10,000 for medical bills on behalf of the insured and thereafter the insured recovers $20,000 from the tort-feasor, the insurer has a lien against the recovery and may collect $10,000. The lien or subrogation rights must be specifically contained in the policy between the insured and the insurer and the insurer must give insureds special notice of the lien or subrogation rights in the policy. The bill contains procedures for perfecting a lien under this provision and requires that an attorney who represents the injured party and who has knowledge of the lien may be personally liable for the lien amount for not honoring it.

The bill also requires the Director of the Department of Insurance to promulgate rules to designate which policies are primary over other policies and to describe the manner in which benefits under

[37] ARIZ. REV. STAT. ANN. §§ 12-581 to 12-594. *But see supra* note 6 and accompanying text.

[38] ARIZ. REV. STAT. ANN. § 12-714 (1993).

[39] Section 5 of S.B. 1055 addresses the problem created principally by Harleysville v. Lea, 410 P.2d 495 (Ariz. 1966), and Allstate Ins. Co. v. Drake, 576 P.2d 489 (Ariz. App. 1978), which apply the prohibition of assignments of personal injury causes of actions to prohibit a subrogation in favor of an insurance company for claims paid.

all policies coordinate. According to the Department of Insurance, the basis for these rules will be existing statutes, rules, and case law. Wherever gaps exist, they will attempt to fill them by using the general policies upon which the current authorities are based.

This provision is subject to the plaintiffs' bar's referendum.

*Landowners' liability; educational, recreational purposes*. Unfortunately, in Arizona many landowners, both public and private, have closed their land to the use of others for fear of liability. Cities and towns began discussing the possibility of closing bike paths and parks because of the costly, too often frivolous, suits being filed. Sections 24 and 25 of S.B. 1055 attempt to allay some of those fears by limiting the liability of public and private landowners who make land and water areas available to the public for educational and recreational purposes, without charge to the public. The bill also provides a mechanism whereby owners of land may be compensated for expenditures incurred in defense against frivolous or purposeless suits.

Because of the great popularity of this provision to many constituencies in Arizona, including the Sierra Club, this provision, not surprisingly, is not subject to the plaintiffs' bar's referendum.

*Report to the governor and legislature*. The bill requires that insurers provide information to the Department of Insurance regarding their litigation expenses and ultimate loss payments over the next three years and that the Department of Insurance submit an analysis of this information to the governor, president of the senate, and speaker of the house on or before December 31, 1996. Despite the fact that the plaintiffs' bar's referendum would eliminate almost all of the provisions which would drive this information filing process, it did not make this section subject to its referendum.

### *Some Observations*

S.B. 1055 was, admittedly, lengthy and complex. Nevertheless, it is very distressing that we have yet to hear any committee testimony or public debate by plaintiffs' bar representatives which does not contain a significant amount of inaccurate information on civil justice issues.

*The point is that a successful reform effort entails effectively addressing misinformation—not an easy task.*

Throughout our efforts on S.B. 1055, we often questioned the basis for the plaintiffs' bar's opposition to reform. Certainly its main concern is protection of its economic base,[40] but a siege mentality seems to transcend this concern.

The economics of the practice of personal injury law has changed drastically in the last generation and has had an enormous and negative impact on the profession. Today we have lawsuit mills whose activities resemble more insurance adjusting than the practice of law.[41] For these lawsuit mills, any limitation on the ability to bring a lawsuit and recover is a direct economic threat to their livelihood. It is understandable then, why they resist reform. The fact that their resistance is understandable, though, makes it no less offensive.

In general terms, the corruption of our civil justice system began with the breakdown of accepted norms of ethics in the legal profession within the last thirty years.[42] For example, plaintiffs' lawyers now go on once-forbidden fishing expeditions for cases with no fear of sanction. One need only scan the typical lawyer television ads for confirmation of this.[43]

Probably the most insidious general factor, however, has been the abandonment by the legal profession of the notion that lawsuits are about personal tragedy, that they are wasteful measures of last resort to be avoided if at all possible. Today, the bar and law schools espouse the notion that litigation is a positive force in our society and should be used to mold public policy.

Other contributing factors have been the relaxation of lawsuit procedures, and the judicial expansion of causes of action. Judges often fancy themselves as social engineers and welcome the opportunity to shape public policy.

Finally, the plaintiffs' bar currently portrays itself as the protector of the downtrodden and, of course, this self-anointed group uses the almighty lawsuit as its sword. Walter K. Olson has put it very well:

---

[40]Arizona state senator Marc Spitzer, a tax lawyer and member of the Arizona state bar, likened the problem to a fox chasing a hare. The fox represents the reform movement and the hare the plaintiffs' bar. If the fox loses, he merely forgoes a meal that day. The consequences for the hare are much dimmer, however. Senator Spitzer hastened to add that S.B. 1055 would have little or no financial effect on the legitimate plaintiffs' bar (as opposed to the lawsuit mills). But apparently it is all for one and one for all for the plaintiffs' bar in Arizona.

[41]We believe Bill Jones' distinction between "trial lawyers" and "litigators" also describes the problem. Jones said: " 'litigators' are a form of beast more voracious than alligators. They feed primarily upon paper, contentious conduct and irrelevant inquiry. They are rarely seen around courtrooms except on discovery motions." William R. Jones, Jr., *Do We Have A Plain, Speedy and Adequate Remedy?*, ARIZ. ATT'Y, Dec. 1990, at 25.

[42]*See, e.g.*, WALTER K. OLSON, THE LITIGATION EXPLOSION: WHAT HAPPENED WHEN AMERICA UNLEASHED THE LAWSUIT (1991).

[43]*Id.* at 19.

> The idea of treating lawsuits as vessels for compensation and deterrence is seductive. In no time at all you get to thinking of them less as a personal tragedy and more as a policy opportunity. You begin to imagine that the more people sue, the more will find happiness; while the more people get sued, the more responsibly everyone will behave for fear of sharing the same fate. The more lawsuits there are, in short, the closer to perfection the world will become. By the 1970's the climate in the law schools had turned around on the subject of litigation, first to ostensible neutrality and then to admiring support.[44]

What the bar fails to acknowledge is that the rest of society is being victimized by their "pious" actions in the form of higher insurance rates, higher consumer prices, and unemployment.

## III. Conclusion

In fighting for civil justice reform, we have learned several lessons.

The first is that *being right is not enough*. The plaintiffs' bar has discovered that even intelligent lawmakers and citizens are easily confused about the purpose and intent of reform measures. Those of us who fight for reform do so, then, with one hand tied behind our backs. We do not seek to misinform, an all-too-easy task, but to illuminate. Moreover, we are not unified in our opinion as to what is worthwhile reform, yet the plaintiffs' bar sings with one voice, and that voice is the status quo.

The second lesson is that *it is sometimes more important how you say something, than what you say*. In today's world, where debates on complex issues are often forged in the media, the use of competent wordsmiths and pollsters is necessary.

The third lesson is that the old cliche, *knowledge is power*, is particularly true in the civil justice reform debate. The plaintiffs' bar excels in using ignorance to their advantage. The only effective retaliation is through knowledge and the ability to educate others.

In the long run, meaningful reform will come more easily when we find a way to bring the bar back to the ethics of yesterday, and the bench back to judging and away from social engineering. In the meantime, we should appreciate the Bill Joneses of the world who buck the trend of so many other trial attorneys.

When faced with a well-financed cadre of professional advocates in the plaintiffs' bar, it seems sometimes as though we are wasting our time. The passage of S.B. 1055 proves that we are not.

[44]*Id.* at 4.

CHAPTER 11

# MICHIGAN: A DECADE OF MEDICAL MALPRACTICE REFORM

REPRESENTATIVE RICHARD A. BANDSTRA

On July 13, 1993, Michigan Governor John Engler signed into law Senate Bill 270, legislation which will significantly affect medical malpractice suits brought in the state of Michigan for years to come. That legislation—Public Act 78 of 1993—was the end of a long and controversial battle between the medical community and the plaintiffs' bar over the nature of the medical malpractice insurance cost problem and the steps needed to address it. This chapter will recount the difficult struggle for effective malpractice liability reform in Michigan.

## I. Round One: The 1986 Reforms

The 1993 legislation was really the third round in this debate. The first had occurred in the early- to mid-1980s.

At that time, the medical community, led by the Michigan State Medical Society and the Michigan Hospital Association, made its first attempt at malpractice reform. That effort was prompted by statistics showing that Michigan physicians were leaving the state and health care costs were rising, both as a result of escalating malpractice insurance premiums. The medical community was joined by the medical malpractice insurers, who argued that the reasons for the high premiums were frivolous lawsuits and extravagant jury awards which, in turn, encouraged high settlement amounts even in cases that did not proceed through trial.

In response, the Michigan Trial Lawyers Association argued that escalating premium levels were not the result of a flawed medical malpractice liability system. Rather, the trial bar blamed the insurance industry for being greedy and inefficient or, alternatively, argued that escalating premiums were simply the result of worldwide cycles in insurance costs.

Both sides, of course, produced a morass of statistics and arguments in support of these general positions. Each side labeled the statistics and arguments of the other as biased and lacking credibility. For most legislators, then, the issue boiled down to whether the medical community or plaintiffs' bar was more trustworthy and who presented the more believable sets of arguments and statistics.

Most Republicans sided with those in the medical community arguing for change, and most Democrats sided with those in the legal community arguing that tort reform was unnecessary. There were, however, important exceptions to this general rule, with some Democrats aligned with the doctors and some Republicans aligned with the plaintiffs' bar. Moreover, on individual controversial issues, such as whether there should be a cap on noneconomic or "pain and suffering" damages, legislators took individual positions which did not sort out along party lines.

The lobbying effort mounted by the hospitals and doctors was significant. It culminated in a "march on Lansing" in October 1985. At a rally attended by thousands of white-coated health care professionals on the lawn of the state capitol, calls were made by legislators and others for significant medical malpractice reform. Because of the balance of power in the house and senate, however, immediate reform did not occur.

The Michigan senate, controlled by the Republicans, was amenable to change and quickly passed legislation that made changes in tort law generally, effecting most of the changes that were championed by the medical community. The battle became pitched in the Democrat-controlled house of representatives. The speaker of the house set up a special ad hoc committee chaired by the Democratic floor leader, purportedly in recognition of the importance of the issue. Many on both sides of the aisle believed, however, that the speaker's true intent was to ensure that changes recommended to the full house would be at least somewhat amenable to the plaintiffs' bar and would not be the kind of significant reform that the health care community was demanding.

The special ad hoc committee proposed legislation which was acceptable to a majority of the house, and it was signed into law as Public Act 178 of 1986. The malpractice portion of the legislation had five basic components. First, it placed a cap of $225,000—to be adjusted annually—on noneconomic damages,[1] with the following exceptions not subject to a cap: where the malpractice resulted in death; where there was an intentional tort; where a foreign object was wrongfully left in a patient's body; where the injury was to a person's reproductive system; where the fraudulent conduct of a

[1]"Noneconomic" damages are those to compensate for losses that do not result in expenditures by plaintiff—such as "pain and suffering," "emotional distress," and the like. "Economic" damages are those that do result in out-of-pocket expense. *See supra* chapter 6.

health care provider prevented discovery of the existence of a potential cause of action; where a limb or organ was wrongfully removed; or where a person lost a vital bodily function. Second, the law required that medical experts testifying in a malpractice case have the same (or a related) specialty as the defendant and that they have devoted a substantial portion of their professional time to practicing, or instructing students, in that specialty. Third, it provided that the statute of limitations for a malpractice action begins to run at the time of the act or omission that was the basis for the claim, and that a malpractice claim could in no case be brought more than six years thereafter. In addition, it required a person thirteen years of age or younger at the time a malpractice action accrued to file suit on or before his or her fifteenth birthday. Fourth, it required the parties to provide security for costs by posting a $2,000 bond or by filing an affidavit of merit or meritorious defense signed by the party's attorneys. Finally, the legislation set forth a process that would allow a party to request dismissal from a malpractice case by filing an affidavit that he or she was not involved in the acts causing the alleged injury.

The medical community's reaction to the 1986 reforms could best be described as grudging acceptance. Many believed that the changes enacted would do little to affect the cost of litigation or insurance premium levels. At the same time, most realized that, given the political realities in the state capital at that time, they had achieved about all that could be reasonably expected.

## II. Round Two: The 1992 Stalemate

### *An Unsolved Problem*

Those skeptical of the changes made in 1986 kept a close watch on the issue for the remainder of the decade. While there was some relief in the rate of escalation of insurance premiums, Michigan continued to suffer under the weight of extremely high premium levels for medical liability coverage. For example, in 1990, the average cost for a hospital insuring against liability on a per-bed basis was $4,600 for the state, and $6,900 for Detroit area hospitals. By 1992, those figures had risen to $5,700 and $8,600 respectively. The Detroit rates are the highest in the United States, with the national average in 1990–92 remaining a constant $1,300.[2] Similarly, individual practitioners in Michigan had to pay extremely high rates for liability coverage as well. For example, in 1992, Michigan

[2]Source: St. Paul Fire & Marine Ins. Co. (1992).

obstetricians practicing in the Detroit area paid an incredible $133,900 for rather minimal coverage of $200,000 per incident, $600,000 per year.[3] In comparison, an obstetrician practicing in Chicago paid only $49,200 for the same coverage, and Los Angeles obstetricians paid only $38,000—less than a third of what their Michigan counterparts had to pay.[4] According to a study on liability insurance costs commissioned by the state of Michigan, the annual medical liability premiums paid in Michigan in 1990 totaled nearly a half *billion* dollars—$251 million for physicians, and $239 million for hospitals. That same amount would cover the liability costs of every physician and hospital in all Canada for two and a half years.[5]

The terribly high cost of malpractice insurance had a significant impact on the provision of medical services in Michigan. The legislature received many complaints about the large numbers of doctors leaving Michigan, often after having been trained at taxpayer expense at a Michigan public university, and about specialty shortages in rural and poor urban neighborhoods. Indeed, more than nine out of ten smaller and rural hospitals reported difficulties in recruiting health care professionals. Some claimed that nearly sixty percent of all Michigan-trained physicians left Michigan to practice medicine in large part because of the exorbitant medical liability rates and what they perceived to be a climate conducive to malpractice lawsuits. Other evidence of the negative impact on Michigan health care was the closing between 1987 and 1992 of one of every ten hospital obstetric units because of the cost of medical liability insurance and the inability of hospitals to find replacement obstetricians.[6]

Not surprisingly, a consensus developed that the 1986 reforms were much too weak to affect significantly the high cost of liability coverage. For example, many argued that the key piece of the enactment reforms—the cap on noneconomic damages—was ineffective since the exceptions had swallowed the rule. They contended that the only cases where noneconomic damages might exceed the set limit of $225,000 were those which involved an injury which was listed among the exceptions, making the rule against higher damage levels totally ineffective. The discretion left to judges regarding expert witnesses' qualifications and other components of the 1986 legislation were similarly criticized as ineffective.

[3]Source: Michigan Hosp. Ass'n et al. (1993).
[4]*Id.*
[5]*Id.*
[6]*Id.*

### *The Hutzel Hospital Case*

Matters came to a head in early 1990 with the infamous Hutzel Hospital case,[7] which created a great deal of discussion and controversy in Michigan's medical, legal, and insurance communities. In that case, a young woman sued Hutzel Hospital, a hospital serving a large number of poor and indigent patients in the Detroit area. The plaintiff, who apparently had received little if any prenatal care, gave birth at the hospital to a child who had serious physical and mental defects. She filed suit with only a vague allegation of malpractice and, after mediation, was awarded $10,000. Both the plaintiff and defendant rejected the mediation, and the case went to trial. At some point after the mediation but prior to trial, the plaintiff discovered an alleged five-minute gap between the time the baby was born and the time the pediatrician's notes indicated that he had first treated the baby. It was this gap, and the plaintiff's allegation that the lack of attention during that five-minute period resulted in the child's injuries, that became the foundation of the plaintiff's case at trial, even though the plaintiff had testified at the mediation that the pediatrician was in the delivery room at the time of birth. The defendants explained the alleged gap by the difference between the watches worn by the pediatrician and the physician who delivered the baby, arguing that the baby was not left unattended.

The plaintiff's lawyer made a lengthy presentation on the damages that the plaintiff and her child had suffered. The defendants apparently chose not to respond to the damages argument and argued only the issue of liability. The jury found for the plaintiff, and awarded the plaintiff $19 million plus interest, for a total judgment of $31 million. The parties then entered into a negotiated settlement and agreed that the plaintiff should receive $10 million, to be divided equally between the attorney, the mother, and the child.

The Hutzel Hospital case became notorious in the medical, legal, and insurance communities. It also became for many a symbol of what was wrong with the system, and became both a catalyst and rallying point for liability reform.

### *The 1991–92 Struggle*

At the beginning of the 1991–92 legislative term, the medical community came forward with a new plan to supplement the 1986 malpractice reforms. In addition to the notoriety of the Hutzel Hospital case, proponents of change saw two other encouraging developments. First, a new governor had been elected, John Engler, who

[7]Ahmad v. Hutzel Hosp., No. 86-625595-NM (Wayne County Cir. Ctr.).

was firmly in support of more significant change in the malpractice area and had worked toward that end as the president of the Michigan senate. As governor, Mr. Engler remained committed to an aggressive legislative agenda in a number of areas, including medical malpractice reform.

The second, and perhaps more encouraging, development was the formation of the Michigan Medical Liability Reform Coalition. In the fall of 1990, spurred on in part by the Hutzel Hospital case, the Michigan State Medical Society, Michigan Hospital Association, and Michigan Association of Osteopathic Physicians and Surgeons came together and agreed to give top priority to achieving medical liability reform. They pooled their resources with the three malpractice liability insurers in the state, and formed the Coalition. The Coalition eventually was joined by sixty-five to seventy-five other organizations—including the state chamber of commerce and many other influential business organizations—that were interested in addressing the serious problems facing medical services providers in Michigan.

The Coalition was important because it underscored the importance of medical liability reform as an economic and job-development issue. While previous efforts towards reform could be branded as the simple selfish agenda of a single special interest group, that damning label would not fit most members of the Coalition. Instead, legislators had to recognize that medical malpractice costs were one of the many reasons that *business costs generally* in Michigan were higher than elsewhere. Accordingly, they were encouraged to understand that medical malpractice reform was not an issue that the medical community alone was interested in. Rather, it had a real impact on the state's economy and on the creation and retention of jobs for the individual constituents that each legislator served.

In 1991, the second round of liability reform began with the introduction, on behalf of the Coalition, of legislation patterned after the Medical Insurance Cost Reduction Act (MICRA), a series of tort reforms enacted in California in 1975. The California legislation had included the following changes: a $250,000 cap on noneconomic damages; modifications to the collateral source rule to prevent plaintiffs from receiving double recovery from primary defendants and insurers or other sources; mandatory periodic (versus lump-sum) payments of future damages; and a sliding scale for plaintiff attorneys' contingent fees to prevent "jackpot" windfalls in high-judgment cases. The changes in California, which were upheld as constitutional in 1986, resulted not only in lower premiums, but also in improved delivery of health care to California residents. For example, the average cost of ob-gyn malpractice insurance premiums in California increased 97% from 1983 to 1989. While this may seem high, the national average during those same years jumped more than 248%. Also in 1983, California ob-gyn premiums were almost 50% higher than the national average—$14,834 versus $10,946. By 1989, ob-gyns in California were paying $29,238 while the national average had risen to $38,138. Not surprisingly, the reduced cost of malpractice insurance in California caused the number of ob-gyns practicing without liability insurance to decrease from 4% in 1985 to 1% in 1989—well below the national average of 3%.[8]

More importantly, the California reforms reduced from 15.5% in 1985 to 11.9% in 1990 California ob-gyns who had decreased the number of their deliveries as a result of the risk of malpractice; the percentage who decreased the level of high-risk obstetrical care also dropped from 33.8% in 1985 to 23.8% in 1990; and, finally, the percentage of those who made the most dramatic change of all—dropping obstetrics entirely—decreased from 11.3% in 1985 to 9.4% in 1990. The Coalition and other proponents of additional reform were thus able to argue, based on the successful California experience with MICRA, that the legislation they were promoting had already been successfully implemented in a large leading state.

With a new governor in Michigan, a proven legislative package, and the Hutzel Hospital case providing a striking illustration of the need for change, medical malpractice reform seemed a likely prospect when it surfaced during the 1991–92 term. As expected, the medical malpractice bill quickly sailed through the senate. The political makeup of the house, however, had not changed much since 1986. Moreover, the chair of the committee to which the bill was assigned was an ardent foe of any attempt to limit lawsuits for injuries. As a result, the bill languished without a hearing until the spring of 1992.

It was an election year in 1992, and the Democratic speaker of the house was eventually pressured into allowing a discussion of the medical malpractice bill among legislators, notwithstanding the committee chair's reluctance on the issue. An ad hoc group of three legislators, two Democrats and one Republican, was assigned to meet with the competing interest groups to try to work out an agreement that all concerned could live with.

Unfortunately, these efforts were unsuccessful. The Michigan Trial Lawyers Association successfully injected a number of issues into the discussion which were not included in the legislation passed by the senate and which were considered extraneous by proponents of medical malpractice reform. For example, the MTLA argued that if health care providers were to be afforded protection from severe

[8]Source: Michigan Hosp. Ass'n et al. (Aug. 1992).

economic liability through a cap on noneconomic damages, they should be required to provide proof of insurance or some other ability to make payment on any limited damage awards against them. The medical community was unwilling to acquiesce to a "financial responsibility" mandate since, in many specialties, insurance coverage was virtually unavailable or available only at such a high cost that it was economically infeasible to purchase it. The same kinds of irreconcilable disputes also arose in a number of areas the legislation did address. Since the speaker's marching orders had been to work out a compromise that both sides could agree to, these disputes became a recipe for failure.

The usual complexity and controversy surrounding medical malpractice reform was exacerbated by the fact that 1992 was not only an election year, but an election year with especially high stakes. The Democrats who had controlled the Michigan house of representatives for a quarter-century were beleaguered by the firm control the Republicans had over the state senate and the governor's office. At the same time, Republicans were staging a hearty and optimistic effort to gain the six seats needed in order to take over control of the house following the 1992 election. The medical malpractice issue surfaced in a number of the campaigns where targeted Democratic incumbents were being aggressively challenged by their Republican opponents. With that occurring across the state, even those Democrats sympathetic to the need for medical malpractice reform were unable to break party lines on procedural issues like the discharge vote necessary to bring the legislation to the floor for a full debate and vote. The bill stayed in committee and died at the end of the year.

## III. Round Three: The 1993 Reforms

### *A Favorable Setting*

In the November 1992 elections, the house Republicans did very well and almost succeeded in their quest for control of the chamber. After recounts were completed in a number of razor-thin election victories across the state, the final result was a chamber equally divided, with 55 Democrats and 55 Republicans elected.

Thus, the first order of business for the new term was crafting a shared power agreement under which medical malpractice and other contentious issues would be processed. The elected leaders of the two caucuses negotiated an agreement which named them cospeakers, each presiding over the house floor in alternate months. Cochairs for each standing committee were also chosen from each caucus; each party's chairpersons were in charge of their respective committees during the months when the speaker of the other party presided over the floor. An equal number of members were selected to each committee from each caucus, and the rules provided that, while a majority was needed to report a bill to the floor, each speaker had a specified number of "extraordinary voting privileges" which could be used to get legislation out of committee upon a tie vote. These rules almost ensured that the medical malpractice legislation would not again die in committee, since the Republican cospeaker was committed to seeing the issue reach the floor for full debate.

Under these circumstances, the health care community again had high hopes for reforming Michigan's malpractice laws. The governor's office and senate remained in control of those sympathetic to the issue and the need for change. In addition, the shared power agreement in the house would almost certainly allow reform legislation to get out of committee in some fashion or another. In the full chamber, a majority of legislators, including a number of Democrats, would be in support.

Furthermore, medical malpractice was surfacing as a legislative issue that would receive high priority. Representatives of the governor's office and the house and senate Republican caucuses met prior to the beginning of the legislative term in January 1993 to compose a legislative agenda which would receive the concerted efforts of all three groups. Since medical malpractice had become such a galvanizing force in so many legislative races the preceding fall, the issue surfaced high on that agenda. All in all, everything looked promising for the Medical Liability Reform Coalition as the third round of reform efforts commenced.

*The Struggle Begins Again*

As in the two previous attempts at substantial liability reform, the medical malpractice bill that was introduced in the senate, SB270, was quickly passed. The senate-passed version of SB270 was sweeping in the changes that it proposed. Perhaps most significantly, the bill placed a $250,000 flat cap on noneconomic damages with no exceptions for more serious injuries involving the brain or spinal column or injuries to the reproductive system. Economic damages remained uncapped under this as well as all subsequent versions of SB270. In addition, the bill implemented a sliding scale on the amount of the contingency fees that lawyers could be awarded, beginning at 40% for smaller cases and decreasing to 10% for larger ones; required that expert witnesses be board-certified in the same specialty as the defendant, and have spent 80% of the past year in active practice or teaching; required the plaintiff to show that his or her injury was more probably than not caused by the defendant's negligence and barred plaintiff from recovering for loss of an opportunity to survive or failure to achieve a better result;[9] mandated a 20% rollback in premiums for malpractice insurers; allowed interest to accrue only on that portion of the judgment which the plaintiff would actually receive, and not on the attorney fee or costs; provided for time limits on presuit notification, access to medical records, and filing of affidavits of meritorious suit and defense; and provided that any cause of action brought on a child's behalf that arose on or before the child's eighth birthday had to be filed by the child's tenth birthday, and that after age eight, the appropriate statute of limitations would apply.

The Democratic and Republican cochairs of the house judiciary committee to which SB270 was assigned both felt that the issue had festered long enough and were committed to reporting a bill to the full house for debate. After hearing from interest groups on both sides, they concluded that nothing would satisfy everyone and that, instead of working toward an unobtainable consensus, they would simply put together a bill to which they personally agreed and have their committee report it to the floor without amendment.

As a result, the bill which came out of the house committee was a much scaled-back version of that which had been reported from the senate. Some of the most significant differences were that the house-passed version:

1. Imposed a two-tiered cap: $500,000 for ordinary malpractice, and $1 million where the malpractice resulted in death, permanent disability resulting from injury to the brain or spinal cord, or permanent loss or damage to the reproductive organs resulting in the inability to procreate. The $1 million cap also applied where there was alteration, destruction, or falsification of a medical record.
2. Provided that the caps would be reduced by half if the defendant had medical malpractice insurance or other proof of financial responsibility.
3. Implemented a contingency fee arrangement where the plaintiff's attorney would receive 15% of the settlement if entered into prior to mediation; 25% of the settlement if entered into after mediation but before trial; and 33-1/3% if the case went to trial.
4. Required that an expert witness be board-certified in the same or "substantially similar specialty" as the defendant, and required the expert to have devoted a substantial portion

[9]*See* discussion of Falcon v. Memorial Hosp., *infra* p. 194 & n.10.

(instead of 80%) of his or her time in the preceding year to active clinical practice or instruction.

5. Provided for the same standard of proof as the senate-passed version except that it did not bar a plaintiff from recovering for failure to achieve a better result.
6. Required the plaintiff's affidavit of merit and defendant's affidavit of meritorious defense to be signed by the attorneys instead of a health care professional, as the senate-passed version provided.
7. Included an arbitration provision for cases with a projected dollar value of less than $75,000.
8. Increased the statute of limitations provision in cases involving children from age eight to ten, and included an exception for injury to the child's reproductive system.
9. Provided that the malpractice legislation would not be enacted unless a package of bills reforming Michigan's physician discipline system was also enacted.

Not surprisingly, neither side liked the committee-passed version. Overall, the Coalition believed that the committee substitute did not go far enough, especially considering the years of effort they had put into securing significant reform and the support they were confident they had among a majority of the legislators in both chambers. The Coalition found especially offensive the increased caps on noneconomic damages and the requirement that physicians maintain malpractice liability insurance. The plaintiffs' bar continued to argue that no changes to existing law were necessary and that even the committee substitute severely and unfairly compromised the rights of injured patients.

The Republican leadership of the house agreed with the medical community that the committee-passed version of SB270 was insufficient to address the concerns which prompted the legislation in the first place. At the same time, the senate-passed version of the bill was thought to be too broad and potentially detrimental to the rights of injured patients in a number of areas and probably not acceptable to a majority of house members.

The Republican speaker, therefore, assigned the Republican floor leader to meet with representatives of the medical community and its insurers to craft a compromise between the house committee and senate version of the bill which would address their real concerns without unfairly compromising the rights of plaintiffs. That compromise differed most significantly from the previous versions of SB270 in that it:

1. Maintained the committee substitute's two-tiered framework for the cap on noneconomic damages, but reduced the amount

of the cap to $250,000/$500,000 and eliminated the requirement that physicians maintain malpractice liability insurance. In addition, the compromise eliminated the death and altered-records exceptions of the committee substitute and added an exception for malpractice resulting in impaired cognitive capacity that ends the plaintiff's ability to live independently.

2. Rejected the changes proposed by both previous versions of SB270 concerning contingency fees and retained the existing law.
3. Retained the requirement in the senate-passed version that the affidavits of merit and meritorious defense be signed by an expert witness rather than the committee substitute's requirement that the parties' attorneys sign it.
4. Reached a middle ground on the requirement that an expert be engaged in the practice or teaching of their specialty by requiring the expert to have spent "the majority" of their time in the previous year practicing or instructing. In addition, the compromise eliminated the "substantially similar" language of the committee substitute and so required that the expert be board-certified in the same specialty as the defendant.
5. Concerning the statute of limitations for children, the compromise followed the age limit of the senate-passed version (i.e., eight years of age), but included the committee substitute's exception for an injury to the child's reproductive system.
6. Limited plaintiff's recovery in actions alleging loss of an opportunity to survive or achieve a better result to those cases where the opportunity was greater than half. This compromise effectively incorporated into statute the decision in *Falcon v. Memorial Hospital.*[10]
7. Retained the tie-bar to the physician discipline bills.

*Last Steps*

This final version of the bill was debated at length by the full house. Numerous amendments were offered by legislators who felt

[10] 462 N.W.2d 44 (Mich. 1990). In that case, a nineteen-year-old woman suffered a pulmonary embolism during childbirth and died. The plaintiff did not allege that the embolism was caused by the malpractice, but that the physician's failure to treat the embolism probably deprived the woman of a 37.5% chance of surviving the embolism. The defendant claimed that the woman's chance of surviving was only about 2%. A very divided court held that the plaintiff could sue for loss of an opportunity to survive and in doing so recognized a new cause of action in Michigan. Nonetheless, five of the seven justices ruled that the action could survive only where it was more probable than not that the defendant's negligence caused the injury. The three dissenters appeared especially troubled by the prospect that allowing recovery in cases where the likelihood of survival was less than 50% would put courts in the rather absurd position of allowing plaintiffs to recover for injuries that they probably

the final version went too far in limiting the rights of plaintiffs. No significant amendment to the bill was adopted, however, and it was sent back to the senate for concurrence.

The senate, which had passed a much more aggressive version of medical malpractice reform earlier, was at first leery of concurring with the amendments that had been made in the house. Nonetheless, the Medical Liability Reform Coalition itself successfully argued that the compromise version of SB270 was the best bill that could be passed by the house. Accordingly, the senate reluctantly concurred in the house amendments.

The final battle revolved around whether the legislation should have immediate effect. Under the Michigan constitution, unless two-thirds of the legislators in both houses vote for immediate effect, legislation does not become effective until ninety days after the end of the year in which it is passed. The senate was able to secure a two-thirds vote; the house was not despite repeated efforts. Accordingly, the legislation took effect in Michigan on April 1, 1994.

## IV. Conclusion

In sum, efforts at medical malpractice reform in Michigan were ultimately successful, notwithstanding a decade of strong resistance by the plaintiffs' bar. In retrospect, four factors appear to have been crucial. First, there existed—and the proponents of reform stressed—the compelling insurance cost differences between Michigan and other states for malpractice coverage. Second, a high-profile medical malpractice case dramatized and brought the issue home for many legislators. Third, a broad coalition was formed of interest groups beyond medical care providers in support of the effort, underscoring that soaring malpractice costs were bad not only for doctors, but for Michigan business generally. And, finally, the combined leadership in the senate, house, and governor's office made the issue a legislative priority. All of these elements were needed to make medical malpractice reform in Michigan a reality.

never sustained. The compromise allowed an action for "loss of an opportunity to survive," but only in cases where the opportunity was greater than 50%.

CHAPTER 12

# MISSISSIPPI: PRODUCT LIABILITY AND PUNITIVE DAMAGES

SENATOR WALTER A. GRAHAM*

## I. Introduction

In 1993, Mississippi became the first state since 1988 to enact significant civil justice reform legislation.[1] This action culminated a multiyear effort by legislators, private citizens, and businesses to restore fairness to the Mississippi civil justice system.

Civil justice became a serious legislative issue in Mississippi during the mid-1980s. The Mississippi business community believed that existing product liability laws, in particular, were detrimental to the state's economy and discouraged innovation and competitiveness. As a result, during the past several years a host of civil justice reform bills were introduced in both houses of the Mississippi legislature.

Proponents of these tort reform measures believed then and now that a uniform federal law is best suited to solve the product liability crisis. There is also an urgent need for a uniform punitive damages standard. Such laws do not, however, exist in the United States. Since Mississippi was unwilling to wait for Congress to act on these important issues, the legislature passed House Bill 1270 during its 1993 Regular Session.

The enactment of this legislation accomplished two important objectives. First, it provided clear standards which apply to product liability lawsuits. Interested parties will now know with some degree of certainty what rules govern their activities. Second, it established standards and procedural safeguards for courts and juries to follow when considering punitive damages claims.

This chapter will discuss how this bill came to be enacted, and then describe in greater detail what the new law does, especially with respect to punitive damages.

---

*The author would like to recognize the following people for their contributions to this chapter: former Senator Bob Montgomery of the law firm Montgomery, Smith-Vaniz & McGraw; former Senator Ellis Bodron; and Mary B. Davis.

[1]Soon after Mississippi enacted its legislation, the Arizona, North Dakota, and Texas legislatures also adopted major tort reform statutes.

## II. How the Bill Was Passed

In 1989, the Mississippi business community supported comprehensive civil justice reform legislation that would have codified existing state law and enacted several commonsense provisions that have been adopted in other jurisdictions. This sensible legislation reflected mainstream legal doctrine and received strong support from both the business and legal communities. Unfortunately, this legislation died on the house calendar because of its failure to be considered before a procedural deadline for adopting legislation.

Advocates of reform were also stymied in 1990, 1991, and 1992. A broad range of tort reform bills was introduced, with no favorable results. During the 1991 legislative and gubernatorial campaigns, tort reform was a key issue in several races. In several legislative races and in the governor's race, the proponents of tort reform prevailed.

In 1993, civil justice reform was again a key issue before the legislature. A comprehensive product liability and punitive damages reform bill (H.B. 1270) was introduced in the house on January 18, 1993, and was referred to the Judiciary-A Committee. The committee, which is chaired by Representative Mike Mills, held hearings on January 26 and 27 and received testimony from the bill's supporters and opponents. The bill was reported from committee on February 2, and passed the house, with minor amendments, on February 9 by vote of 97 to 25.

H.B. 1270 then moved to the senate. In previous years, all product liability reform legislation was referred to the Judiciary Committee, where it died due to strong opposition by the trial lawyers. A key difference in 1993 was that Lieutenant Governor Eddie Briggs, a civil justice reform supporter, referred the bill to the Insurance Committee, which is chaired by Senator Jim Bean. On February 16, 1993, the Insurance Committee held a hearing on H.B. 1270 and favorably reported the bill on February 17, 1993. Later that same day, H.B. 1270 passed the senate without amendment by a vote of 43–6. Governor Fordice signed the bill into law on February 18.[2]

The swiftness with which H.B. 1270 was considered and passed by the legislature is a clear indication of the broad support this measure received from a well-organized and united coalition of Mississippi citizens and businesses. The enormously positive effect these groups had on the successful effort to enact H.B. 1270 cannot be overstated.

Business and other groups that supported H.B. 1270 included the Mississippi Manufacturers Association, the Mississippi Economic

[2]*See* MISS. CODE ANN. § 11-1-63 & -65 (Supp. 1993).

Council, Mississippians For A Fair Legal System (M-FAIR), wholesale and retail merchants, insurance companies and agents, and the American Tort Reform Association. Opposition to civil justice reform efforts came primarily from labor unions and the Mississippi Trial Lawyers Association. Health care providers, while expressing an interest in civil justice reform, concentrated their efforts on legislation directly affecting them, such as shortening the statute of limitations governing claims against health care providers and strengthening the evidentiary requirements necessary to establish medical malpractice.

The most visible organization supporting the bill was M-FAIR. Former Senator Glen Deweese served as chairman of M-FAIR and was instrumental in bringing together over two thousand small businesses, citizens, and others interested in enacting civil justice reform legislation. M-FAIR members were extremely successful in their efforts to contact legislators and urge them to support H.B. 1270. Roadside billboards, toll-free telephone lines, grass-roots communications, television advertisements, and other techniques were also effectively utilized by M-FAIR to generate additional public support for this important measure.

The effectiveness of these groups was seen most clearly when the Mississippi Trial Lawyers Association (MTLA) agreed not to oppose H.B. 1270. This group had in previous years vehemently opposed any product liability reform proposals. In 1993, however, MTLA decided to remain neutral in the civil justice reform battle. It is possible that MTLA determined that H.B. 1270 was a fair and rational bill, but MTLA also may have recognized that this measure was receiving overwhelming public support and that it was not politically wise to oppose it. Whatever the reason, MTLA's position of neutrality helped to ensure the passage of H.B. 1270.

After the trial lawyers withdrew their opposition and prevailed upon the labor unions to moderate their opposition, legislators in both houses who had previously opposed product liability and punitive damages legislation voted in favor of H.B. 1270, noting that the trial lawyers association and business community both agreed on the bill's beneficial result.

## III. What the Bill Says

As noted, H.B. 1270 addresses two basic civil justice reform issues, namely product liability and punitive damages.

With respect to *product liability*, the new law does the following: codifies the rule that a manufacturer should not be liable unless a product contains a defect and the defect causes the claimant's harm; provides that liability should not be imposed for harm caused by products that are inherently dangerous if the risk is recognized by the ordinary consumer and cannot be eliminated without substantially reducing the product's usefulness; provides that companies are not required to warn of dangers that were not known or knowable at the time of manufacture; bars damages if a product's danger is obvious or if the injured person knew of the danger and voluntarily exposed himself or herself to it; and bars liability in a design-defect case unless there was a feasible alternative design that would have prevented the alleged harm.

In addition, the bill also requires manufacturers who are found liable to indemnify product sellers for legal costs and damages if the seller had no control over the manufacture, design, packaging, or labeling of the product; was not aware of the product's defect; and made no express warranty.

With respect to *punitive damages*, the new law: allows punitive damages to be awarded only if plaintiffs provide clear and convincing evidence that the defendant acted with actual malice, committed actual fraud, or was guilty of willful, wanton, or reckless disregard for the safety of others; requires the trier of fact to decide whether compensatory damages will be awarded and the amount of those damages before deciding liability for and the amount of punitive damages, and bars punitive damages in the absence of compensatory awards; identifies the factors that juries should consider in determining the amount of punitive damages; and provides immunity from punitive damages for innocent retailers and wholesalers who had no control over the product's design, manufacture, packaging, or labeling.

The punitive damages reforms were especially interesting, and bear further discussion.[3] Punitive damages under Mississippi law are penal in character and thus require compelling evidence of especially egregious behavior in order to warrant their imposition.[4] Recognizing this situation, the new law provides that the right to punitive damages must be shown by clear and convincing evidence. This represents a change in existing Mississippi case law, which previously required proof by a preponderance of the evidence.

The clear and convincing burden falls somewhere between the "preponderance of the evidence" standard commonly used in civil cases and the "beyond a reasonable doubt" standard used in criminal cases. Almost half of the states that permit punitive damages require

[3]For further discussion of the punitive damages issue and, especially, the role of the *courts* in effecting needed reforms, *see supra* chapter 5.—Editor's note.

[4]*See, e.g.*, Tideway Oil Program, Inc. v. Serio, 431 So. 2d 454, 460 n.1 & 467 (Miss. 1983); Fowler Butane Gas Co. v. Varner, 141 So. 2d 226, 233 (Miss. 1962).

proof by clear and convincing evidence.[5] This change in the burden of proof should reduce the number of cases in which punitive damages are awarded.

The new law also establishes the substantive standard for awarding punitive damages. The legislature intended to make clear that negligence was not enough, and that the plaintiff must show that the defendant acted with actual malice, committed actual fraud, or showed by its conduct a willful, wanton, or reckless disregard for the safety of others. This is similar to the standard earlier applied by Mississippi courts.[6]

H.B. 1270 provides for bifurcation of the trial, so that a plaintiff's compensatory damages claim is considered before the jury hears any evidence concerning punitive damages. This procedure, which has been adopted in several other states,[7] is intended to prevent evidence that is relevant only to the issue of punitive damages from improperly inflaming a jury as it considers the plaintiff's entitlement to compensatory damages.[8]

The new law makes clear that the judge must decide whether the proof of malicious, fraudulent, or willful, wanton, or reckless behavior is sufficient to allow the jury even to consider the issue of punitive damages. This provision is consistent with existing Mississippi law.[9] The law also elaborates on existing case law and identifies factors to be considered in assessing punitive damages, including the financial condition of the defendant, the degree of wrongdoing, the defendant's knowledge of harm and motivation, and the duration of any misconduct.

While present Mississippi procedure clearly provides for trial court review of the amount of a punitive damages award by way of post-trial motions,[10] H.B. 1270 makes clear that before entering judgment the court must determine that the award is reasonable in light of the facts of the case and the need for future deterrence of similar conduct. In actual practice, this may result in delay in entering a punitive damages judgment until after typical post-trial motions and briefing, since trial courts might prefer to have the benefit of counsels' argument on this issue. The provision serves to emphasize the trial court's post-trial review duty, and indeed *requires* the court to

[5]One state, Colorado, requires proof beyond a reasonable doubt. COLO. REV. STAT. § 13-25-127(2) (1989).

[6]*See, e.g.*, Defenbaugh & Co. v. Rogers, 543 So. 2d 1164, 1167 (Miss. 1989).

[7]*See, e.g.*, GA. CODE ANN. § 510.263 (1992).

[8]*See, e.g.*, Jesco, Inc. v. Shannon, 451 So. 2d 694, 704 (Miss. 1984).

[9]*See, e.g.*, Andrew Jackson Life Ins. Co. v. Williams, 566 So. 2d 1172, 1182 (Miss. 1990).

[10]*See* MISS. CODE ANN. § 11-1-55 (1992).

review any award of punitive damages and to consider certain factors in that review.

The new law requires the court to consider certain factors as it reviews the propriety of any award of punitive damages. The factors, which are almost identical to those approved by the United States Supreme Court,[11] include the relationship between the amount of punitive damages and the harm likely to have been caused, the degree and duration of the wrongdoing, and whether other punitive damages awards have been made as a result of the same conduct. Mississippi courts have struggled when called upon to evaluate the propriety of the size of a punitive damages award. The new law should provide clearer guidance to the courts, and should ensure in every case that there is a reasonable relationship between the punitive award and harm likely to have resulted or that actually resulted from the defendant's conduct.

Thus, H.B. 1270 will help ensure that punitive damages are awarded only in those instances in which they are deserved. The higher burden of proof for punitive damages claims should mean intensified examination of evidence by the court, resulting in the submission of fewer cases to the jury on the issue of punitive damages. The bifurcated proceeding eliminates the potential unfairness to a defendant and confusion on the part of the jury that can arise when evidence relevant only to the issue of punitive damages is introduced at the same time as evidence concerning compensatory damages. Bifurcation also allows trial counsel and the judge to focus on the relevant issue in each phase of the proceeding, resulting in the reduction of trial error and fewer appeals. Trials will be shorter, because punitive damages evidence will be presented only if actual damages are awarded. And in some cases, if actual damages are awarded, the parties will settle the punitive damages issue.

[11] *See* Pacific Mutual Life Ins. Co. v. Haslip, 111 S. Ct. 1032, 1045 (1991).

CHAPTER 13

# NORTH DAKOTA: TWO-STAGE SUCCESS

REPRESENTATIVE JOHN DORSO

The tort reform effort in North Dakota had two stages, with major activity in 1987 and again in 1993. This chapter will outline why and how we were able to accomplish a very difficult task.

## I. Basic Lessons

There are three basic lessons to be learned from the North Dakota experience in civil justice reform.

### *Don't Get Bogged Down with Numbers*

The cost of insurance is a principal force driving tort reform. Be it liability or health insurance, tort reform is considered part of the solution to the rising cost.

But what *is* the cost? It is very hard to find quantifiable data for many issues. Most people involved in the debate want legislators to assign dollars to the problem and equate money to legislative solutions.

We tried to avoid that. No one believes the other side's numbers anyway. The numbers are meaningful only if both sides agree that they are accurate. There is, unfortunately, no such agreement, and the result is an argument about numbers and not the real problem. In some instances, people opposing reform will try to shift the debate to accuracy of the numbers as a means of shifting attention away from the real issues at hand.

Here is an example. Insurers argue that the increase in premiums for liability is based on the size and number of awards for damages. When underwriters rate a policy, that is part of the risk equation. The trial lawyers on the other side vehemently disagree. They contend that the real driving force in rate increases is the insurance companies' greed for profits. If you can get verifiable data on either of the above, you're doing a lot better than we did.

We decided to go with what we could prove. Our insurance commissioner verified that rates were skyrocketing and gave us percentage increases for previous years. He also informed us that liability concerns were making it difficult to obtain insurance coverage, or making the cost prohibitive and causing some products to be withdrawn from the market. Most importantly, the commissioner knew—as did the legislature—that a crisis was approaching and the citizens of North Dakota wanted a solution.

### *Build a Broad Coalition*

A second lesson also involves the manner in which we addressed the whole civil justice reform issue, and may provide other legislators with some ideas for the efforts in their states. We approached the problem from a number of different perspectives so as to gain the support of as many different sectors of society as we could. By involving as many groups as possible, we were able to develop an effective coalition.

To set the stage for the coalition we built, you need to know a little about North Dakota and its legislature. We are a small state of 630,000 people, the legislators have no personal staff, and our constituents know how to find us and they make their concerns known. Our legislature meets for four months every two years, and we don't have a lot of time to beat the issues to death. Most importantly, we are a citizen legislature. Teachers, farmers, and business men and women make up the vast majority of both houses. Currently, only four of the 152 members in the legislature are attorneys, three serving in the senate and one in the house. Three of the four have multifaceted practices which do not rely on trial work.

Who were the building blocks in our coalition?

The *political subdivisions* (counties, cities, park districts) were finding insurance hard to get and very expensive. We received their support by putting legislation in place for the North Dakota Insurance Reserve Fund, which is a quasi-private insurer of governmental entities.

The *hospitality industry* was tapped through our tourism bureau. They had a crisis in dram shop insurance, and we put some liability provisions in place for them.

The *business community* in general became involved for obvious reasons. We enlisted the help of the Greater North Dakota Association and our state chamber of commerce to coordinate the coalition. We also made a commitment to economic development to go hand in hand with this effort.

*Medical providers,* both hospitals and doctors, were demanding action. Ob-gyn specialists were leaving our state and some hospitals were closing maternity wards. In a sparsely populated state having trouble getting doctors, we needed them as much as they needed us.

Our *courts* were bogged down in civil litigation. The judges were asking for more money from the state treasury. We agreed to an intermediate court of appeals for a short period of time until we determined if the reforms would work.

The above already gave us a pretty good coalition, but we added an unlikely group. A number of us began a dialogue with the state bar association. We ascertained that the term "lawyer" does not necessarily mean "trial lawyer." We were able to convince the attorneys that do corporate work, estate work, and other specialties that their interests were not necessarily the same as the trial lawyers association. The state bar did not take a stand on our program, thus leaving the trial lawyers on their own.

Let me digress here a bit to inject a caveat. We were careful not to get into "lawyer bashing." We had allies in the legal profession who taught us terminology, gave us the right questions to ask, and were a quiet but effective resource for us. For all intents and purposes, they were the silent members of our coalition.

### *Consider a Two-Stage Strategy*

At the beginning of this chapter, I mentioned that we enacted legislation in 1987, and again in 1993. This was also part of the plan. In 1987, a number of bills were enacted, and then in 1993 additional legislation was enacted that extended and expanded the earlier reforms. By having a seven-year sunset on our 1987 initiatives, we were forced to step back and review the reforms. To some extent, this helped in the negotiations with the trial bar. The two stages are discussed in greater detail below.

## II. What We Passed

### *The 1987 Reforms*

H.B. 1571, passed in 1987, provided for a modified comparative fault system in all tort cases, with the exception of product liability. Under modified comparative fault, a plaintiff may recover damages from each defendant in proportion to the percentage of fault of the defendant; the damages are, however, reduced in proportion to the fault attributable to the plaintiff. In other words, the bill provided that the liability of each party is "several" only and not "joint." In addition, a plaintiff may not recover any amount if the plaintiff's fault is as great or greater than the combined fault of all other persons contributing to the injury. Finally, the bill provided for periodic payment of judgments and a reduction of judgments for collateral source payments (i.e., an elimination of double recoveries). These parts of the legislation were slated to sunset June 30, 1993.

A number of other provisions enacted in 1987, however, were not subject to the sunset provision. These included a requirement for a bifurcated trial when punitive damages are sought, and limits on the liability of those persons selling a product but not actively engaged in the manufacturing or assembling of the product. In addition, awards in excess of $250,000 for economic damages can be reviewed by the judge at the request of the defendant. On finding that the award does not bear a reasonable relation to the economic damages proven at trial, the court can reduce the amount.

The legislation included provisions limiting municipal liability to protect board members, volunteers, and employees of political subdivisions. The legislation also capped the liability of political subdivisions and removed statutory language allowing political subdivisions to be held liable for punitive damages.

Volunteer immunity was established for those who provide services or perform duties on behalf of nonprofit organizations, and the legislation also provided protection for volunteer athletic coaches and officials. The protection applies only to those who act in good faith in the course of their duties, and their actions must not constitute willful misconduct or gross negligence. Similarly, "Good Samaritan" protection is provided to those rendering emergency aid or assistance, unless the party's acts or omissions constituted intentional negligence or gross misconduct.

Additionally, the 1987 legislation provided for award of attorney fees to the prevailing party if a claim for relief is deemed frivolous.

### *The 1993 Reforms*

The 1993 legislation, S.B. 2351, eliminated the sunset provision that applied to portions of the 1987 reforms. In addition to making permanent the earlier provisions, S.B. 2351 provided for a significant and comprehensive improvement in North Dakota's product liability law within the concept of modified comparative fault. The bill provides that liability will be imposed only if: the product was defective because it deviated from the manufacturer's specifications or performance standards; the product was defective because it failed to contain adequate warnings or instructions; the product was defectively designed; or the manufacturer or seller breached an express or implied warranty on which the person using the product relied.

The legislation also contains a number of important provisions relating to punitive damages. It allows any party to a lawsuit to bifurcate issues relating to punitive damages from issues relating to compensatory damages, provides that evidence of a defendant's financial condition is not admissible in determining punitive damages, and limits punitive damages to twice the amount of compensatory damages or $250,000, whichever is greater. The legislation prohibits informing juries of the limits on punitive damages and requires the court to reduce any jury award in excess of the limit. The legislation also requires the trier of fact in punitive damages cases to consider the nature of the defendant's conduct, the relationship between an award of punitive damages and the harm caused or likely to result from the defendant's conduct, the knowledge of the defendant, the profit gained from the wrongful conduct, and criminal sanctions imposed on the defendant for the same conduct.

While the 1993 reform was a success, there were a few desirable provisions that had to be dropped from the final bill. The only difficulty the bill encountered was in the senate. The senate's judiciary committee has seven members, and at the time three of them were lawyers. The committee removed from the bill three provisions discussed below, dealing with a statute of repose, assumption of risk, and malice determination in punitive damages awards, respectively.

North Dakota passed a statute of repose in 1987, but the state's supreme court issued a decision in support of a challenge to the law's constitutionality. The decision in the senate to remove the statute of repose was somewhat bolstered by opponents pointing to the recent court decision.

Assumption of risk served as a complete defense under a provision contained in the original bill. The provision would have prevented recovery in a product liability case if a party was aware or should have been aware of the risk of injury or death.

Current North Dakota law allows punitive damages to be awarded for actual or "presumed" malice, fraud, or oppression. The deleted provision would have eliminated the "presumed" category.

Nonetheless, overall our 1993 efforts were politically very successful. Support in the house was particularly strong. In fact, once the bill passed out of the senate's judiciary committee, no further changes were made nor were any obstacles to its passage raised. The bill enjoyed bipartisan support in both the Democrat-controlled senate and the Republican-controlled house. In fact, more Democrats supported the bill than opposed it, in both the house and senate.

As we approached the 1993 session, the same coalition we had built in 1987 again drew together. This time it was better organized, much to the credit of the Greater North Dakota Association and the state chamber of commerce. The political subdivisions were more effective, because the North Dakota Insurance Reserve Fund was a success and became the voice for them. An added twist was the economic development people. As an outgrowth of our working with them in 1987, they became more active. In 1993, with their help, we also added product liability reform to the package of reforms.

Besides all this, by 1993 we had a group of legislators committed to the project. Some of us had ties to business, some to the bar, others to the medical profession. One person who deserves special credit is Representative Lynn Aas of Minot. Representative Aas is a retired hospital administrator with a law degree who served on the house judiciary committee and became the point person during the session. More than anyone, he is responsible for the compromises which finally ensured passage of the package.

## III. Conclusion

What can we learn from this? First, it is difficult or impossible to be successful without a coalition of many different groups. Second, put together a package containing a number of different pieces of legislation dealing with distinct specific interests in the tort area. Third, lawyers can be allies—just find the right ones. Fourth, get a nonpartisan organization outside the legislature to work with it and coordinate the efforts of the private sector.

Here is something else I learned going through this process: Justice is many things to many people, depending on their perspective. But one constant is that most people expect a commonsense result from our system of laws. If there is a "Darth Vader" in the equation, it is the trial lawyers. They are worthy adversaries. Don't let them do what they do so well.

A legislator, country lawyer, and state's attorney from western North Dakota, Representative John Mahoney, uses this story from Victor Hugo when ending the prosecution of some cases.

> I wonder if any of you folks have read Victor Hugo's account of the octopus. He tells us of how the octopus doesn't have fangs and poison to defend itself like a snake, nor claws like a lion, nor teeth like an alligator. But it does have what could be called an ink bag, and to protect itself when it is attacked it lets out a dark fluid from this bag, thus making all of the surrounding water dark and murky, enabling the octopus to escape into the darkness.

Trial lawyers are noted for their ability to emit ink. Don't get confused by the murky water. Stay focused on your objective. Keep your coalition focused. We won because we were not only right but because we kept our constituents' sense of fairness always in our perspective.

CHAPTER 14

# TEXAS: "THE BEST FIGHT IN TOWN"

SENATOR JOHN T. MONTFORD*

## I. Introduction

Until the mid-1980s, not many people were widely conversant with the term "tort reform." Now, it is widely used in the news media, among legislators, and by many others. Indeed, tort reform has become an umbrella term for the quest to improve the tort litigation component of our civil justice system at the state and federal levels.[1] In some respects tort reform is generic, geographically and otherwise;[2] in other respects it is specific to various segments of our society, and can be indigenous to a given locale, such as Texas.[3]

Tort reform "Texas style" was enacted in June 1987.[4] It is not as

---

 An earlier and longer version of this chapter first appeared in a 1988 issue of the *Houston Law Review*. *See* John T. Montford & Will G. Barber, *1987 Texas Tort Reform: The Quest for a Fairer and More Predictable Texas Civil Justice System*, 25 HOUS. L. REV. 59 (1988).

[1]*See* HOUSE/SENATE JOINT COMM. ON LIABILITY INSURANCE AND TORT LAW AND PROCEDURE, MAJORITY REPORT (filed with the 70th Texas Legislature, January 1987) [hereinafter MAJORITY REPORT].

[2]*See id.* at 1–4, 224–48. "The liability insurance crisis is a national phenomenon: the problems of affordability and availability are not restricted to particular states or geographical regions. It is a crisis that varies by degree from state to state." *Id.* at 224. *See also Hearing on Tex. S.B. 287, 290, 329, et al. Before the Senate Comm. on Econ. Dev.*, 70th Leg. 27–28, 38–39 (Mar. 9, 1987) (transcript of tape 1 available from Senate Staff Services Office and the author of this chapter). "[T]his is a national problem. [Texas is] one of 50 component units generally of these problems . . . ." *Id.* at 39 (testimony by former Chairman of the Texas State Board of Insurance, Lyndon Olson).

[3]*See* MAJORITY REPORT, *supra* note 1, at 1–168.

[4]The 1987 Texas tort reform laws consist of (1) Act of June 16, 1987, ch. 2, 1987 Tex. Sess. Law Serv. 71 (Vernon) (Tex. S.B. 5, 70th Leg., 1st Called Sess; formerly Tex. S.B. 287, 70th Leg., Reg. Sess.) [hereinafter Omnibus Tort Reform Law or Bill]; (2) Act of June 16, 1987, ch. 33, 1987 Tex. Sess. Law Serv. 99 (Vernon) (Tex. S.B. 6, 70th Leg., 1st Called Sess; formerly Tex. S.B. 290, 70th Leg., Reg. Sess.) [hereinafter Prejudgment Interest Tort Reform Law or Bill]; (3) Act of June 16, 1987, ch. 4, 1987 Tex. Sess. Law Serv. 101 (Vernon) (Tex. S.B. 7, 70th Leg., 1st Called Sess.; formerly Tex. S.B. 329, 70th Leg., Reg. Sess.); (4) Act of June 16, 1987, ch. 370, 1987 Tex. Sess. Law Serv. 3581 (Vernon) (Tex. S.B. 202, 70th Leg., Reg. Sess.); (5) Act of June 17, 1987, ch. 424, 1987 Tex. Sess. Law Serv. 3943 (Vernon) (Tex. S.B. 260, 70th Tex. Leg., Reg. Sess.); and (6) Act of June 16, 1987, ch. 1, 1987, Tex. S.J. Res. 26, 70th Leg., Reg. Sess., 1987 Tex. Sess. Law Serv. No. 8, A-7 (Vernon). The associated 1987 Texas insurance reform laws consist of: (1) Act of June 16, 1987, ch. 1, 1987

much tort reform as proponents sought;[5] it is more than opponents wanted to see passed.[6] Approximately half of the smorgasbord of tort reform recommendations of the House/Senate Joint Committee on Liability Insurance and Tort Law and Procedure (hereinafter Interim Study Committee) to the seventieth state legislature survived the legislative process and passed as modified versions of those proposals. The tort reform proposals enacted addressed contentious issues like frivolous pleadings and claims, venue, comparative responsibility and joint and several liability, exemplary and punitive damages, liability of corporate directors and officers, liability of public officials and governmental entities, liability of governmental contractees, prejudgment interest, charitable immunity, accelerated and direct appeals, and liability standards in cases involving vaccines and drugs. All in all, the 1987 tort reform laws constituted the most significant legislation ever enacted in Texas with respect to civil actions for personal injury, death, and property damage. At the bill signing ceremony, then-Governor William P. Clements stated, "This legislation sends a positive signal to the business community that we are serious about holding down the cost of doing business in our state."[7] As was discussed in floor debate on the issue,[8] the legislation was designed to make the Texas civil justice system fairer and more predictable, so that economic development and growth are encouraged and liability insurance becomes more affordable.

One of the key factors leading to the decision to launch an effort to reform the Texas civil justice system was the Texas Supreme

Tex. Sess. Law Serv. 1 (Vernon) (Tex. S.B. 2, 70th Leg., 1st Called Sess.; formerly Tex. S.B. 291, 70th Leg., Reg. Sess.); (2) Act of June 16, 1987, ch. 5, 1987 Tex. Sess. Law Serv. 103 (Vernon) (Tex. S.B. 8, 70th Leg., 1st Called Sess.; formerly S.B. 688, 70th Leg., Reg. Sess.); and (3) Act of June 16, 1987, ch. 6, 1987 Tex. Sess. Law Serv. 107 (Vernon) (Tex. S.B. 9, 70th Leg., 1st Called Sess.; formerly Tex. S.B. 175, 70th Leg., Reg. Sess.).

[5]*See* Tort Reform Recommendations 1-60 [hereinafter Recommendations] in MAJORITY REPORT, *supra* note 1, at 4–6, 13–17, 168–223. Former Senator J.P. Word, president of the Texas Civil Justice League, was moved to comment that: "When compared with the program we advocated, the reform package doesn't look like much. When compared with present law, there is significant progress." Memorandum from J.P. Word to the Board of Directors of the Texas Civil Justice League 2 (June 10, 1987) (on file with University of Houston Law Center Library) [hereinafter League Memorandum].

[6]*See Hearings on Tex. S.B. 287 Before the Senate Comm. on Econ. Dev.*, 70th Leg., Reg. Sess. 7-12 (Mar. 2, 1987) and 1-18 (Mar. 5, 1987) (transcripts of tapes 1 and 2 available from Senate Staff Services Offices and the author of this chapter). The Director of Texans for Civil Justice, lead opponents of tort reform, called the compromise a "disgrace." Robert Elder, Jr., *Reforms Hurt Trial Lawyers,* TEX. LAW., June 8, 1987, at 26; Tommy Jacks, *Commentary,* TEX. LAW., June 22, 1987, at 19.

[7]*See* Bruce Hight, *Governor Touts 13 New Laws as "Tools" to Bolster Economy,* AUSTIN AM.-STATESMAN, June 17, 1987, at B2.

[8]Debate on Tex. S.B. 287 on the Floor of the Senate, 70th Leg. 14–15 (May 6, 1987).

Court. According to the Interim Study Committee's Majority Report, one of the reasons why the Texas civil justice system had lost as much predictability as it had was attributable to activism by the supreme court during the 1980s, which resulted in proplaintiff expansions of Texas tort law.[9] The conclusions of that report included:

> While the problems plaguing Texas liability insurers and their customers are partly the result of aggressive competition and the cyclical nature of the industry, the industry has also been a victim of fundamental changes in tort law over the past several years. Unusually high jury awards, court construction of liability policies far beyond their original intent, and *activist courts have created a legal environment of unpredictability. Far-reaching decisions by the Texas Supreme Court, redefining the parameters of risk and liability, have eroded the ability of insurers to accurately predict the frequency and magnitude of their losses.* Without reasonable predictability in the law, stability, availability, and affordability in the liability insurance market remain elusive goals.[10]
>
> *Far-reaching decisions by the Texas Supreme Court have redefined many of the basic tenets of the tort law in a way that has increased the unpredictability of the Texas civil justice system.*[11] As a consequence, the availability and cost of liability insurance has been adversely affected. Insurers are concerned about potential unforeseen past liability, the magnitude of future liability based on the possibility of more redefinitions of tort law by the supreme court, and the increasing propensity of the supreme court to push tort law in a direction opposite to that clearly indicated by the legislature.[12]
>
> Unlike other forces that affect the liability insurance industry over which the legislature has no control, such as fluctuations of the stock and bond market or the income earned on insurance industry investments, *the legislature can play a crucial role in restoring a reasonable amount of predictability to the civil justice system.*[13]

In opening statements made at the public hearings on tort reform, speakers echoed the concerns raised in the Majority Report about the activist court. I commented that the tort reform issue cuts to a very basic concept of separation of powers, and that the legislature, not the supreme court, is the proper forum to address issues that are so vitally important to our socioeconomic structure.

---

[9] Majority Report, *supra* note 1, at 8–13, 93–96, and 100–122.

[10] *Id.* at 93 (emphasis added).

[11] The Interim Study Committee cited several cases, including Whitworth v. Bynum, 699 S.W.2d 194, 197 (Tex. 1985) (declaring the Texas Automobile Guest Statute unconstitutional); Cavnar v. Quality Control Parking, Inc., 696 S.W.2d 549, 553–54 (Tex. 1985) (expanding prejudgment interest to personal injury/death cases); Duncan v. Cessna Aircraft Co., 665 S.W.2d 414, 428–29 (Tex. 1984) (adopting a pure comparative causation system for product liability and combined negligence–product liability cases); Sanchez v. Schindler, 651 S.W.2d 249, 253 (Tex. 1983) (expanding wrongful death recoveries by parents and subsequently others). Majority Report, *supra* note 1, at 10–12, 100–14.

[12] Majority Report, *supra* note 1, at 95 (emphasis added).

[13] *Id.* at 93 (emphasis added).

Tort reform did not become a reality in Texas without a full test of the legislative process. Indeed, the task of passage seemed insurmountable at times, particularly in view of the prowess of the Texas Trial Lawyers Association.[14] In reviewing my files, I counted at least nine times that the package of bills was pronounced "dead," two of these declarations made "officially," by the press.[15] The reform legislation was, however, always resuscitated by an unexpected twist or turn of events. What follows is my firsthand account of the Texas Tort Reform Act's course through the halls of the Texas legislature, where I had the privilege of being involved, along with my colleague, Senator Kent Caperton (D-Bryan), in virtually every minute of the fight. I hope the reader finds this to be an informative and candid account of the Texas tort reform legislative process.

## II. Players and Strategies

*"The Best Fight in Town"*

I was a conscript in the battle for tort reform in Texas. Frankly, I am not proud of my reluctance, prior to the convening of the seventieth regular session of the Texas legislature in 1987, to get involved in the tort reform fight. In fact, I had not given tort reform a lot of thought since I made a feeble attempt in the sixty-ninth session with a structured settlement bill that never got out of committee.[16]

All of my political confidants urged me to stay out of this fight because it was destined to heat up and, according to most seasoned advisors, there would be no winners. Furthermore, the philosophical alignment of the Texas senate for the seventieth session was such that an informed vote count showed that anywhere from eleven to sixteen of the state's thirty-one senators would vote against tort reform. With these odds, the prospects for passage seemed impossible or, at best, improbable. It was, by all tests, a political hot potato, and if anyone introduced tort reform without securing passage that member would wind up in the unenviable position of making both sides mad.

[14]As I use the term "trial lawyers" in this section I am referring to the plaintiffs' bar, including members of the Texas Trial Lawyers Association. Of course, the defense bar are trial lawyers, but not as this term is used herein.

[15]*See* Bruce Hight, *Tort Reform Appears Dead as Session Ends,* AUSTIN AM.-STATESMAN, June 1, 1987, at B2; Steve McGonigle, *Plans to Revamp Tort System Fail,* DALLAS MORNING NEWS, June 2, 1987, at 8A.

[16]Tex. S.B. 1149, 69th Leg. (1985).

All of these factors dampened my enthusiasm. And yet, it was clear the fight was coming. I could sit on the sidelines and not get involved, but I believed my constituents expected more of me than this. Moreover, I had become personally disenchanted with a number of Texas Supreme Court decisions, which I felt left the perception that in Texas civil cases there was no longer a level playing field for litigants.[17] Then, quite unexpectedly, in mid-December 1986, I got a call from George Christian.[18] He asked if we could meet to discuss my getting involved in the looming tort reform battle. We agreed to meet later that month at the capitol.

Next to the "Quorum Club," a local gathering place frequented by politicians, perhaps more bills have reached consensus in the "Linoleum Club," a dingy-looking cafeteria in the basement of the Texas capitol, than in any other place in Austin. It was there, on December 22, 1986, that the pro–tort reform Texas Civil Justice League, represented by George Christian and Jerry "Nub" Donaldson,[19] first asked me to carry the tort reform legislative package in the Texas senate. I had been involved in a number of legislative battles with Christian and Donaldson. They presented me with a fairly convincing case why I should sponsor tort reform in the senate, and I communicated my concerns to them about the legislation. After we had discussed the pros and cons of the package, I specifically recall a comment made by Christian that, more than any other, stuck in my mind: "It's the best fight in town, Senator." Before I got into the fray, however, I wanted to know more about the Texas Civil Justice League.

### *The Texas Civil Justice League*

The beginnings of the Texas Civil Justice League can be traced to the Texas Medical Association's unsuccessful lobbying efforts on behalf of several tort reform bills during the 1985 legislative session. As a result of the failure of those bills, several interested professions, businesses, and health care groups formed a post-session coalition to discuss a concentrated legislative offensive on the tort reform issue and the changing composition of the Texas Supreme Court. This was the origin of the Texas Civil Justice League.

---

[17]For a similar perspective, *see* Robert D. D'Agostino, *The Decline of the Law in the Texas Supreme Court,* 2 BENCHMARK 171 (1986) (state courts are becoming increasingly activist and unpredictable, and result-oriented decisions have replaced the rule of law; no longer can a litigant rely on precedent or even legislative enactment as setting parameters of allowable conduct).

[18]George Christian is a political consultant in Austin and former press secretary to President Lyndon Johnson.

[19]Donaldson is a prominent Austin lobbyist and attorney.

From the outset, the League's participants realized they faced formidable opposition from the Texas Trial Lawyers Association ("Trial Lawyers"). If their organization was to be effective, it had to be first-rate. By the fall of 1985, what had been at first a rather loose-knit coalition of diverse business interest groups was becoming a well-funded, powerful grassroots organization. The seventieth legislative session was scheduled to begin in January 1987, and by the fall of 1986, the League's members were fighting mad and ready to do something about liability insurance premiums, coverages, cancellations, and a civil justice system which was perceived as replete with raw deals for parties who were sued as defendants in civil cases.[20]

The League was the prime mover of tort reform legislation. Its strong point continued to be an extraordinary grassroots organization. Its biggest problem was that it lacked the influence and momentum of the most powerful and best-financed lobbying arm in the capitol, the Trial Lawyers. Business interests, both large and small, had for the past several years been out-funded and out-lobbied by the Trial Lawyers.

### *The Texas Trial Lawyers Association*

The Texas Trial Lawyers Association starts fights and normally finishes them. Tort reform was a fight the Trial Lawyers did not start but surely wanted to finish, and finish as early in the seventieth session as possible. For years, the Trial Lawyers, under the leadership of Phil Gauss as its executive director, had steadily built a power base in Austin that was second to none.

To the Trial Lawyers, tort reform threatened a system it had worked hard to build. For years, the Trial Lawyers had placed enormous financial backing behind plaintiff-oriented candidates for the Texas Supreme Court, in an effort to change the philosophy of the court. In my view, the election of plaintiff-oriented candidates to the court significantly changed the odds for Texas tort litigants to the point that there was no longer a level playing field for litigants.

The Texas Trial Lawyers also had a line of defense against any drastic legislative revision of the tort laws. This defense concentrated on the Texas senate, where the Trial Lawyers were effective because they gave strong support and large contributions to their favored candidates. They were well aware that eleven votes against rule

[20]Memorandum from George Christian to John Montford (July 17, 1987) (on file with University of Houston Law Center Library).

suspension in the senate could kill any bill,[21] so they worked hard to maintain a solid block of at least eleven votes.

By December 31, 1985, the Trial Lawyers had so out-maneuvered the defense bar and the business lobby that Texas was heralded as a "plaintiff's paradise."[22] Ironically, it was the rash of plaintiff-oriented decisions[23] that triggered deeper legislative involvement in the tort reform movement and spurred significant momentum within the League.

The Trial Lawyers chose Senator Kent Caperton (D-Bryan) as their standard bearer, although, as events unfolded, it became clear that he was not a mere spokesman for any one group. Caperton is a formidable adversary in any arena. In my opinion, he was one of the most agile members of the senate in debate. It was clear that obtaining meaningful tort reform in Texas in 1987 would require a sustained, all-out effort.

### *The Anti–Tort Reform Strategy*

From the viewpoint of the proponents of tort reform, the Trial Lawyers' strategy in opposition to tort reform was simple and forthright: kill the package. This strategy was to be carried out by the following tactical plan: (1) form a group consisting of consumer advocates rather than lawyers, finance it, and use it to offset the League's grass-roots organization and advertising capability; (2) kill the bills in the senate committee to keep the members from getting cut up politically by a floor fight and a record vote; (3) in the event the package made it to the senate floor, prevent it from being brought

[21]Senate Rule 32(b) (adopted by the 70th Leg., Jan. 21, 1987) allows the senate to suspend Rule 12, which requires the senate to consider bills, resolutions, and other business in the order in which they are introduced. Because Rule 32(b) requires a vote of two-thirds of the senate (which consists of 31 members) to suspend the order of business, only 11 votes are required to block rule suspension. In practice, this regular calendar rule is usually suspended, and bills are routinely considered out of turn. The rule essentially imposes a supermajority requirement on consideration of bills on the senate floor. EUGENE W. JONES ET AL., PRACTICING TEXAS POLITICS 298 (4th ed. 1980); CLIFTON MCCLESKEY ET AL., THE GOVERNMENT AND POLITICS OF TEXAS 170 (6th ed. 1978); THOMAS M. SPENCER, THE LEGISLATIVE PROCESS, TEXAS-STYLE 68–70 (1981).

[22]Stephen J. Adler, *The Texas Bench: Anything Goes,* AM. LAW., Apr. 1986, at 13.

[23]*See* William P. Barrett, *"The Best Justice Money Can Buy,"* FORBES, June 1, 1987, at 122 (Texas elects the judiciary and the biggest and most reliable contributors to judicial campaigns are Texas lawyers; the system has great potential for corruption); Ken Case, *Blind Justice,* TEX. MONTHLY, May 1987, at 134–38, 195–98 (Texas Supreme Court justices regularly help out their close friends and violate court rules by discussing the merits of pending cases with people outside the court); Paul Burka, *Heads, We Win, Tails, You Lose,* TEX. MONTHLY, May 1987, at 138–39, 206 (by making large contributions to judicial campaigns, Texas plaintiffs' lawyers have taken over the Texas Supreme Court and rewritten state law to favor their clients).

up by blocking rule suspension;[24] (4) stall the package to the fullest extent possible so that, in the event it did reach the floor in the senate, it could be killed by a filibuster; (5) permit no constitutional amendments to the "open courts" provision of the Texas Constitution;[25] and (6) shift the blame for the problems in the system to the insurance companies by insisting on insurance reform, instead of tort reform, as being the cure for the civil liability insurance crisis.

To assist in the implementation of their strategy, the Trial Lawyers formed the "Texans for Civil Justice" organization to counteract the effects of the pro-tort reform group Texas Civil Justice League. With such similarity in names, there was much confusion in the public about which group had which role. The Texans for Civil Justice group ran anti-tort reform television and newspaper advertising campaigns of a type that had been used to dilute legislative tort reform efforts in both Arizona and Florida. Interestingly, this expensive advertising campaign fell flat in Texas because it came too late. Because of a number of ironies, the Trial Lawyers' well-planned, well-organized strategy ultimately failed to stop tort reform in the seventieth regular session of the legislature.

### *The Pro–Tort Reform Strategy*

Like the Trial Lawyers, the League adopted a simple and straightforward strategy. It was to divide and conquer, and then place such enormous constituent pressure on the members of the legislature that they ultimately would be forced to take a stand. If this plan did not work, there was the ever-present threat of a special session.[26]

The pro–tort reform forces also had the findings of an interim study committee on their side. On January 22, 1987, Senator Grant Jones and Representative Mike Toomey released the report of the Joint Committee on Liability Insurance and Tort Law and Procedure, which was signed by eight of the committee's ten members. The report called for thirty sweeping changes in the state's civil justice

[24]*See supra* note 21.

[25]TEX. CONST. art. I, § 13. In Nelson v. Krusen, 678 S.W.2d 918 (Tex. 1984), the Texas Supreme Court declared that certain applications of the two-year statute of limitations for medical malpractice actions were unconstitutional under the Texas Constitution's open courts provision. *Id.* at 923. *See also* Comment, *The Current Status of the Open Courts Provision and the Discovery Rule in Texas: In a State of Limbo after* Krusen, 16 TEX. TECH. L. REV. 765, 774–80 (1985).

[26]Governor William Clements repeatedly declared that he would call a special session on tort reform if the legislature failed to pass "meaningful" reform. *See* John C. Henry, *Governor Threatens Special Session on 2 Issues,* AUSTIN AM.-STATESMAN, Apr. 1, 1987, at B1.

system and twenty-two major revisions in the regulation of the insurance industry. To no one's surprise, Senator Caperton and Representative James Hury (D-Galveston) filed a minority report that attempted to focus the issue on insurance reform rather than on tort reform.

In implementing the strategy for the passage of tort reform, there were a number of decisions that had to be made, and made quickly. In which house should passage first be sought? Could the lieutenant governor be persuaded to refer the package to a favorable standing committee? Should the bills be grouped into an omnibus bill or filed as a series of separate bills and proposed constitutional amendments? What were the chances, given the alignment of votes in the senate, for the passage of any constitutional amendments, which require approval by two-thirds of the membership? Who would comprise the pro–tort reform negotiating team? When I assumed the responsibility of carrying the senate tort reform package on January 27, 1987, I assumed the responsibility of addressing these issues and implementing the pro–tort reform strategy.

## III. How the Fight Was Won

### *The Opening Salvo*

On January 13, 1987, Lieutenant Governor Bill Hobby gaveled the senate to order, convening the seventieth regular session of the Texas legislature. Tort reform bills were filed contemporaneously in both houses, but the battle for tort reform was destined to be fought in the senate. The League did not anticipate any major problems in the house since 50 of the 150 house members were Republicans and almost that many were conservative Democrats. It was clear that the senate was to be the legislative battlefield for tort reform. On February 3, 1987, Senators Ray Farabee, Grant Jones, and I introduced in the senate the legislative package for tort and insurance reform, a package containing one proposed constitutional amendment and seven separate bills.

Filing these seven bills came after extensive discussions over whether we should file one omnibus bill or several "single-shot" bills. In the end, both courses were pursued and, ultimately, both an omnibus bill and separate bills for each topic were referred to committee. The difficulty in attempting to pass separate bills was that the regular order of business rule, which required a two-thirds vote for each bill, would have to be repeatedly suspended. If the bills were not topically grouped with sufficient constitutional basis,[27] the opponents of tort reform could effect a "round-robin" strategy on rules suspension and effectively block bills from coming up by switching off votes. In other words, some "surplus" opposition members could vote for suspension of the regular order of business rule on particular tort reform measures without jeopardizing the eleven votes needed to block rules suspension. Opponents could trade off "supporting" particular measures, tell their constituents they voted for tort reform, and still effectively block rules suspension.

### *The First Turning Point: The February 3, 1987, Meeting*

The first turning point in the passage of tort reform in the senate came on February 3, the day the package was filed. The initial confrontation took place in the evening hours in the lieutenant governor's office; the subject was the proper committee to which the package should be referred. The rumor around the capitol was that the bills would go to the Senate State Affairs Committee, whose chairman, Ray Farabee, was carrying the charitable immunity portion of the tort reform package. It was clear, however, that the potential existed for this committee to kill the package on a 7–6 vote.

Lieutenant Governor Bill Hobby summoned Jones, Farabee, and me to his office late that afternoon. Also at the meeting were Senators Ike Harris (R-Dallas), chairman of the Economic Development Committee, and Kent Caperton, captain of the anti–tort reform group. Caperton strongly urged that the package be referred to State Affairs, contending it would get a fairer hearing because that committee represented a better cross-section of the senate. The pro–tort reform camp vehemently disagreed, arguing that it would not be in anyone's best interests to have this package die in committee. Farabee added

[27]The Texas constitution contains a "one subject rule": "No bill . . . shall contain more than one subject, which shall be expressed in its title." TEX. CONST. art. III, § 35. For a discussion of the history and construction of this constitutional requirement, see TEX. CONST. art. III, interp. commentary (Vernon 1984):

> The purpose of the title-subject provision is threefold: First, it is designed to prevent log-rolling legislation, i.e., to prevent the writing of several subjects having no connection with each other in one bill for the purpose of combining various interests in support of the whole. Second, it prevents surprise or fraud upon legislators by means of provisions in bills of which the titles give no intimation, and which might therefore be overlooked and carelessly and unintentionally adopted. Third, it permits the people to be fairly apprised of the subjects of legislation under consideration, so that they may have an opportunity of being heard, if they so desire.

that the people of Texas were collectively behind this issue, particularly in view of the liability crisis. Everyone except Caperton concurred that the package should be referred to the Economic Development Committee where, in our view, it stood the best chance of being favorably reported to the floor of the full senate.

Bill Hobby is a person of few words. After each of us had presented his case, Hobby made his decision: "I've made up my mind. The package will go to Economic Development. Thank you, ladies and gentlemen." The battle lines were drawn, the die was cast. The real street fighting over tort reform had begun.

### *The Senate Economic Development Committee*

The referral of the tort reform package to the Senate Economic Development Committee sent shock waves throughout the capitol, the lobby, and the press.[28] The Trial Lawyers viewed the committee assignment as a major setback. It derailed their initial strategy. If a person could pick a date that represented the beginning of the end for the Texas Trial Lawyers' opposition, it would have been February 3, 1987, the date the bills were referred to committee.

The Economic Development Committee opened hearings on the legislation before a packed senate chamber on March 2, 1987. The Trial Lawyers had by this time regrouped and done their homework. They succeeded in getting a large number of injured claimants, together with most of their sons, daughters, secretaries, investigators, and spouses, to assemble in the capitol wearing buttons and carrying placards saying "Prove It."[29] The contingent arrived early and occupied all of the chairs in the senate chamber as well as most of those in the gallery. By the time the pro–tort reform Texas Civil Justice League's large crowd showed up, there was no place left to sit.[30]

The hearings were volatile and the testimony often emotional, creating what the press termed a "circus-like atmosphere."[31] Doctors, engineers, lawyers, businessmen, consumer groups, public officials, and virtually every segment of the population had representatives in attendance. Chairman Harris's biggest problem was maintaining order. On one occasion when Attorney General Jim Mattox was testifying against some aspects of tort reform, I retorted that

[28]*See* Bruce Hight, *Tort Law Assignment Draws Fire,* AUSTIN AM.-STATESMAN, Feb. 5, 1987, at B2.

[29]*See* Fred Bonavita, *Fans, Foes of Tort Reform Testify,* HOUSTON POST, Mar. 3, 1987, at 9A.

[30]*See* Dave McNeely, *Gallery Packing Becomes Latest Salvo in Tort Reform Battle,* AUSTIN AM.-STATESMAN, Mar. 3, 1987, at B2.

[31]*See* Bonavita, *supra* note 29.

we were going to pass tort reform in spite of him. The gallery erupted in such an outburst that Harris lost his temper trying to calm the crowd and recessed the hearings.

On March 12, 1987, the committee completed the public hearing phase and Chairman Harris gave each side two weeks to produce compromise bills through negotiation. All bills were sent to subcommittee in the meantime. Our initial canvas of the committee showed that we could vote out a strong package with a margin of eight to three. This prediction set the Trial Lawyers scrambling, particularly when a vote tally sheet was "inadvertently" left on the table in the committee room.

### *The Negotiations*

The negotiations on tort reform were the most rigorous sessions in which any of the senators had ever participated. Perhaps the most important factor in bringing about the passage of tort reform was the character of the negotiating teams assembled by both sides, which consisted of the most skillful negotiators who could be assembled in Texas. The quote that best summed up the negotiating teams was made by Senator Harris who, after one totally exhausting day, quipped to Caperton and me, "You both have good negotiating teams but Kent's are a lot more fun than yours."

Caperton's negotiating team consisted of Mike Gallagher, former president of the Texas Trial Lawyers Association, Austin trial lawyer Broadus Spivey, and Corpus Christi trial lawyer Bill Edwards. Working in the wings were Tommy Jacks, an Austin lawyer especially knowledgeable in consumer law, Mike Perrin, who was Mike Gallagher's law partner, Jim Kronzer, dean of the plaintiffs' bar, and Joe Longley, an expert in Texas law on deceptive trade practices.

Our lead negotiator was Morris Atlas, a lawyer from McAllen, Texas. Joining him was Will Barber, the defense bar's answer to Jim Kronzer, Professor Hadley Edgar from Texas Tech University, and Professor Bill Powers of the University of Texas School of Law.

The bulk of the negotiations took place in the anteroom adjacent to the lieutenant governor's office, under his watchful eyes and ears. Many sessions ended in stalemate after extremely bitter exchanges. At one point we became so frustrated that Harris, Caperton, and I left the capitol in disgust and met at Harris's apartment. At this time, Harris asked for our vote tally sheets to get an update on the voting alignment in the senate. When he totaled them, they added up to forty-one senators. The Texas senate has only thirty-one members; apparently ten members had committed to both sides. We returned to the capitol more stalemated than ever.

Our negotiating sessions lasted exactly one month longer than the March deadline Chairman Harris had imposed on us. We worked around the clock, night and day, Saturdays, Sundays, and holidays. With no compromise reached, the pro–tort reformers asked Chairman Harris to docket the bills and call for a vote in the committee to increase pressure for a compromise bill. On April 27, 1987, a total of seventeen bills and five constitutional amendments was approved by the committee and favorably reported to the full senate. This brought more pressure on the members of the senate to encourage the negotiators to reach a compromise.

The major sticking points were the placing of a cap on punitive damages, the sixty percent (plaintiff's own negligence) bar rule against recovery, and the establishment of a threshold for joint and several liability. At one point we spent two weeks haggling over one percentage point for the threshold of joint and several liability. We could not agree whether the threshold (for any one defendant) should trigger at "more than twenty percent" or "less than twenty percent" of responsibility. We spent the same amount of time haggling over whether "more than sixty percent" responsibility would bar recovery, as distinguished from "less than sixty percent."

### *The Second Turning Point: Enter Jamail, the Referee*

Since the senate had been selected as the battlefield for tort reform, it was here that the genius of Bill Hobby came into play in a second crucial way, through his choice of referees. Hobby called Caperton and me in after we had reached our fourth impasse in five days in negotiating sessions. To my surprise, Hobby stated he was intent on bringing noted Texas trial lawyer Joe Jamail into the tort reform fight. I will never forget looking at him and thinking to myself, "Governor, have you lost your mind?" In retrospect, it has become clear that he knew exactly what he was doing. Jamail is like a human magnet radiating shock waves. As Jamail first recounted to me his proposals on what tort reform should be, the age-old maxim "politics makes strange bedfellows" became embossed in my mind forever. What Jamail indicated he was willing to support in the way of tort reform may well have been more than we could ever have passed out of the senate.

Under Hobby's direction, Jamail was probably the best bargain of a referee the legislature of Texas ever had. Every time the negotiators reached an impasse, Jamail showed up and attempted to work out the problem. He was persistent in his demand that we get a bill. As an example, one of the major obstacles to passage was that our side had held out for the establishment of a shorter statute of limitations on minors. Jamail persuaded Hobby that this measure posed too great an impasse and that we could never get the remainder of the package passed as long as that section remained. Hobby called us in and said that provision needed to go in order to get the negotiations off high center. It went out the window that afternoon like used dishwater.

In the early morning hours of April 30, the two negotiating teams reached a compromise. So many drafts of the compromise bill were floating around that we finally had the Legislative Council[32] start marking the drafts with the times they were turned out. The bill that finally went to the floor was dated 1:57 a.m., April 30, 1987. Shortly after the package was reported out of committee, Senator Bob Glasgow (D-Stephenville) began to complain, alleging that the authors of the compromise were not able to explain it to him the night before. He was right—the negotiators were so tired that we did not even feel like trying to explain the complex agreement that night.

The stage was finally set for a senate floor debate. Key points in the Senate compromise included a sixty-one percent bar rule (i.e., "more than sixty percent"), and a "less than twenty percent" threshold for joint and several liability in the case of an innocent plaintiff. Strong environmental language was written into the joint and several liability section of the compromise.

### *The Third Turning Point: The Committee of the Whole*

A third major factor in the passage of tort reform, after Hobby's decisions to refer the package to the Senate Economic Development Committee and to bring Jamail in to break deadlocks, was Hobby's referral of the negotiated package to a "Committee of the Whole Senate" prior to the package being taken up on the floor. This move had the effect of sending up a giant trial balloon and allowing everyone to express concerns prior to floor debate.

This move completely deflated the opposition. Since we had struck an agreement on the bill, our negotiating teams fully supported the package in the Committee of the Whole. Gallagher, Atlas, Jamail, and Edwards all spoke in support of the package.[33] It was going to

[32]The Legislative Council is an agency of the legislative branch of the state government created to serve the legislature by investigating, compiling reports, and disseminating information on issues of interest to the legislature. TEX. GOV'T CODE ANN. §§ 323.001, 323.006 (Vernon Supp. 1987). The Council attorneys are the principal draftsmen of legislation during the session. The Council consists of the lieutenant governor as chairman, the speaker of the house of representatives as vice-chairman, and other members of the Texas legislature. *Id.* § 323.001.

[33]Since the meeting of the Committee of the Whole was technically a public hearing, persons other than members of the senate were permitted to participate in the debate.

be politically tough for any senator to vote against the package when it came up for consideration by the full senate on May 6, 1987.

By this time, the Trial Lawyers were in large part divided. A primary concern of theirs, as well as of Caperton, was that if the compromise package was passed out of the senate there was no assurance that the house would not load the package up with proposals that would effectively negate the senate's proudly negotiated product. By supporting the compromise on which their own members had signed off, the Trial Lawyers might be completely outmaneuvered in the long run. The Trial Lawyers' concern was compounded by the fact that Representative Toomey, sponsor of the house tort reform package, had made statements to the press to the effect that all the tort reformers wanted to do was get some bill out of the senate, and that then it would be written the way the house wanted it to be written. But we in the senate made the point that our side had made a commitment to defend reasonably the senate bill. If we had not, there would have been no tort reform. We were therefore determined not to hang Caperton out to dry. In the Texas senate, a deal is a deal.

After fending off numerous unwanted amendments, S.B. 287, the tort reform omnibus bill, passed the senate by a vote of 28–3 on May 6, 1987. Also passing were single shot bills dealing with prejudgment interest, railroad venue, charitable immunity, and insurance reform, as well as a proposed constitutional amendment confirming the legislature's power to define governmental functions of municipalities. Frankly, most of us in the tort reform battle never believed that we would make this much progress in passing a tort reform bill in the seventieth regular session.

### *Consideration by the House of Representatives*

We found ourselves in a very awkward position in the Texas house of representatives. We had no guarantees about what the house would or would not do, and we were not in a position to accept significant house modifications to the package. We were clearly unable to speak for the house or to represent that we had a deal all the way through the house. In retrospect, the failure to include the house in the negotiations on the senate package proved to be a mistake, a matter which became clear when the bills ultimately went to conference committee.

The biggest problem with the house's taking up tort reform after the senate was a building resentment on the part of the house members for all the work that had been done without their involvement. A delicate balance had to be maintained or the entire package would be derailed. If the house returned the package with significant changes, the whole compromise would be effectively killed and a special session would be the inevitable result. Mike Toomey knew this. He had cochaired the Interim Study Committee on Tort and Insurance Reform. He had been everybody's choice in the tort reform movement for house sponsor. He had been a knowledgeable, tenacious lawyer who devoutly believed in the cause he was championing. He still does. He made a believer out of me.

On May 14, 1987, the House State Affairs Committee approved an altered version of the senate tort reform bill with significant changes. On May 21, 1987, the house overwhelmingly passed its version of the tort reform package. The house bill included a fifty-one percent bar rule, compared with the senate's sixty-one percent rule, and a twenty-five percent threshold for joint and several liability, as compared with the senate's "less than twenty" percent threshold. It had no provisions for an innocent plaintiff. These, together with some other matters, were the major differences in the two packages.

*Conference Committee*

In accordance with our agreement with Caperton reasonably to defend the senate bill, we asked the senate to refuse to accept the house amendments, and to send the bill to conference committee. The bill was sent to a conference committee consisting of Senators Harris, Caperton, Don Henderson (R-Dallas), and Hector Uribe (D-Brownsville). The house conferees were Toomey, Bruce Gibson (D-Cleburne), Pat Hill (R-Dallas), David Cain (D-Dallas), and Steve Wolens (D-Dallas). Hobby's appointment of Henderson as one of the senate conferees proved fortunate for tort reform. Earlier in the session, he had sponsored and passed a tort reform-oriented bill that enabled shareholders to limit liability of corporate directors. Henderson turned out to be a significant player in reaching a compromise.

The committee's pace was slow and, as chairman, I was criticized at first for not calling the respective issues for a vote. I deferred doing so in order to try to resolve the house and senate differences; I did not want to jeopardize passage of the bill by calling for a vote prematurely. Finally, on Saturday, May 30, less than seventy-two hours before the close of the regular session, I started calling issues to a vote in order to narrow the differences between the house and senate. By this time I was being openly criticized by Wolens for trying to ram the legislation down the house conferees' throats.

As we entered the last forty-eight hours of the session, both sides were exhausted, time was running out, and tempers were short. As the clock wound down, we were hopelessly deadlocked on the issues of comparative responsibility, threshold percentages for joint and several liability, and the inclusion of the Deceptive Trade Practices Act under the purview of the tort reform package.[34] Representative Hill insisted on rewriting the senate's prejudgment interest provisions, claiming that the senate version was too complex and burdensome for judges and party litigants to deal with.

As the conferees convened in the old Supreme Courtroom in the capitol on Sunday, May 31, the press pronounced tort reform "dead" for the seventieth session.[35] The senators went to see Hobby, and Toomey went to see house speaker Gib Lewis. Hobby and Lewis began directly participating in negotiations. At one point Lewis walked out after having a confrontation with Caperton. Hobby, too, lost his temper on one occasion when Gilbert Adams, the president of the Texas Trial Lawyers Association, attempted to convince him that the package should be allowed to die. Hobby's response was, "If this package doesn't pass this session of the legislature, you are going to see some real tort reform in the special session." All seemed lost. We urged that the conferees continue working around the clock in an attempt to beat the deadline of *sine die*.[36] As we moved into the last legislative day for the seventieth session, we decided to give it one more try. A large crowd of lobbyists, lawyers, and interested parties gathered outside the lieutenant governor's conference room. By this time, we were negotiating in teams of two because the press was continuously monitoring for violations of the Open Meetings Act.[37] Some members of the press watched us like hawks and took our names as we went in and out of the lieutenant governor's conference room, apparently hoping to catch a quorum present in a closed meeting.

Around 7:00 p.m., the conferees were down to three issues: a "sixty" vs. "sixty-one" percent bar rule against recovery in products

[34]Some advisors feared that plaintiffs could circumvent the tort reform measures by bringing an action for breach of warranty under the Deceptive Trade Practices Act (DTPA). This issue remained a concern, and eventually became the subject of an interim study committee. Reform of the DTPA was achieved in the seventy-first legislative session in 1989. *See infra* p. 228.

[35]*See* Bruce Hight, *Tort Reform Appears Dead as Session Ends*, AUSTIN AM.-STATESMAN, June 1, 1987, at B2; Steve McGonigle, *Plans to Revamp Tort System Fail*, DALLAS MORNING NEWS, June 2, 1987, at 8A.

[36]"*Sine die*" means final adjournment. BLACK'S LAW DICTIONARY 1242 (5th ed. 1979). A regular session of the Texas legislature cannot last longer than 140 days. TEX. CONST. art. III, § 24. After the *sine die*, or adjournment, of each regular session, no senate rules or legislative provisions permit further action on a bill until it is reintroduced as a new bill in the next legislative session.

[37]TEX. REV. CIV. STAT. ANN. art. 6252-17 (West Supp. 1987) (repealed Sept. 1, 1993). Section 2 of the Act provided that "[e]xcept as otherwise provided in this Act . . . every regular, special or called meeting or session of every governmental body shall be open to the public."

or strict liability cases, a "twenty" vs. "twenty-one" percent threshold for joint and several liability, and a "ten" vs. "eleven" percent joint and several liability threshold where the plaintiff was without fault. At that point, Hobby asked Caperton to step back into his office. We will never know what Hobby said to him, but whatever it was, Caperton returned, uttered a heavy sigh, and said he would go with the house percentages if we would exclude the Deceptive Trade Practices Act from the provisions of the tort reform package. At that time it was agreed that the Deceptive Trade Practices Act would be the subject of an interim study.

*Off to the Races: The Report to the Floor*

It was 8:20 p.m., June 1, 1987, when the conferees struck a deal. We were unfortunately within the filibuster zone. The session was to end at midnight, and a filibuster could kill the hard-won tort reform package. Rumors had circulated earlier in the day that a group of dissident Trial Lawyers were assuring their colleagues that they could get the bills killed. We quickly canvassed the senate conferees, except for Uribe whom we were unable to locate. All four said they would sign the conference committee report. We had a serious problem, as it was now 8:41 p.m. and the legislative council still had to proof, print, and distribute copies of the conference committee report and compromise bill to 31 senators and 150 house members before we could go further. I would then have to obtain recognition on the floor of the full senate and move to adopt the conference committee report. The Legislative Council did yeoman's service in cranking out the finished product. What would have ordinarily taken three days they accomplished in two hours. These were, however, the longest two hours of my life.

At about 9:20 p.m., we got wind of an impending filibuster by Senator Craig Washington (D-Houston). We again enlisted the help of Joe Jamail, asking him to try to reason with Washington. We located Washington, sat down in the front of the chamber, and went over the bill line by line with him. He told us he was still undecided about what he was going to do, but we noticed that he had already put on his designer snakeskin tennis shoes, which certainly indicated to me he had already made up his mind.[38]

At about 10:40 p.m., I was recognized on the floor to make a motion that the senate concur in the conference committee reports on the tort reform package. Senator Ted Lyon (D-Rockwall), who, along with Washington, had consistently voted against tort reform

[38]It is common practice for a senator to wear tennis shoes when about to filibuster, since he or she will have to remain standing for a long time.

throughout the session, raised a number of questions on the report. At about 11:31 p.m., Washington stood up and started to talk, and the session ended on his filibuster. Some of us preferred to call it a "minibuster" since he only had to talk for the twenty-nine minutes remaining until midnight, when time ran out on the seventieth regular session—and on the bills.

An interesting thing about serving in the Texas legislature is that things can change completely in a split second. We were about to witness as rapid a turn of events as has perhaps ever been seen in the Texas legislature. At about 10:40 p.m., during Lyon's protracted question and answer session, Hobby, Jones, and Farabee gathered at my desk. We summoned George Bayoud, a top aide to Governor William P. Clements, to the floor. Hobby suggested that we walk over to the governor's office and request an immediate special session to take up tort reform. We went, we asked, it was granted. Washington's filibuster had bought the tort reform opponents just two additional days.

## IV. Victory

Governor Clements issued his proclamation calling the special session in the early morning hours of June 2, 1987, calling a special session to convene at 11:00 a.m. the same day. This time the bills were reintroduced as Senate Bills 5, 6, and 7. The bills were back on the floor of the full senate before anyone had time to get a good night's rest. They were in the identical form that the conference committee had agreed on. Two pieces of the package—Senate Joint Resolution 26 and Senate Bill 202, relating to charitable immunity—had passed during the regular session and did not require reintroduction in the special session.

The house anxiously awaited the arrival of our bills. For seven hours, Senator Washington relentlessly propounded questions in the senate, going over every line of every page of every provision of every bill. At about 6:40 p.m. on June 2, 1987, Washington sat down. By 6:45 p.m. we had the bills out of the senate. Jones' insurance reform package, which we had agreed would be kept in tandem, likewise resisted amendments and passed out of the senate.

The house was scheduled to take up the bills the morning of June 3, 1987. The house took less than ten minutes to concur in the senate package. Caperton and I exchanged accolades, thanked each other, and sat down. We had come a long way since the opening of the seventieth session.

On June 16, 1987, Governor Clements signed the Texas tort reform bills into law. As he signed these measures, he stated, "It took a lot of work—and a little extra time—but the legislators did what many thought would be impossible. They passed meaningful tort reform."[39] Tort reform was now a reality in Texas. It was indeed the "best fight in town."

*Editor's Note*

Since the 1987 legislation, there have been additional developments in Texas tort reform.

In 1989, the legislature passed a bill sponsored by Senator Montford amending Texas's Deceptive Trade Practices Act to provide that plaintiffs could not bring an action for breach of warranty under that act.

In 1993, two major reforms were enacted. "S.B. 2," also sponsored by Senator Montford, was signed by Governor Ann Richards on March 4, 1993, and took effect August 30, 1993. It provided that a court may decline jurisdiction of an action on the basis of the doctrine of forum non conveniens for death or injury caused by acts or omissions occurring out of state. "S.B. 4" was signed by Governor Richards on March 4, 1993, and took effect September 1, 1993. It contained a comprehensive series of product liability measures, including: (1) in suits against product manufacturers for defectively designed products, plaintiffs must prove that, at the time the product was manufactured, there was an economical and technologically safer alternative design that would have prevented or significantly reduced the risk of injury without impairing the utility of the product; (2) in suits against innocent retailers and distributors of products, the product manufacturer will be required to indemnify and hold harmless the retailers or distributors for any damages, costs, and attorney fees incurred in the defense of a product liability suit, except for any loss incurred as a result of the seller's conduct; (3) a fifteen-year statute of repose for product liability lawsuits against manufacturers or sellers of manufacturing equipment, unless the manufacturer or seller expressly represents that the product has a useful life of longer than fifteen years; and (4) if the product is a common consumer product known to be inherently unsafe by the ordinary consumer,[40] a manufacturer or seller of the product shall be immune from a product liability action.

[39] *See* Mark Sanders, *Tort Reform, Other Measures Signed by Governor,* HOUSTON POST, June 17, 1987, at 12A.

[40] The bill lists a variety of products, "such as sugar, castor oil, alcohol, tobacco, and butter, as identified in Comment i to Section 402A of the Restatement (Second) of Torts."

# AUTHORS

**REPRESENTATIVE RICHARD A. BANDSTRA** is the Republican Floor Leader of the Michigan House and has long been deeply involved in medical malpractice reform. He was a key player in all three rounds of the debate discussed in his chapter and drafted the bill that became law in 1993.

**MARK A. BEHRENS** is an associate in the law firm of Crowell & Moring in Washington, D.C. Mr. Behrens obtained his J.D. from Vanderbilt University in 1990, where he served as Associate Articles Editor of the *Vanderbilt Law Review* and received an American Jurisprudence Award for achievement in tort law. He received his B.A. from the University of Wisconsin-Madison in 1987.

**GRIFFIN B. BELL** was Attorney General under President Carter and is now a partner at King & Spalding in Atlanta. He also served on the U.S. Court of Appeals for the Fifth Circuit from 1961-76.

**SAMUEL A. BRUNELLI** has been Executive Director of the American Legislative Exchange Council since 1988. Prior to this, he served as Director of Intergovernmental Affairs at the U.S. Department of Education and, before that, established and operated Brunelli Farms, a multimillion dollar agricultural operation, and served as a consultant to the agricultural and energy industries. Many will remember Mr. Brunelli from his days as a professional football player with the Denver Broncos.

**SUSAN CHARLTON** is Counsel to the Majority for the Arizona State Senate. She received a B.A. in government from Smith College in 1986 and a law degree from the University of Arizona College of Law in 1989. Ms. Charlton has been with the Arizona Senate since 1991. Prior to her current position, she served as Policy Advisor and Counsel to the Minority.

**REPRESENTATIVE JOHN DORSO** was elected to the North Dakota State House in 1984. He is currently serving his second term as Chairman of the House Industry, Business, and Labor Committee, and his fifth term as a member of the House Transportation Committee. Representative Dorso is the owner of two small businesses in North Dakota.

**JOSEPH K. DOSS** is an associate in the law firm of Covington & Burling in Washington, D.C. He obtained his A.B. from the College of William and Mary in 1979 and his J.D. from George Mason University in 1984. Mr. Doss's practice includes providing legal counsel in matters relating to product liability law and federal regulation of foods, drugs, and other consumer products, and he has been active in several successful efforts to enact state tort reform legislation. Prior to joining Covington & Burling in 1990, Mr. Doss served as assistant general counsel for the Nonprescription Drug Manufacturers Association.

**MATTHEW P. EASTUS** has been an associate in the trial department of Baker & Botts, L.L.P., in Houston, Texas, since 1992. Mr. Eastus practices primarily in the field of labor and employment law. He received his J.D. in 1992 from the University of Virginia, where he was a member of the editorial board of the *Journal of Law & Politics* and was inducted into Phi Delta Phi. Mr. Eastus graduated magna cum laude and with honors in the liberal arts in earning a B.A. in journalism and political science in 1989 from Southern Methodist University, where he was also a member of Phi Beta Kappa.

**CLAUDIA WILSON FROST** is a partner in the trial department of Baker & Botts, L.L.P., in Houston, Texas. Ms. Frost received her J.D. magna cum laude in 1982 from the University of Houston Law Center, where she was editor-in-chief of the *Houston Law Review*. She has a general civil trial and civil appellate practice, with emphasis on securities, business torts, ERISA, and oil and gas litigation. She has served on various state and local bar association committees, has given CLE presentations on many subjects around the country, and is board-certified in civil trial law and in civil appellate law by the Texas Board of Legal Specialization.

**SENATOR WALTER A. (PUD) GRAHAM** of Mississippi was elected to the State Senate in 1984 and to the position of President Pro Tempore in 1993. He is also currently serving as Chairman of the Rules Committee. After attending Delta State University, he established a farm supply business and has been in that business ever since. He was recently presented with the Thomas Jefferson Award by the American Legislative Exchange Council in recognition of his leadership role in the passage of major tort reform legislation in Mississippi.

**SENATOR JOHN GREENE** is President of the Arizona State Senate, where he represents District 24. Senator Greene received his bachelor's degree in political science from the City University of New York at Hunter College in 1969, his J.D. from St. John's University Law School in June 1972, where he was the Research Editor of the *St. John's Law Review*, and a masters of law degree in taxation from New York University School of Law in 1979. He has been a practicing tax and business lawyer for over twenty years. Senator Greene is a recipient of the Arizona State Bar Foundation's Pro Bono Award for "extraordinary contributions by an Arizona attorney in making legal services available to persons who otherwise could not afford them." In August 1992, the American Legislative Exchange Council gave Senator Greene its 1992 Outstanding Legislator Award for his "outstanding leadership as a key member of its Task Force on Civil Justice."

**MARTIN J. HATLIE** currently is the Director of the American Medical Association's Department of Professional Liability and Insurance, where he has responsibility for coordinating the AMA's initiatives on tort reform, liability insurance, and risk management issues. He is also the Director of the Health Care Liability Alliance, a national coalition whose members include many physician organizations and organizations representing the insurance, health care, and manufacturing industries. In addition, he is the principal staff liaison and coordinator of the activities of the AMA/Specialty Society Medical Liability Project, a coalition of more than thirty national medical societies formed in 1986 to address liability concerns on behalf of organized medicine. He serves on the boards of trustees of the Anesthesia Patient Safety Foundation and the American Tort Reform Association and as AMA liaison to the board of the Physician Insurers Association of America. Mr. Hatlie is a graduate of Carleton College and received his law degree in 1982 from Boston College Law School.

**JOHN L. HOWARD** is Senior Corporate Counsel with Tenneco Inc. Prior to that, he served as Counsel to Vice President Quayle, where he was particularly active on civil justice reform issues. Mr. Howard has also served as Associate Deputy Attorney General at the Department of Justice; Legal Counsel to the Chairman, Merit Systems Protection Board; Special Assistant to the General Counsel, Consumer Product Safety Office of Personnel Management; and Deputy Prosecutive Attorney for the 30th Judicial Circuit in Indiana. Mr. Howard received a B.S. with honors from Indiana University School of Business, a J.D. from the Indiana University School of Law, and an LL. M. with the highest honors from George Washington University.

**DAVID HRICIK** has been an associate in the trial department of Baker & Botts, L.L.P., in Houston, Texas, since 1988. Mr. Hricik has a general civil trial and civil appellate practice, with emphasis on patent litigation and legal malpractice litigation. Since 1990, Mr. Hricik has also been an Adjunct Professor of Law at the University of Houston, where he teaches legal writing. He received his J.D. cum laude in 1988 from Northwestern University School of Law, where he was Note & Comment Editor for the *Northwestern Journal of International Law & Business*. He holds a B.A. in English magna cum laude from the University of Arizona.

**KARLA KINDERMAN** is an attorney with the American Medical Association's Office of General Counsel, Department of Professional Liability and Insurance. She also serves as a staff liaison for the AMA/Specialty Society Medical Liability Project, a coalition of more than thirty national medical societies formed in 1986 to address liability concerns on behalf of organized medicine. Ms. Kinderman received her B.A. from the University of Dayton, J.D. from the University of Louisville, and LL. M. from the Loyola University of Chicago School of Law, Institute for Health Law.

**CHRISTOPHER LANDAU** is an associate in the Washington, D.C., office of Kirkland & Ellis. A 1989 graduate of Harvard Law School, he also served as law clerk to United States Supreme Court Justices Antonin Scalia and Clarence Thomas.

**JAMES D. MILLER** is the head of civil litigation in the Washington, D.C., office of King & Spalding. He specializes in litigation involving medical devices, foods, pharmaceuticals, and medical research, including product liability and intellectual property issues. His law degree is from Yale Law School, where he was an editor of the *Yale Law Journal*.

**SENATOR JOHN T. MONTFORD** of Texas began his elected service to the public in 1979 when he was elected Lubbock County Criminal District Attorney. In November 1982, he was elected to the Texas Senate, where he has served as Chairman of the Senate State Affairs Committee and is now Chairman of the Senate Finance Committee. Senator Montford has won numerous awards in his highly successful legislative career. He received his B.A. from the University of Texas in 1965 and J.D. from the University of Texas in 1968.

**U.S. REPRESENTATIVE JOHN EDWARD PORTER** of Illinois is serving his eighth term in the United States House of Representatives. He is founder and cochairman of the Congressional